LEGENDARY
CARS

CARS THAT MADE HISTORY
FROM THE EARLY DAYS TO THE 21ST CENTURY

WHITE STAR PUBLISHERS

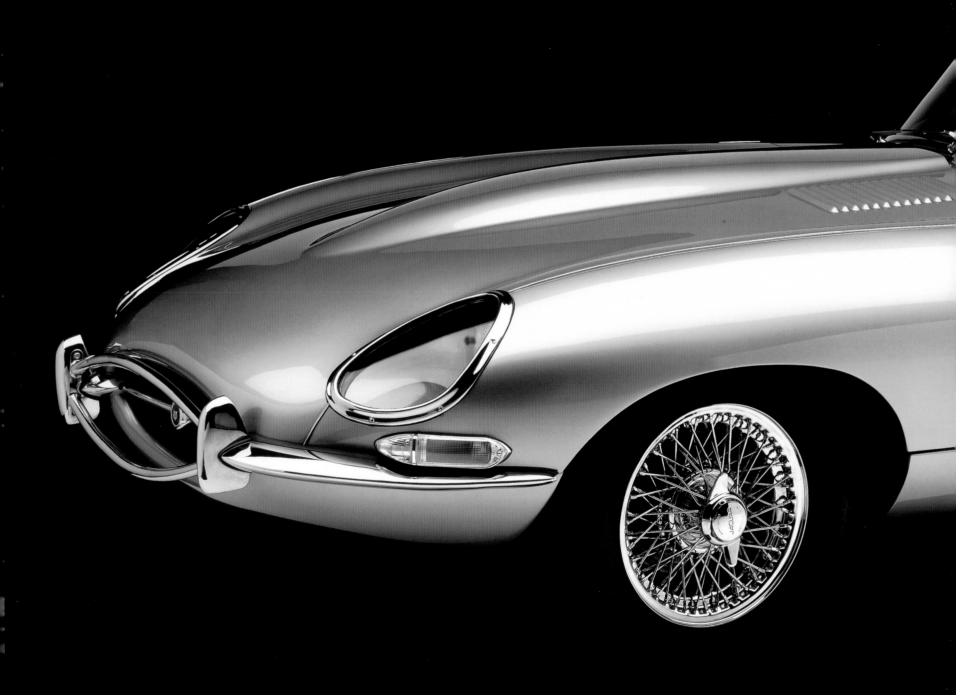

CONTENTS

1 EDSEL FORD SELECTED THE SLEEK GREYHOUND AS THE MASCOT FOR THE MARQUE.

2-3 THE LATE 1930S TALBOT LAGO HAD A SHAPE THE FRENCH CALLED "GOUTTE D'EAU."

4-5 THE MID-1950S MERCEDES-BENZ 300SL, KNOWN AS THE "GULLWING".

6-7 JAGUAR'S ICON OF THE 1960S – AND, IN FACT, FOR THE AGES – WAS THE XK-E.

8-9 THERE HAVE BEEN FEW CARS AS AUDACIOUS AS THE DODGE VIPER OF THE 1990S.

10-11 A JAGUAR WAS THE EMBLEM USED BY THE CAR COMPANY OF THE SAME TIME.

12-13 ROLLS-ROYCE INTRODUCED THE SECOND GENERATION OF ITS SILVER CLOUD IN 1959. THIS „DROPHEAD COUPE" WAS POWERED BY A NEW V8 ENGINE.

PREFACE

For much longer than you might imagine, people have eagerly awaited the opportunity to drive a motorized vehicle.

Long before the Industrial Revolution made such things possible, Homer and da Vinci dreamed of mechanically propelled vehicles.

Steam-powered devices looking much more like locomotives that had escaped their tracks than anything we might now accept as a motorcar were "driven" on roads in China, Europe and North America, in some cases more than a century before Karl Benz and Gottlieb Daimler and Emile Levassor built what we now recognize as the first automobiles.

With his mass-produced Model T made from standardized parts, Henry Ford put the world on wheels. By the end of its production in 1927, half of all the cars ever built had been Model T Fords.

Automakers from Europe - and Japan - sailed to Michigan to study Ford's production and assembly systems, then returned home and adopted the techniques to local conditions.

Cars proliferated. No longer were they only transportation toys for the wealthy classes. Whether Model T, Citroën Torpedo, Austin Seven, Fiat Topolino, Volkswagen Beetle or Toyota Corolla, they were affordable, could be used for everyday transportation by seemingly anyone of more than the most modest of means.

But just as people aspired at first just to own a car, almost immediately after achieving that goal they dreamed of owning not just a car, but a special car. A car that looked better. A car that went faster. Especially a car that would do both of those things. Cars, at least some very special cars, took on legendary status.

To be legendary is to be considered remarkable enough to take on mythic, even heroic proportions, to be celebrated and acclaimed, even to become part of the cultural tradition.

Such cars are the focus of this book.

15 THE MERCEDES-BENZ 540K DISPLAYS THE EXQUISITE DETAILING THAT WENT INTO THE HIGH-END AUTOMOBILE IN THE 1930S. THE CAR DREW ITS POWER FROM A SUPERCHARGED, INLINE EIGHT-CYLINDER ENGINE DESIGNED FOR RACING BY FERDINAND PORSCHE.

A Quick Drive Through Early Automotive History

Years before he painted the Mona Lisa, Leonardo da Vinci was drawing dream machines, some that flew – even a parachute-like apparatus to escape them when they didn't — and some that moved along the ground under their own power, two large and counter-balanced springs feeding each other and providing power to propel one of da Vinci's auto-mobile vehicles.

Centuries later, schoolboys in Europe, the United States and Japan would be scolded by their teachers for doing much the same thing, for drawing pictures of exotic or even ordinary cars and for dreaming of where and how fast those cars might transport them.

"The inventor of the automobile has had more influence on society than the combined exploits of Napoleon, Genghis Khan and Julius Caesar," renowned American sociologist William Ogburn wrote in 1938, when the automobile was just beginning to make its cultural impact.

More than a millennium before da Vinci dreamed of a mechanically propelled vehicle, Homer wrote in the Iliad of "living wheels" rolling under their own power from place to place "around the bless'd abodes."

British scientist, mathematician and philosopher Roger Bacon speculated about the possibilities of auto mobile vehicles two centuries before da Vinci drew them.

There are reports that two French Jesuit missionaries constructed steam-powered vehicles in China in the mid-17th century, though automotive historians tend to point to the steam tractor built in 1769 by Swiss engineer Nicholas Cugnot as the automotive Adam. Cugnot's contraption was huge, and designed to pull cannon for the French military, and it reportedly crashed out of control and into a wall while still under development.

Steam locomotives pulled rail cars along metal tracks and steam also provided the power for vehicles such as the carriages English engineer Richard Trevithick built as early as 1801. American inventor Oliver Evans drove self-propelled dredging machines driven on streets in Philadelphia as early as 1805.

Steam would continue to provide power to many early automobiles. The Locomobile was a steamer and the best-selling automobile in the United States in 1901. The Stanley Steamer won worldwide acclaim in 1906 when it set a land speed record of 127.66 miles per hour on the sands at Ormond Beach, Florida.

So who really invented what we now accept as the modern automobile, the vehicle that Ogburn says had such a dramatic effect on culture and societies?

In 1895, American inventor and lawyer George B. Selden was granted a U.S. Patent on a car powered by an internal combustion engine, even though he wouldn't build such a vehicle until 1904 and even though such vehicles already were being built in Europe when Selden applied for his patent.

The internal combustion engine is a machine in which gasoline or another flammable liquid or gas mixes with air and is ignited; causing an explosion that pushes a piston down within a cylinder. As the piston moves, a pivoted rod connected to it turns a shaft, which, in turn, can be connected in a variety of ways to a wheel.

Pistons move up and down, driveshafts are turned, wheels go around and around and the vehicle that carries all of these things can be steered down the street.

Patents were granted on such engines in the United States in 1844 to Smart Perry of

18-19 KARL AND BERTA BENZ AND FAMILY NEEDED TWO OF KARL'S CARS TO GO ON THIS FAMILY OUTING IN 1891. BENZ WAS ONE OF THE INVENTORS OF THE MOTOR CAR.

19 TOP THESE ARE THE DRAWINGS BENZ INCLUDED IN HIS APPLICTION FOR THE PATENT, WHICH WAS AWARDED TO HIM IN 1886.

19 BOTTOM GOTTLIEB DAIMLER DRIVES HIS VIKTORIA IN 1886. THE VEHICLE WAS A HORSE CARRIAGE ON WHICH DAIMLER MOUNTED A MOTOR AND GEARS TO TURN THE WHEELS.

New York and in 1860 in France to a Belgian, Etienne Lenoir, who devised a method for using a battery, coil and spark plug to ignite the air/fuel mixture. Lenoir's was the first such engine to be commercially viable.

Then, in 1876, Nickolas August Otto, a German who had been experimenting with engines similar to those by Perry and Lenoir, devised a way to compress the fuel/air mixture inside the cylinder, enabling the engine to run more smoothly by having the cylinder make four strokes (rather then the former two) during the combustion cycle. Otto's piston moved to draw in the fuel/air mixture, then back to compress it before it was ignited, forcing the piston to move again. Finally, exhaust gases were forced out of the engine as the piston returned to its original position, ready to draw in another squirt of the fuel/air mixture.

Because Alphonse Beau de Rochas of Paris had described a similar four-stroke engine in 1862, Otto was not allowed to patent his Otto Silent Engine, and thus his design entered the public domain, where others worked to on improvements. Among them were Germans Karl Benz, Gottlieb Daimler and Rudolph Diesel. It was Diesel who developed an engine that used pressure rather than an electrical spark to ignite the fuel/air mixture.

In 1886, Benz mounted a two-cycle, gasoline-burning engine on a three-wheeled chassis and produced what is considered the first true motor vehicle. Later that same year, Daimler, who had worked for Otto and now was working with engineering genius Wilhelm Maybach, developed an improved four-stroke engine that he put on a four-wheeled carriage chassis and created what is largely accepted as the first true automobile. Daimler's motorcar was capable of traveling at speeds in excess of 10 miles per hour.

But it was Benz who was the first to build cars in quantity, selling more than one thousand four-wheelers by 1898, primarily in France, Germany and England, but even a few in the United States, where the bicycle-building brothers Charles and Frank Duryea read about Benz and his work and by 1893 were among the first Americans to

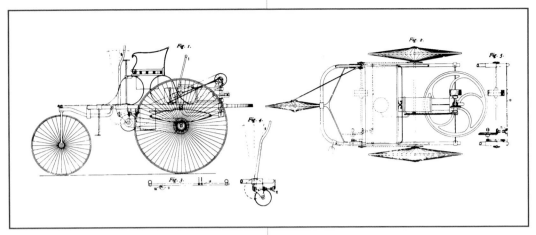

houette also allowed motorcars to carry even larger and more powerful engines.

Levassor proved the worthiness of this design by racing his car, and by winning. First, he defeated 12 other internal combustion cars as well as eight steam-powered vehicles in the 78-mile Paris to Rouen race in 1894, then driving without sleep for two days to beat 21 other vehicles in the race from Paris to Bordeaux and back

the following year.

France became the center of the auto industry, at least until 1904, when its production was surpassed by that in the United States.

Henry Ford wasn't the first American to build an automobile, but he revolutionized the process by which they were built, and in the process he put the world on wheels.

build motorcars for sale.

While Germans Benz and Daimler may have invented the motorcar, it was Emile Levassor of France who built the prototype for the sort of cars that would be driven for decades into the future. Levassor and coachbuilder René Panhard mounted an engine with its cylinders positioned vertically and at the front of the carriage instead of under its seats or at the rear. This new sil-

Although the Duryeas were first, and also won the first American auto race, held on the streets of Chicago, Alexander Winton, a young Scotsman who had immigrated to American and was building bicycles in Cleveland, Ohio, emerged as the most successful of the earliest American carmakers and auto racers, and proved the viability of the motorcar by driving one of his from Cleveland to New York in less than 48 hours. In 1901, Ransom E. Olds of Lansing, Michigan, who had been building cars since 1897, introduced his Curved-Dash Oldsmobile, which would become the first American car built in quantity as well as quality. Olds' factory produced some 2500 of the small runabouts in 1902, 4000 more the following year and more than 5500 in 1904. Olds' car featured precisely machined and interchangeable parts produced by Henry Leland, who had learned about producing parts in both high quality and high volumes while working at the U.S. Armory in Springfield, Massachusetts. Leland and a partner later opened a machine shop in Detroit, and Leland would become the engineering genius behind Cadillac, "the standard of the world," and then would found Lincoln. It was under Leland's reign at Cadillac that Charles Kettering invented the self-starter in 1911. Until then, the internal combustion engine's crankshaft

20 AMERICAN AUTOMOTIVE PIONEER HENRY LELAND POSES WITH HIS PERSONAL CAR, A 1906 CADILLAC MODEL H COUPE OSCEOLA. LELAND BUILT THE ENGINES FOR THE FAMED CURVED DASH OLDSMOBILES, THEN FOUNDED HIS OWN CAR COMPANY, CADILLAC, IN 1902. LELAND LATER SOLD CADILLAC TO WHAT WOULD BECOME GENERAL MOTORS AND IN 1920 FOUNDED ANOTHER CAR COMPANY, LINCOLN, THAT HE LATER SOLD TO FORD.

20-21 THE MODEL R BECAME FAMOUS AS THE CURVED DASH OLDSMOBILE AND WAS THE FIRST AMERICAN CAR PRODUCED IN QUANTITY. THE COMPANY SOLD 2100 OF ITS RUNABOUTS IN 1902, 4000 A YEAR LATER (SHOWN IS ONE OF THE 1903 MODELS) AND MORE THAN 5500 IN 1904.

had to be hand-cranked to get the car running, and it could be a dirty if not dangerous proposition. Kettering had developed an electric motor for use on cash registers and he adapted it to turn over a car's engine, thereby ending the brief popularity of electric cars that drew their power not from petroleum-burning engines but from storage batteries. Despite their limited range, such cars had been especially popular with women drivers.

21 TOP IN 1905, TWO CURVE DASH OLDSMOBILES - OLD SCOUT AND OLD STEADY - RACED FROM NEW YORK TO PORTLAND, OREGON TO PROMOTE THE GOOD ROADS CONVENTION. DWIGHT HUSS AND MILFORD WIGLE WON $1,000 BY COMPETING THE JOURNEY IN OLD SCOUT IN 45 DAYS, FINISHING SEVERAL DAYS AHEAD OF PERCY MEGARGEL AND BARTON STANCHFIELD.

The person who truly applied mass production techniques to the building of automobiles was Henry Ford, who built his first Quadricycle in 1896 and finally earned financial backing to start a car company by upsetting the famous Alexander Winton in a race in 1901.

By 1908 Ford's company was successful enough that he could realize his dream of building an inexpensive car available to the masses.

Painted black because that color dried more quickly, Ford's Model T flowed along his assembly line at the rate of as many as 1000 a day. This was a stark contrast to auto manufacturing in Europe, where craftsman and coachbuilders constructing cars one at a time was still the norm. Many European companies sent engineers to Michigan to study Ford's production operation.

By 1913, the last year of full-scale auto production in Europe before war wracked the continent, more than two-thirds of the world's cars were being built in the United States and more than half of those were

Model T Fords. The Model T was the workhorse among horseless carriages. It could go seemingly everywhere, and it did. It won races across the North American continent, became a best-selling car even in Europe, where Ford's British branch was that country's largest automaker.

When an earthquake in 1923 shattered the railroad line between Tokyo and Yokohama, the Japanese government ordered 1000 Model Ts to transport passengers. (Ford and General Motors both set up auto plants in Japan enjoyed near monopolies until late in the 1930s, when Japan acted to encourage domestic automakers.)

Some 125,000 Model Ts were called into service to carry Allied troops in World War I and even Lawrence forsook his camels to use Ford's cars to transport troops across the Middle Eastern desert.

The needs of wartime military supplies encouraged European automakers to modernize their production facilities.

After the war, Citroën used more modern production methods to launch the Type A Torpedo in 1919. Automotive historian

James Flink notes that the Torpedo sold for about a quarter of the price of the typical pre-war European car and that in 1920 Citroën sold almost 20,000 Torpedoes, making it Europe's first mass-produced and popularly priced model and forcing other European automakers to produce similar vehicles. Britain's Austin Seven was such a car, and was built not only in England but elsewhere, even Japan and America, under license.

22 TWO YEARS AFTER ITS INTRODUCTION, THE MODEL T WAS RESTYLED FOR 1911 WITH NEW FENDERS, RADIATOR, WHEELS, AXLES, STEEL INSTEAD OF WOOD BODIES AND EVEN A NEW ENGINE.

22-23 BY 1919, ELECTRIC (RATHER THAN HAND-CRANK) STARTERS WERE STANDARD ON FORD'S MODEL T SEDANS AND OPTIONAL ON OPEN CARS SUCH AS THIS RUNABOUT ROADSTER. THE ELECTRIC PACKAGE INCLUDED FORD'S FIRST INSTRUMENT PANEL, WITH AMMETER, CHOKE AND IGNITION/LIGHT SWITCH AND A PLACE FOR A DEALER TO INSTALL A SPEEDOMETER.

23 BOTTOM HENRY FORD SHOWS ONE OF HIS CARS TO AMERICAN ESSAYIST JOHN BURROUGHS (FRONT SEAT) AND THOMAS EDISON. BEFORE BUILDING CARS, HENRY FORD WORKED FOR THE DETROIT BRANCH OF THE EDISON ELECTRIC COMPANY. IT WAS EDISON WHO ENCOURAGED FORD TO PURSUE HIS AUTOMOTIVE DREAMS.

But the post-war recession was hard on European auto sales, and it didn't help European automakers that Ford and GM were building more cars on foreign soil that French and German automakers were producing combined. In their massive book Cars 1930-2000, the trio of authors points out that no European automaker had the potential to produce 100,000 cars a year in the decade of the 1920s

THE BODIES CARRIED by Ford's Model T and most of the other early motorcars were little more than flat-cornered boxes placed to cover mechanical parts or to hold the driver and passengers. But style was coming quickly to the streets.

Under the flamboyant William Durant and then with skilled businessman Alfred

Sloan in charge, General Motors challenged Ford's domination by combining several automakers under one umbrella and by offering its customers something other than a single and all-black model.

In 1926 GM hired Harley J. Earl, who had been building custom cars for Hollywood stars, and within a year he had established the first true auto company design department, GM's Art and Color Section. Earl's 1927 LaSalle was widely considered to be the first series-built production car that had been consciously designed rather than merely engineered.

Particularly in Europe, engineers had built experimental cars to explore the possibilities of enhancing the aerodynamics of the motorcar. But in 1938 Earl would design

the first automotive "dream car." His Buick Y-Job, named after a term for experimental aircraft, was a concept car that explored the potential for aesthetic automotive design. In addition to its enhanced design, the car had an electric-operated power convertible top and power windows.

Much like Earl's father's operation in southern California, European coachbuilders had been crafting custom bodies for expensive cars for wealthy clients for many years, just as they had made horse-drawn carriages and coaches before the horseless age of transportation began.

Isotta Fraschini, Hispano-Suiza, Maybach, Alfa Romeo and many other automakers built stout chassis on which coachbuilders from Italy, Germany, France,

England and elsewhere created custom bodies for their clients.

Though much fewer in number compared to the vehicles of mass production, these works by companies such as Saoutchik, Touring, Zagato, Murphy, Le Baron and many more were exquisite in their design and detail.

But these hand-built cars required constant maintenance. The chauffeur's work was a full-time job, whether he was driving or oiling or polishing or tinkering with finicky mechanical parts.

For the automobile to have a wider audience, it needed to be easier to operate and to maintain. It also needed to have a passenger compartment that was closed from inclement elements.

Through the 1920s automakers made such improvements. Hand-cranked engines gave way to electric starters. Enhanced lighting made driving at night less arduous.

Brakes were improved. Tire technology advanced. So did road building, with Italy's autostrade of the late 1920s becoming the prototype for the super highway of the future. More powerful engines now had a place to be exercised.

"The automobile was at last emerging for good from its initial role as a rich man's plaything," write the authors of Cars. "Women drivers, hitherto a rarity outside the United Sates, were becoming more numerous in other countries...."

However, they continue, "The state of the art in 1930 was not vastly different from that of 1920."

But things were improving. Engines were becoming more powerful. The transmission of that power to the wheels was smoother. Suspensions were improved. Cars were getting better, and a new wind was getting ready to blow across the automotive horizon.

24-25 CESARE ISOTTA AND ORESTE FRASCHINI STARTED BUILDING CARS IN MILAN, ITALY IN 1899. IN 1910, ISOTTA FRASCHINI WAS THE FIRST AUTOMAKER TO EQUIP ITS CARS WITH FOUR-WHEEL BRAKES. ITS VEHICLES, SUCH AS THIS 1929 MODEL, WERE LARGE LUXURY CARS SOLD AS ROLLING CHASSIS, COVERED WITH COACH-BUILT BODIES AND FAVORED BY ROYALTY AND MOVIE STARS.

25 TOP HISPANO-SUIZA WAS THE NAME SWISS-BORN MARC BIRKIGT GAVE TO THE AUTOMOBILE-MAKING COMPANY HE AND A PARTNER FOUNDED IN BARCELONA, SPAIN IN 1904. IN THIS IMAGE CAN BE ADMIRED THE MODEL H6B PRODUCED FROM 1922 TO 1933.

26-27 VOLKSWAGEN REKINDLED AN ICON AND A RETRO REVOLUTION IN 1999 WHEN IT LAUNCHED THE NEW BEETLE, A CAR THAT UPDATED CLASSIC STYLING CUES AND APPLIED THEM TO A MODERN CHASSIS.

28-29 THE EXOTIC F40 WAS THE LAST CAR UNVEILED BY ENZO FERRARI BEFORE HIS DEATH. THE CAR WAS NOT ONLY THE MOST OUTRAGEOUSLY DESIGNED FERRARI TO DATE, IT ALSO WAS THE FASTEST.

30-31 THE Z3 WAS BMW'S MODERN INTERPRETATION OF THE CLASSIC EUROPEAN ROADSTER, THOUGH THIS NEW GERMAN SPORTS CAR WAS BUILT IN THE UNITED STATES FOR ALL MARKETS.

A Fresh Wind:
Aerodynamics rounds
off those boxy bodies

1932/1944

Driving was a dirty and dangerous chore in the early days of the automobile.

Engines started with hand-operated cranks that often kicked back, breaking hands and fingers. Early engines spewed oil and exhaust on driver and passengers. About all the pioneering automobilists had for protection were goggles, gloves and coverall "dusters." These truly were horseless carriages, little more than a wheeled frame with an engine, a fuel tank, a seat and a steering tiller (eventually to be replaced by the steering wheel).

Before long, however, wood or metal boxes were placed around the mechanical components. Soon, a larger box was built around the seats that held the driver and passengers, sometimes with a canopy-like cover that offered some shade but very little protection from the elements, whether weather or road dust and debris. In time, lights, fenders, spare wheels and storage boxes for tools needed to keep the car running were attached to the various structures. Eventually the entire passenger compartment was enclosed with a hard roof and glass windows. But except for the curved fenders, round light fixtures and perhaps a small peak to the metallic box that covered the engine, the lines of the early motorcars were flat, straight and upright. There were exceptions (there always are). In 1899, Frenchman Camille Jenatzy became the first to exceed 100 kilometers per hour (62 miles per hour) when he built an electric-powered car that basically looked like a torpedo mounted on a four-wheeled frame.

Since late in 1898, Jenatzy and fellow Frenchman Gaston de Chasseloup-Laubat had been trading the speed record back and forth between their electric vehicles.

Chasseloup-Laubat's Jeantaud also was amazingly aerodynamic, though tall, and looked like an inverted canoe with a knife-like nose and a tapered tail. As their back and forth pursuit of speed escalated — to nearly 63… more than 66… nearly 70…and then to more than 91 kilometers per hour, Jenatzy finally built his torpedo-like vehicle, Jamais Contente (Never Satisfied) and used its aerodynamic advantages to help shatter the 100 km/h barrier with a top speed of 105.26 (65.79 miles per hour).

While the two Frenchmen fought their high-speed battle, most pioneering automakers were busy simply trying to develop and build cars that were mechanically and perhaps even commercially viable to be concerned much with style or significant speed. Besides, any speed faster than a horse-drawn carriage was considered downright reckless by many people.

Even the custom coachbuilders and their wealthy clients would be concerned more at first with luxury, preferring show to go.

Certainly those who raced cars would come to realize the advantage of reducing frontal surface, of replacing vertical surfaces with more streamlined shapes and of lowering their car's center of gravity, but their primary mission was to prove to the public the validity of the motorcar as an efficient, reliable and perhaps even rapid means of transport. Jenatzy's speed record would stand for nearly three years, though when it was shattered, it was by nearly 15 km/h (10 mph).

Hungarian engineer Paul Jaray undertook if not necessarily the first then certainly the most significant early study of how aerodynamic improvements could enhance the motorcar – just as they had watercraft and aircraft.

From 1914 until 1923, Jaray was a chief designer of Zeppelin airships, but he also used his wind tunnel to experiment with automotive designs. By the early 1920s, he was building experimental cars with teardrop shapes instead of flat surfaces. He also devised mathematical formulae to predict how much horsepower would be needed to overcome aerodynamic resistance and achieve specific speeds.

In addition to his work in Europe, Jaray established an American company, Jaray Streamline Corporation, and soon his work was influencing automotive designs on both sides of the Atlantic.

A Fresh Wind: Aerodynamics rounds off those boxy bodies

33 THE CORD 810 HAD SUCH A LOW STANCE THAT DESIGNER GORDON BUEHRIG COULD DISDAIN THE USE OF RUNNING BOARDS TO CREATE AN AMAZINGLY MODERN VEHICLE.

35 IN 1933, GENERAL MOTORS, OLDSMOBILE BRAND ISSUED A SALES BROCHURE PROMOTING THE ELEGANCE OF ITS NEW OLDSMOBILE 8 TWO-DOOR CONVERTIBLE COUPE.

1932/1944

FIAT 508 BALILLA

The industrialization of Italy truly began to roll in the final years of the 19th century when Giovanni Battista Pirelli started his tire company, Camillo Olivette began building typewriters, Guido Donegani created the Montecatini chemical firm and Giovanni Agnelli and associates founded the *Societa Anonima Fabbrica Italiana de Automobili Torino* – FIAT — to build motorcars.

Fiat was founded on July 1, 1899 and before the end of the year had built its first car, powered by a 3.5-horsepower, two-cylinder engine. Within two years, Fiat was among the first to establish modern automotive architecture by placing engines at the front of the carriage with seats for the driver and passengers toward the rear.

Under Agnelli's leadership and an early move from craft-based workshops to mass production techniques, Fiat dominated the Italian automotive market; its cars accounted for 80 percent of auto sales in Italy by the outbreak of World War I, when Fiat's engineering efforts expanded greatly as it built aircraft, ships, railroad locomotives and trucks.

To expand its auto production, Fiat commissioned engineer Giacomo Matte-Trucco to design a new factory on the south side of Turin (Torino). His Lingotto was a futuristic masterpiece. Completed in 1922, it was Italy's first building made from reinforced concrete. Its five floors stretched some two kilometers in length and were built around a series of interior courtyards that were open to the sky. Topping this strong structure was not a normal sort of roof, but a rooftop automotive test track with paved lanes that looped around the full length of the building and featured banked turns at each end.

In 1932, Fiat launched two new and important models, the 518 Ardita and the 508 Balilla.

The Ardita was a high-performance sedan, capable of speeds of 115 km/h (more than 70 miles per hour) and was Fiat's first car designed with an independent radiator grille.

But the breakthrough car that year would be the Balilla, which translates from the Italian as "plucky little one."

The Balilla looked more like an American import than a typical European motorcar, and it would do for Italy what Henry Ford's Model T had done for America: it put the average family on wheels. No longer was motoring an exclusive enjoyment for the well to do. Many families could afford a Balilla, a compact vehicle that was priced at less than 11,000 lire, yet had a durable, short-stroke, 20-horsepower, four-cylinder engine that could propel it to speeds of 85 km/h (more than 50 mph) while using only

eight liters of fuel per 100 km. "Tariffa minima," Italians proclaimed at the car's low cost of operation.

The Balilla was available in three versions: a two-door coupe (Berlina), a torpedo (a slightly more streamlined touring car), or a spider (convertible).

A 36-horsepower, two-seat Sport version, the 508S, was added for the 1934 model year and soon coachbuilders such as Ghia, with its Millemiglia coupe, and Touring, with its low-slung roadster, were creating their own racy bodies for the chassis.

Even with Italy's economy still depressed, Fiat sold some 41,000 Balillas in the first two years of car's production. The Balilla would be built under license in Germany, Poland, Czechoslovakia, Spain and France. Its successor, the 1937 Fiat 1100, or *Nuova Balilla*, would provide the basis for a line of Fiats that would remain in production until 1955.

38 TOP A CONVERTIBLE JOINED THE FIAT BALILLA FAMILY IN 1937. THE BALILLA COULD BE PURCHASED WITH COUPE, TOURING CAR OR CABRIOLET BODYWORK.

38-39 SIDE CURTAINS PROVIDED PROTECTION FROM INCLEMENT WEATHER WHEN THE BALILLA'S CONVERTIBLE TOP WAS UP.

39 IN 1934, MARCELLO DUDOVICH'S ADVERTISING POSTER PROCLAIMED THE NEW BALILLA FOR EVERYONE, AND ESPECIALLY FOR A "LADY OF CLASS."

TATRA 77

esseldorfer Wagenbau-Fabriks-Gesellschaft began building railroad coaches in 1853. By 1897 it was producing central Europe's first automobile, the Präsident (President), designed by engineer Hans Ledwinka and powered by a 2-cylinder Benz engine. By 1900 the company was building its own engines.

After World War I, the Austro-Hungarian Empire was carved up and the former Nesseldorf became Koprivnice, Czechoslovakia. The car company took its new name from the Tatra Mountains, the range where it had tested many of its products.

Ledwinka's first Tatra was the Tatra 11, notable because it was built around an 11-cm (4.3-inch) steel-tube spine rather than a standard chassis and featured independent suspension. Ledwinka's engines ranged from an air-cooled boxer 4-cylinder to 6-cylinders and even a V12.

Tatra later built the 70, a luxury limousine, and in 1932 introduced the 57, a handsome sedan.

But what made Ledwinka and the Czech automaker most famous was the Tatra 77 introduced in 1934. The Tatra 77 was a pioneer in unit-body motorcar architecture, but what really set it apart was its long-tailed, high-finned aerodynamic design with an air-cooled V8 mounted behind the rear axle. Ledwinka and his associate Erich Uberlacker were convinced that putting the engine at the rear would enhance aerodynamics, would reduce power losses inherent with a long driveshaft and would improve traction because the engine's weight was close to the wheels that powered the car.

40 THE TATRA 77 HAD NO REAR WINDOW. HOWEVER, ITS DRIVER COULD GLIMPSE THE ROAD BEHIND THROUGH LOUVERS ON THE LARGE ENGINE COVER, THOUGH EVEN THAT VIEW WAS SPLIT BY THE CAR'S LONG REAR TAIL FIN.

41 WHILE THE PURSUIT OF IMPROVED AERODYNAMICS RESTRICTED THE DRIVER'S REAR VIEW, THE WRAPAROUND WINDSHIELD AND A LOW FRONT HOOD PROVIDED A GOOD LOOK AT THE ROAD AHEAD OF THE 1934 TATRA 77.

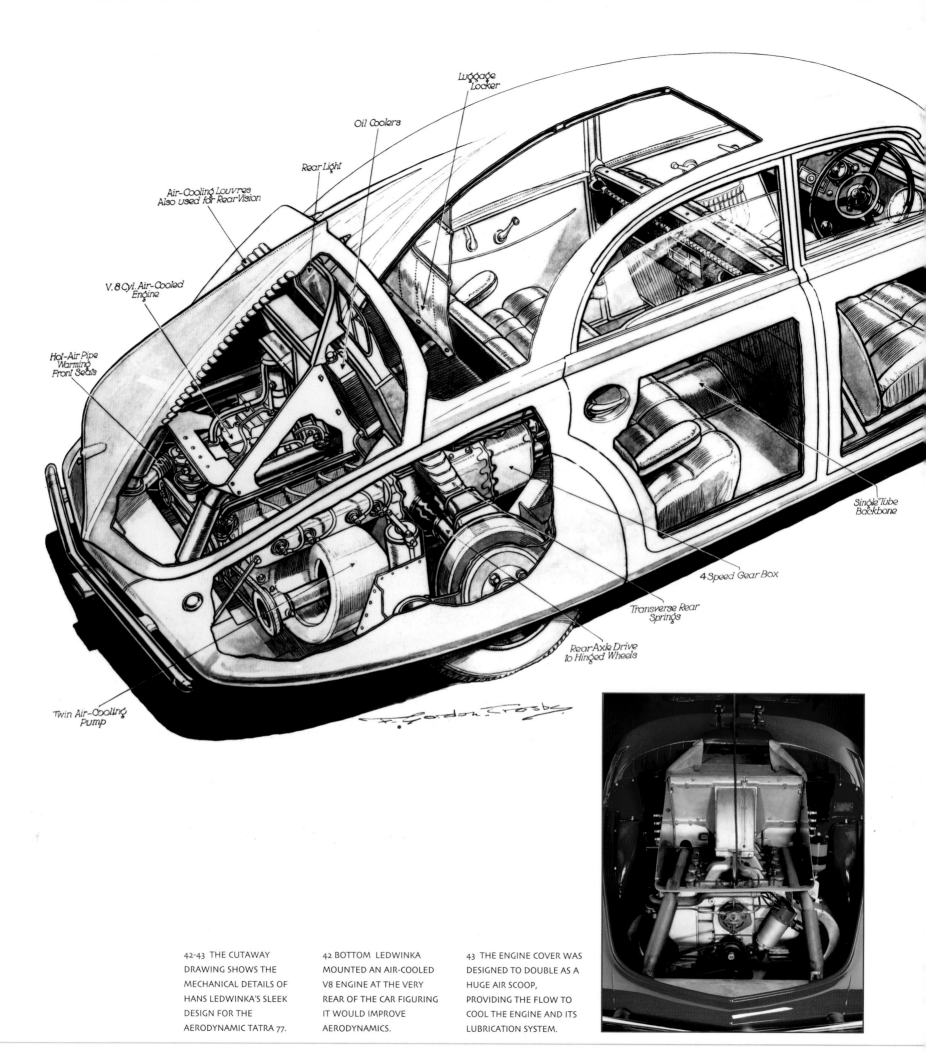

Luggage
Locker

Oil Coolers

Rear Light

Air-Cooling Louvres
Also used for Rear Vision

V.8 Cyl. Air-Cooled
Engine

Hot-Air Pipe
Warming
Front Seats

Twin Air-Cooling
Pump

F. Gordon Crosby

Single Tube
Backbone

4 Speed Gear Box

Transverse Rear
Springs

Rear Axle Drive
to Hinged Wheels

42-43 THE CUTAWAY
DRAWING SHOWS THE
MECHANICAL DETAILS OF
HANS LEDWINKA'S SLEEK
DESIGN FOR THE
AERODYNAMIC TATRA 77.

42 BOTTOM LEDWINKA
MOUNTED AN AIR-COOLED
V8 ENGINE AT THE VERY
REAR OF THE CAR FIGURING
IT WOULD IMPROVE
AERODYNAMICS.

43 THE ENGINE COVER WAS
DESIGNED TO DOUBLE AS A
HUGE AIR SCOOP,
PROVIDING THE FLOW TO
COOL THE ENGINE AND ITS
LUBRICATION SYSTEM.

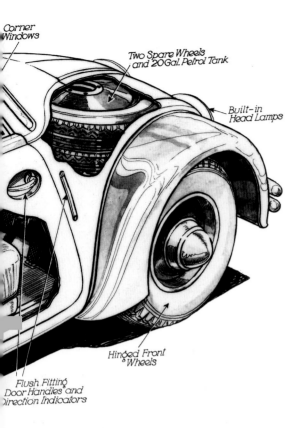

Corner Windows

Two Spare Wheels and 20 Gal. Petrol Tank

Built-in Head Lamps

Hinged Front Wheels

Flush Fitting Door Handles and Direction Indicators

To modern eyes, the Tatra 77 looks as if someone took a Volkswagen Beetle and converted it into a stretched limousine, adding a tall dorsal tail fin. (Tatra would file suit against Volkswagen, claiming its design had, indeed, been copied. It would take until 1967 for Tatra to win a judgment of some three million German marks).

The Tatra 77 was built on a Tatra 11-style tube, except this one forked near its rear to hold the V8 engine. And this tube was long; the car had a 122.8-inch (312-cm) wheelbase. The car itself stretched 212 inches (5.4 meters) from its blunt nose to the tip of its tail. The car had a revolutionary and steeply ranked and wrap-around windshield and the front trunk, which contained the spare tire, chassis lubrication system and room for luggage, curved abruptly. This gave the driver an excellent view of the road ahead. But the Tatra 77 had no rear window. Instead, its rear section featured a long, sloping engine cover with a tall single fin designed to enhance stability at higher speeds. Thus, the driver had no view of what was behind the car.

The Tatra 77 was powered by a 3.0-liter V8 that provided 60 hp. With the car's aerodynamic qualities – including a coefficient of drag of just 0.21 – the car was capable of speeds up to 85 mph (more than 135 km/h). A year later, the engine was enlarged to 3.4 liters and 70 hp for the Tatra 77A, which had third headlamp.

The three-lamp design carried over to the Tatra 87, the company's last pre-war car, which was in production from 1937 until 1950. This model had a shorter wheelbase and lighter engine and, at least in prototype form, featured an unusual cockpit with the driving position in the middle of the front seat.

Tatra's string of exotically streamlined cars ended with the Tatra 603, which was in production until 1975.

CITROËN TRACTION

André Citroën is credited with many things, among them introducing mass production to the European auto industry, as well as being the first with all-steel bodies, with car insurance for his customers, and for making front-wheel drive a practical way to propel an automobile. Traction Avant is French for front drive ("traction in front").

Citroën was the grandson of wealthy Dutchman Roelof Limoenman, who changed the family name from Limoenman to Citroën, and was the son of a Paris diamond dealer Levi Bernard Citroën. André studied engineering until 1898, and then started a company that produced gears in a design patented by his uncle. By 1908 Citroën was consulting with automaker Mors and eventually took over the bankrupt company.

Citroën visited the United States to learn about more efficient production techniques and learned much while visiting Henry Ford's car making complex. Citroën built armaments for France during World War I, and afterward converted his factory to automotive production. The Citroën badge features what appear to be double chevrons but the design actually

44 CITROËN'S LINEUP FOR 1934 INCLUDED THE 7, FIRST IN THE LINE OF TRACTION AVANT MODELS, AS WELL AS THE 11, SIMILAR TO THE 7 BUT SLIGHTLY LARGER, AND THE 22, A PROTOTYPE WITH A 100-HORSEPOWER V8 ENGINE.

44-45 THE LOW-SLUNG DESIGN AND SINGLE STEEL-SHEET BODY OF THE 1934 CITROËN TRACTION AVANT ELIMINATED THE NEED FOR RUNNING BOARDS.

45 TOP ANDRE CITROËN (FAR RIGHT) VISITED THE UNITED STATES TO LEARN MORE EFFICIENT AUTOMOTIVE PRODUCTION METHODS FROM HENRY FORD (LEFT).

7 4 CYL. **11** 4 CYL. **22** 8 CYL.

CITROËN
TRACTION AVANT

AVANT

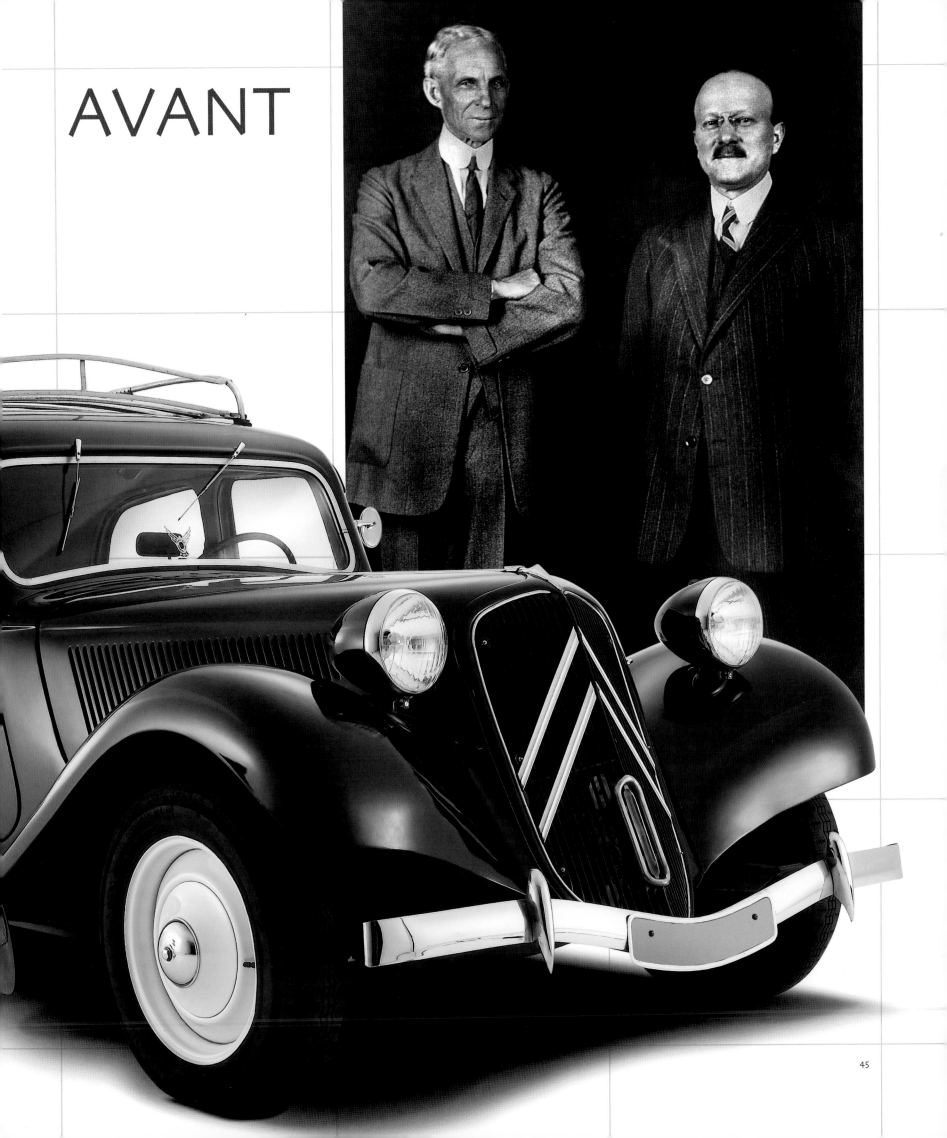

is meant to recall the teeth on the gears his first company produced.

Citroën's first cars were conventional for the time, but with mass production they were very numerous, and Citroën was eager to draw attention to them with various publicity stunts, including international endurance drives through Asia, Africa and North America, sky-writing airplanes and putting the company's name up in lights on the Eiffel Tower.

In 1934, Citroën launched the Traction Avant, a rakish, low sedan officially known as the Citroën 7CV, or "Seven" for short, which used its front-wheel power to pull the car forward instead of its rear wheels to push it. Front-wheel drive had been used on some luxury cars, but Citroën thought its "road-holding" capabilities could be applied to the mass market. The 7CV had a monocoque steel body with a separate front subframe that held the engine, trans-

mission and suspension. With its engine's weight over the wheels providing traction, front-wheel drive was sure-footed. With its wheels pushed toward the car's corners and with a lower center of gravity, thanks in part to the lack of a long, central driveshaft running between front and rear axles, the architecture also provided a lower center of gravity.

The lack of a tunnel through the passenger compartment also meant a roomier, more com-

fortable interior for those riding along. However, like so many businesses of the era, Citroën suffered the financial shock wave that began with the U.S. stock market crash of 1929. Citroën was virtually broke when he died in 1935, soon after completing a new factory to build the 7CV. To get the car into production, the tire-making giant Michelin had to step in and take a majority interest in Citroën's car-making company. In fact, Michelin underwrote

the Seven's launch. Powered by a 1.3-liter 4-cylinder engine, the Traction Avant was slow in accelerating, but could achieve a top speed of 60 mph (nearly 100 km/h). Citroën would continue its Traction Avant series well into the 1950s. By the end of the production run, more than 750,000 front-wheel drive cars had been sold, including the II Legère and long-wheelbase 11 Normale, the first cars to ride on Michelin's revolutionary radial tires.

46 THE GRILLE OF THE 1934 TRACTION AVANT WAS EMBLAZONED WITH THE DOUBLE CHEVRON EMBLEM, A REMINDER OF CITROËN'S HERITAGE AS A MANUFACTURER OF GEARS.

47 TRACTION AVANT MEANS THE FRONT WHEELS BOTH STEER AND PROPEL THE CAR, LEAVING MORE ROOM IN THE REAR OF THE VEHICLE TO ACCOMMODATE PASSENGERS, LUGGAGE AND THE SPARE TIRE.

MERCEDES-BENZ 540K

T he automobile companies founded by Gottlieb Daimler and Karl Benz combined in 1926. Together, they would produce some of the most spectacular vehicles of the era.

Arriving at Mercedes-Benz about this same time was Ferdinand Porsche. Porsche stayed only a couple of years before leaving to open his own engineering company – and to create not only spectacular Auto Union racing machines but the people's car, the Volkswagen, which would surpass Henry Ford's Model T as the best-selling vehicle of all time. Though he wasn't there long, Porsche had a significant impact on Mercedes-Benz, both in terms of its awesome racing cars and its amazing road machines, those produced while he was there and those built on their foundation after he left.

Daimler's son, Paul, had worked to apply aero engine supercharging to passenger car motors.

Combining supercharging with Porsche's engines and automotive design genius created new horizons.

Mercedes-Benz 26/120/180 Model S was technically a sports car, though much longer, larger and heavier than what modern eyes accept as a sports car.

Porsche created an alloy-block, six-cylinder engine with overhead camshaft and when supercharged this 6.8-liter engine generated 180 horsepower, propelling the large Mercedes-Benz S to speeds of more than 100 miles per hour (160 km/h). Only some 300 of these S series cars were built, and many were used primarily for racing, with victories in everything from Grands Prix to the Tourist Trophy and from mountain climbs to the Mille Miglia. The engine was enlarged to 7.1 liters for the SS, and special short wheelbase and lightweight versions, SSK and SSKL, respectively, were propelled by as much as 300 horsepower.

Porsche also developed an inline eight-cylinder engine for Mercedes-Benz racing cars. After he left, the straight-eight architecture was used in a new line of road cars that carried forth the heritage of the S cars but now combined relatively sporty dynamics – as sporty as a 5000-pound car could be in the 1930s – with truly elegant, even timeless proportions and luxurious amenities.

First came the 500K (K for kompressor, the German word for compressor, the technical term for supercharger) in 1934. The 500K was powered by a 5.0-liter eight-cylinder engine that pumped out 160 horsepower, enough to carry the large and elegant two-seater to speeds of more than 100 miles per hour (165 km/h) on its all-independent suspension. In 1934, the engine was enlarged to 5.4 liters for the 540K, with 180 horsepower and a top speed of 170 km/h, a speed easily attainable on Germany's new autobahn highway system. To maintain such speeds,

Mercedes equipped the 500K and 540K with four-speed transmissions. But what truly set the cars apart were their designs. Engines were mounted behind the front axle so hoods were incredibly long and provided a large palette for bright work trim. Front fenders were large curved-metal sculptures that flowed back toward the car's sloping tail section, which like the engine cover served as a canvas for bright and artistic trim.

CHRYSLER AIRFLOW

For some 20 years, Carl Breer, Fred Zeder and Owen Skelton were Chrysler's famed "Three Musketeers," the trio of engineers responsible for the line of vehicles built by Walter P. Chrysler's company. Like other cars of the era, Chryslers were basically two square-cornered steel boxes carried on a ladder-framed chassis. The large box protected passengers from foul weather and road debris. The smaller one covered the engine. Fenders were curved, but not much else. Breer, who had built his own steam car as a teenager and who studied engineering at Stanford University, became head of research at Chrysler in 1925.

He also became intrigued by airplanes and wondered if aeronautics might improve automotive efficiency. Breer contacted aviation pioneer Orville Wright, who suggested that

FLORIDA HIGHLIGHTS

SKETCHED IN AND AROUND MIAMI BY FLOYD DAVIS

THE NATION'S SOCIAL CAPITAL moves South. And social leaders coming for rest find themselves caught in a furious round of revelry...the gayest season Florida has seen since the Twenties.

LONG ISLAND MALLET STARS arrive *via Airflow* to try the turf of Florida's leading polo center ...the scenic Phipps Fields at Gulf Stream. The Sunday games are always gala events.

YACHTSMAN CARTER divides his life between boat and DeSoto Airflow III. "Every one," he says, "should have the safety of Airflow's genuine hydraulic brakes, steel unit frame-and-body."

THE MOTORING THRILL THAT'S STILL UNMATCHED

TWO YEARS AGO, DeSoto introduced the famous Airflow car...predicted that *all* cars would follow its lead.

Today, its scientific weight distribution...equalized springing...seating for six...are still the most talked-about features in cars. And many are the efforts to copy them.

But any DeSoto owner will quickly tell you...America's lowest-priced Airflow car is *still* years ahead.

Spend a few minutes with DeSoto's Airflow III. Feel the utter relaxation of travel that's silent, swift and sure ...on any road, at any speed. Test the economy of its Gas-Saver Transmission. See the charming intimacy of its custom-styled interiors...the new beauty of its extended front and modern trunk.

Sedan or coupe, $1095, list at factory, Detroit. Special equipment extra. Ask about the new 6% Time Payment Plan.

DE SOTO Product of the Chrysler Corporation

Airflow III
Companion Car to Airstream DeSoto

MIAMI'S SPORTING calendar is studded with sailing events, which reach their climax in the annual St. Petersburg Race, held late in March.

DANCING AT THE DEAUVILLE...and demonstrating the mode in wide-cut evening frocks. Slippers are in vivid reds, greens and blues.

Breer build a small wind tunnel and use it to test wooden, scale-model cars. He did, and among the discoveries was that the typical car had better aerodynamic qualities when placed in the tunnel backward. Breer also consulted with Norman Bel Geddes, who had done some groundbreaking work in aerodynamic automotive design. Experimenting with tapered shapes to better manage airflow around and over the car, Breer, Skelton and Zeder designed a prototype vehicle, the Trifon Special, which was named the Airflow after Walter P. Chrysler approved production for 1934 The Airflow's prominent nose had the parabolic curve of an airplane wing, with headlamps not added on but recessed into the bodywork, and with front fenders that presented a similar wing-like profile.

The windshield was laid back into the dashboard of a passenger compartment and trunk

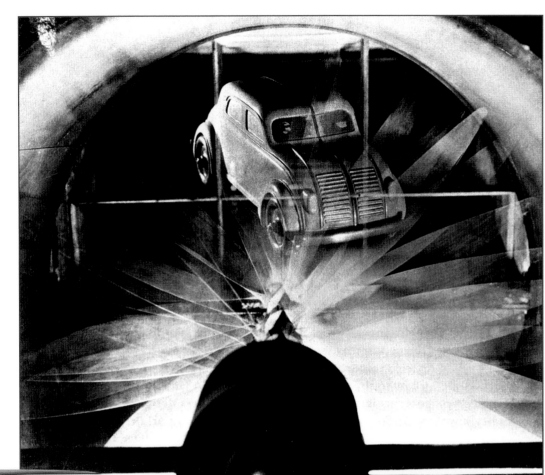

that had a smooth, tapered, teardrop design that was emphasized by covers over the rear wheels. The car was just as revolutionary under its sleek skin. A cage-like steel frame provided structure. To show just how strong the car was, one was pushed over a 100-foot cliff, then was started and driven away under its own power.

To provide sufficient room for passengers within the tapered shape, the engine – a 122-horsepower, 4.9-liter straight eight powerplant – was moved from its typical position between the front axle and passenger compartment to a position over the axle, thus starting a trend that continued through subsequent decades. The aerodynamic car set speed and endurance records at Daytona Beach and averaged more than 18 miles per gallon in a coast-to-coast drive across the United States.

Walter P. Chrysler particularly liked the car's smooth ride and its roomy interior, which featured much wider seats with exposed steel frames, chrome trim on the dashboard and rubber floor mats. He went so far as to call the radically shaped Airflow "the first motorcar since the invention of the automobile."

History might not argue with him, although Chrysler's customers argued with their money. They found the car too radical for their tastes. Although the Airflow was available in five configurations, Chrysler's sales figures plummeted and its DeSoto brand, which only had the Airflow in its dealerships, had its sales drop nearly in half. The Airflow underwent nose jobs and other styling and interior changes in each of the three subsequent years, but the car-buying public simply wasn't ready for such a vehicle and production ended after 1937.

52 CHRYSLER'S AIRFLOW WAS BUILT IN TWO-DOOR COUPE AND FOUR-DOOR SEDAN CONFIGURATIONS, INCLUDING THE LONG-WHEELBASE IMPERIAL AIRFLOW MODEL. SOME VERSIONS OF THE AIRFLOW CAME WITH AN INLINE SIX-CYLINDER ENGINE.

52-53 RACER HARRY HARTZ ESTABLISHED NUMEROUS SPEED AND ENDURANCE RECORDS IN AN AIRFLOW COUPE. THE CAR'S AERODYNAMIC LINES ALSO ENABLED HARTZ TO DRIVE FROM COAST-TO-COAST WHILE AVERAGING MORE THAN 18 MILES PER GALLON.

CORD 810

54-55 THE LOUVERED HOOD OF THE CORD 810 MAY REMIND SOME PEOPLE OF A CASKET, BUT AMONG AMERICAN CAR COLLECTORS, WHETHER COUPE, SEDAN OR CONVERTIBLE, THE 810 REMAINS A CAR "TO DIE FOR."

55 TOP E.L. CORD WAS AMONG THE YOUNGEST OF AMERICAN AUTOMAKERS AND WAS THE FIRST TO FEATURE FRONT-WHEEL DRIVE ON A PRODUCTION CAR, THE CORD L29. A SIMILAR DRIVELINE WAS USED IN THE STUNNING CORD 810.

Errett Lobban "E.L." Cord had made and lost three fortunes by the time he turned 21 years of age. But four years later he had his own auto agency in Chicago and before long investors in the Auburn Automobile Company recruited him to try to lead the company out of debt.

Auburn's predecessor, the Eckhart Carriage Company, was founded in 1874 when Charles Eckhart left the Studebaker brothers and moved across Indiana to start his own carriage-building company. When Charles retired, his sons Frank and Morris took over and in 1900 established the Auburn Automobile Company and built their first car, a one-cylinder, tiller-steered open runabout. By 1919 the company needed help from investors. Five years later, at the time when the 26-year-old Cord was brought in as general manager, production had slipped to only six cars a day. Within two years Cord was company president, had bought the Duesenberg company and assembled a staff that included brothers Fred and Augie Duesenberg as well as designer Gordon Buehrig.In 1929, just before the stock market crash, they launched the Duesenberg Model J, among the most elegant and fastest cars on the road and a car still highly sought after among classic car collectors. Cord also started building cars under his own name, and his first offering, the Cord L29, was the first American production car with front-wheel drive.

Then, for 1936, Cord had Buehrig design another American classic, the Cord 810, "as startling and lovely a car as had ever been designed," is how automotive authority Leon Mandel put it in his book on American cars.

The car originally was designed to be the "baby" Duesenberg, but was labeled as a Cord when it made its debut at the 1935 New York auto show.

"The 810 looked like no other car: so dramatically different was it that Buehrig took out a patent for 'a new, original and orna-

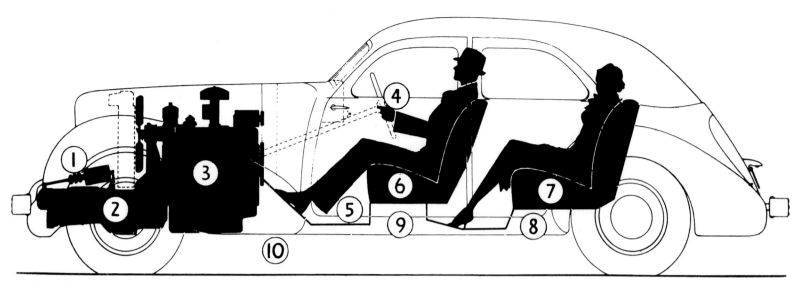

THE CORD FRONT DRIVE EMBODIES MORE NEW FEATURES that contribute to safety and comfort, than any other automobile

mental design for a car'," writes British design dean Penny Sparke, who adds that the 810 and its virtual twin, the supercharged 812, "were two of the most visually striking cars of the époque."

The car had an extended nose that covered the front-wheel drive's mechanical components and was set low between the front fenders. Those arching fenders had headlamps hidden within their bodywork, ready to be cranked into position from controls in the cockpit. The sleekly shaped cockpit was set behind a steeply raked windshield. Because the car was so low-slung, Buehrig's design disdained running boards. With a patterned aluminum dashboard, the car was as remarkable on the inside as on the outside. However, the car's most striking design feature was its long, coffin-shaped hood wrapped by a series of long, parallel and chromed bands.

The Cord 810 powered its front wheels with a V8 engine built by Lycoming, an Auburn subsidiary that made aviation and automobile engines. The 289-cubic-inch (4.8-liter) engine pumped out 125 hp, enough to propel the sleek car to a speed of 100 mph (160 km/h).

Then, for 1937, Cord offered the 812 model with its Lycoming V8 supercharged to 170 hp. But there were problems with the car's transaxle, which tried to jam four speeds into what had been a three-speed gearbox, and with an electro/hydraulic shift controller for which

insufficient time for development and testing time had been allowed.

Even with Cord's enthusiasm, and with some 3000 810 and 812 models in production, the company closed down in the summer of 1937. With kidnapping threats against his family, Cord

fled to England. He later returned to the United States and became prominent in the real estate business in California. But Cord left the car business in style, and years later, New York's Museum of Modern Art included the 810 in its showcase of significant automotive design.

56 TOP CORD PROCLAIMED THE SAFETY AND COMFORT PROVIDED BY THE FRONT-WHEEL DRIVE ARCHITECTURE OF ITS 1936 810 MODEL. THE PROFILE (LEFT) SHOWS THE ENGINE MOUNTED WITH THE TRANSMISSION EXTENDING IN FRONT OF THE FRONT WHEELS.

56-57 GORDON BUEHRIG WORKED FOR DETROIT COACHBUIDERS, THEN STYLED CARS FOR PACKARD AND IN HARLEY EARL'S STUDIO AT GENERAL MOTORS BEFORE DOING THE BOAT-

TAILED 1929 STUTZ LE MANS, SEVERAL DUESENBERGS, AUBURNS AND CORDS, INCLUDING THE "COFFIN-NOSED" 810 (BELOW). HE LATER WORKED FOR STUDEBAKER AND FORD.

57 TOP EVEN THOUGH THE LONG HOOD AND WIDE FENDERS TOOK UP MOST OF THE ROOM, THE CORD 810'S DRIVER AND PASSENGERS CERTAINLY RODE IN STYLE.

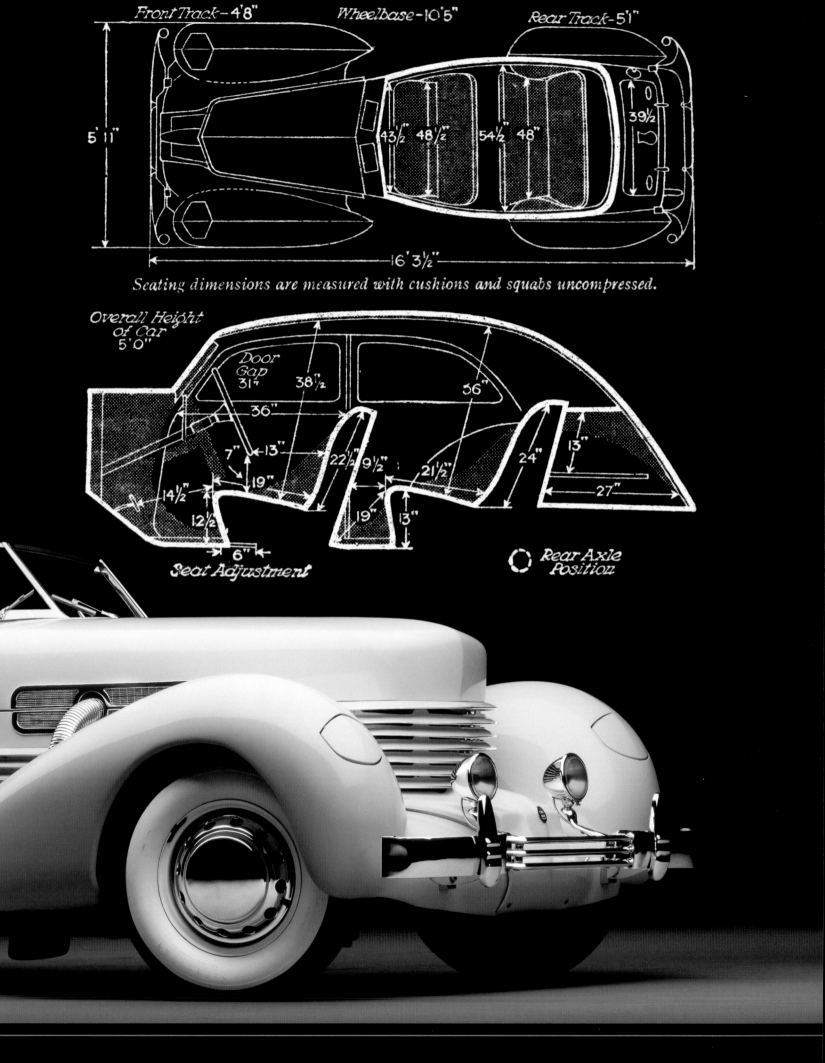

Front Track–4'8"   Wheelbase–10'5"   Rear Track–5'1"

5'11"

43½" 48½" 54½" 48"   39½

16'3½"

Seating dimensions are measured with cushions and squabs uncompressed.

Overall Height
of Car
5'0"

Door
Gap
31"   38½"   56"

36"

7" 13"   22½" 9½"   21½"   24"   13"

14½"   19"   19" 3"   27"

12½

6"

Seat Adjustment   ◯ Rear Axle
Position

BUGATTI TYPE

To say the least, Ettore Bugatti's family was artistic. His father, Carlo, was a famous furniture designer in the late 19th century.

His brother, Rembrandt, was an acclaimed sculpture, especially of animal figures. Ettore's art was sculptural as well. Ettore designed and built beautiful cars, both for the racetrack and the roadway. In her book on the first century of automotive design, professor Penny Sparke wrote that Bugatti's work displayed "an enhanced alignment of function and beauty." His were cars, the professor notes, that visually portrayed their potential for dynamic performance.

Bugatti's son, Jean, inherited his forefathers' artistic skills. Jean took over from his father in 1930 after working with him on the creation of the Bugatti Type 57, a car that automotive historian Roger Barlow said was the rare vehicle that somehow incorporated "the often contradictory goals of superb road holding with reasonable comfort, [of] mechanical sophistication with reliability."

The Type 57 was produced until 1939, the year Jean died when he swerved to avoid a drunk bicyclist who had somehow gotten on a road that had been closed to traffic for the testing of a new, 160 mph version of the Bugatti 57.

The Type 57 made its debut at auto shows in 1933 and was produced in various versions, some powered by a new 135-hp, twin overhead cam, 3.3-liter straight-8 engine that provided 135 hp when normally aspirated and 160 hp when supercharged. The engine was inspired by those built in America by racer Harry Miller. The engine's capabilities were

57SC ATLANTIC

58-59 JEAN BUGATTI USED MAGNESIUM ALLOY TO SCULPT THIS AERODYNAMIC BODY. BECAUSE OF THAT METAL'S LOW MELTING POINT, BODY PANELS WERE RIVETED TOGETHER AND THE RIVETED RIDGES ALONG THE FENDERS AND DOWN THE CENTER OF THE VEHICLE HAVE BECOME A SYMBOL OF HIS ARTISTIC FLAIR.

base reduced from more than 130 inches (3.3 meters) to 120 (just over 3 m) and on a hydraulic front suspension that adjusted damping to fit road conditions and speed. Supercharged versions were called the Type 57SC, the Atlantic.

To make the car as low and as light as possible, Bugatti ran the rear axle through the frame rails and sculpted the Atlantic's body from magnesium alloy, a light material with a melting point too low for the body panels to be welded together in normal fashion.

Instead, Bugatti had them riveted together. In a true stroke of artistic genius, he left the rivets exposed so they formed an exoskeletal spine that ran the length of the car with similar ridges along the tops of the fenders.

With its V-shaped grille set low between the front fenders, a long hood, rounded cabin and kidney-shaped side windows that followed the sloping contour of the roof, the Bugatti Type 57SC Atlantic remains a timeless icon of form and function in automotive design.

demonstrated in 1929 when, from a standing start, a prototype of the Bugatti Type 57 covered 179 km (more than 111 miles) in just one hour.

Though elegant on the road, the Type 57 also was a winner at the track. In 1937, the Bugatti Type 57G, carrying special racing bodywork, won the 24 Hours of Le Mans, lapping the rest of the field and breaking all records while being driven by rookie Jean-Pierre Wimille and veteran Robert Benoist, who retired after the victory.

Two years later, Bugatti was back with its lighter and even more aerodynamic Type 57C, this time with the supercharged engine tuned to provide 200 hp. Despite being as far as three laps behind because of various problems, Wimille, making only his second start in the race, won again, again in record-breaking style, this time with Pierre Veyron as his co-driver.

Jean Bugatti designed several bodies for the Type 57, but none was more spectacular than the Atlantic.

In 1936, Bugatti introduced the S version of the Type 57. This Type 57S rode on a wheel-

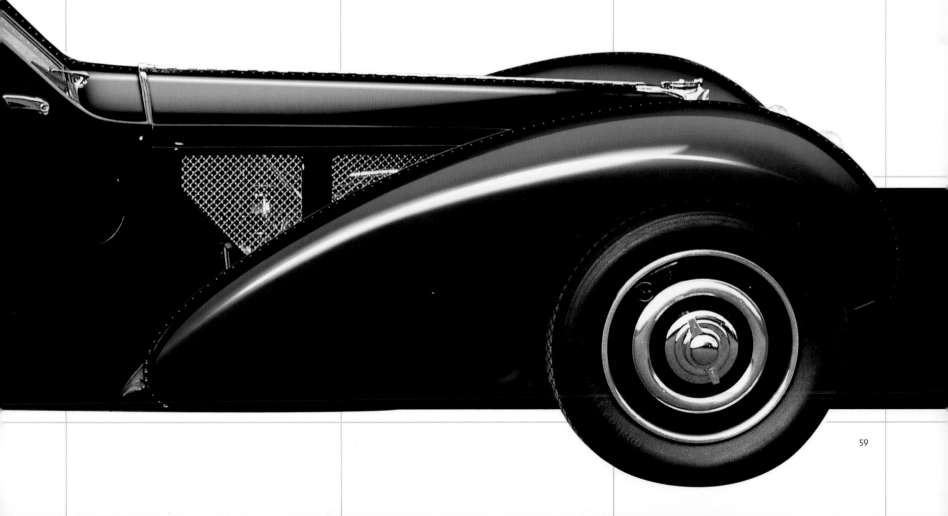

BMW 328

In 1913, German aircraft engineer Karl Friedrich Rapp established a company in Munich to build engines for the still young aviation industry. Three years later, he linked up with airplane builder Gustav Otto, whose father, Nikolas Otto, had invented the 4-stroke internal combustion engine some 40 years earlier.

In 1917, the company was restructured, and its name changed from Bayerische Flugzeug Werke AG to Bayerische Motoren Werke GmbH, now headed by former Daimler manager Franz-Joseph Popp. Popp brought in young engineering genius Max Friz, who improved on Rapp's original designs. Soon the company went public and changed its name to BMW AG, although it retained the blue-and-white propeller logo that dated to the early days of Rapp's efforts.

As early as 1919, motorcycle makers were making use of BMW's 2-cylinder engines, and

when the Treaty of Versailles barred German companies from building aircraft engines for five years, BMW changed its focus. In 1923 it launched its own line of motorcycles. Within a short time, BMW motorcycles were competing in and winning races throughout Europe.

In the late 1920s, with income now from both motorcycles and aviation, BMW took over German automaker Dixi, which had been assembling Austin Sevens under license for Britain's Austin company (Sevens also were being built under license in the United States by Bantam and in Japan by Datsun). When Dixi's license expired, BMW designed and produced its own cars, beginning in 1933 with the 303, the first car to display what would become the BMW automotive design icon – a twin-kidney grille.

In 1936, eight years after assembling its first car and just three years after launching the first car of its own design, BMW rolled out the first of what would be a string of remark-

able vehicles, the 328 roadster. In retrospect, it was the first "ultimate driving machine."

Rudolf Schlelcher and Fritz Fiedler were the design engineers behind the car, which had a tubular cage chassis, independent front suspension, rack-and-pinion steering, hydraulic brakes, as well as an elegant but athletic body and a remarkable inline 6-cylinder engine.

The BMW 328 made its debut in June 1936 in a race at the Nürburgring, where it won with motorcycle racer Ernest Henne at the steering wheel, averaging more than 100 km/h (63 mph). The following year the BMW roadsters won more than 200 events – races, rallies and hill climbs. In 1939, wearing coupe bodywork designed by Touring of Italy, a 328 was fifth overall and first in the small displacement class at Le Mans.

Then, in 1940, 328s finished first, third, fifth and sixth in the Mille Miglia, with Fritz Huschke von Hanstein and Walter Baumer

60 TOP A BMW MOTORCYCLE RIDER, WITH HIS PARTNER HANGING OUT OF THE SIDECAR TO PROVIDE BALANCE, COMPETES IN A RACE IN 1958.

60 BOTTOM ON JUNE 17, 1919, FRANZ ZENO DIEMER FLEW A BI-WINGED AIRCRAFT POWERED BY A BMW ENGINE TO AN ALTITUDE RECORD OF 9760 METERS (32,020 FEET, MORE THAN SIX MILES ABOVE THE EARTH'S SURFACE).

61 AND 62-63 WITH ADVANCED MECHANICAL COMPONENTS AND AN AERODYNAMIC ROADSTER BODY, THE 328 WAS THE FIRST BMW WORTHY OF THE TITLE OF "ULTIMATE DRIVING MACHINE." THE SPORTS CAR SET STANDARDS THAT OTHER AUTOMAKERS WOULD EMULATE.

62 TOP H.S. ALDINGTON'S BMW 328 TAKES FLIGHT ON THE TEST HILL AT ENGLAND'S BROOKLANDS CIRCUIT IN 1937.

64-65 ITALIAN COACHBUILDER TOURING CREATED SPECIAL BODYWORK FOR THE 328 IN

1940, WHICH MINIMAL WINDSCREENS FOR THE RACY SPIDERS. THE FACTORY ENTERED FIVE 328 MODELS IN THE MILLE MIGLIA THAT YEAR, WITH A TOURING-BODIED CLOSED COUPE WINNING.

averaging more than 166 km/h (104 mph). But this was not just a racecar. The BMW 328 was a road car, and set the standard that British and other sports cars would try to emulate. Front fenders were integrated into the car's body and headlamps were set into those fenders. The tall twin grilles were angled slightly back to help the car cut through the air. Running boards were disdained, as were wire spoke wheels.

Propulsion came from Fiedler's 2.0-liter engine, which was fed by three Solex carburetors and featured revolutionary valve train that used standard push rods to activate intake valves with crossover rocker arms opening the exhaust valves. Between 1936 and 1940, BMW would produce some 460 of the remarkable little sportsters, but its engine would continue in production for two more decades.

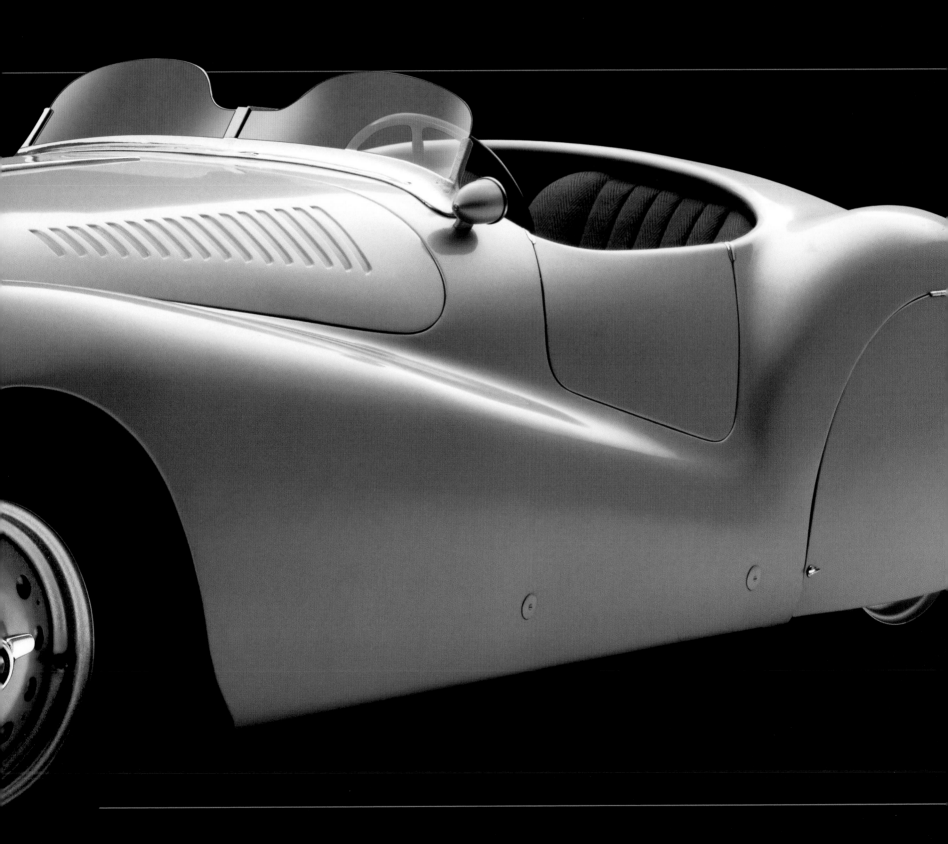

ALFA ROMEO
8C 2900

There are those who have called Vittorio Jano the father of high-performance auto racing. When you consider that the racing versions of the straight-eight engine he crafted for Alfa Romeo won the 24 Hours of Le Mans and the Targa Florio every year from 1931 through 1934 as well as every Grand Prix they entered and from 1932-1937 every Mille Miglia as well, you certainly have to give Jano his due.

Jano's parents had moved from Hungary to Italy, where Vittorio was born in 1891. He worked in his father's blacksmith shop, where they soon started building racing cars. In 1911 Jano went to work as a drafts-

66 TOP ALFA ROMEO USED RACING TO PROMOTE ITS CARS, AND THE 8C 2900 CERTAINLY HAD RACY LINES, AND AN ENGINE BUILT WITH PARTS LEFT OVER FROM ALFA'S DAYS ON THE GRAND PRIX RACING CIRCUIT.

66-67 THE 8C 2900 LONG AND LOW LINES MADE IT LOOK FAST EVEN WHEN IT WAS PARKED. ONCE IN MOTION, A SUPERCHARGED, STRAIGHT EIGHT-CYLINDER ENGINE GENERATED SOME 200 HORSEPOWER.

man at Fiat, again working on racing cars, but now under the mentoring of Carlo Cavalli. Jano became expert at valve design and, working with Swiss chemist Stefano Somazzi, at creating special fuel mixtures that made the most powerful use of those designs. At the end of the 1923 season, racing driver (and future automotive legend) Enzo Ferrari recruited Jano to join Alfa Romeo. The Societa Anonima Lombarda Fabbrica Automoili, or Alfa, was established in 1906 when Italian businessmen bought out French carmaker Alexandre Darracq's Italian operation. By 1915, Nicola Romeo, who had been building drills, air compressors and other heavy equipment, had taken over the company and added his name to

the business, which by 1920 had turned its full attention to automobile production, and to using auto racing to promote its products.

At Alfa Romeo, Jano was able to fully exercise his talents, from beginning to experiment with superchargers to creating what is considered Europe's first true single-seater racing car and to designing cars not only for racing but grand touring machines for regular road use as well.

In 1931 Alfa Romeo launched Jano's newest car, the 8C 2300, with its chassis available in long or short wheelbase versions and for racing or ready for touring car bodywork by Zagato, Touring and a variety of other coachbuilders.

The heart of the car was its straight-eight, 2336-cc supercharged engine. The engine actually comprised two four-cylinder engines, each with its own supercharger

and exhaust system, but joined together and sharing a common crankcase. For the road, the engine provided 155 horsepower and could carry the 8C 2300 to speeds of around 110 miles per hour (180 km/h). When it was introduced, the Alfa Romeo 8C 2300 was considered the fastest road car of its day. Over the course of several years, Alfa built fewer than 200 of its 8C 2300 chassis. Jano also developed a less expensive and less powerful six-cylinder version, the 6C 2300. Then, in 1936, Alfa launched the 8C 2900, which many considered to be the fastest road car of the 1930s. With independent suspension at each wheel, a strengthened chassis and aerodynamic bodywork by various coachbuilders, the 8C 2900 could reach speeds of 185 km/h (115 mph) because its 2905-cc, twin-supercharged straight-eight powerplant was built from the special, high-performance

68 TOP VITTORIO JANO WAS THE ARCHITECT OF ALFA ROMEO'S RACING PROGRAM AND ALSO OF THE A SUCCESSION OF REMARKABLE ROAD CARS, INCLUDING THE 8C 2900, WHICH WAS AVAILABLE IN LONG OR SHORT-WHEELBASE VERSIONS.

68-69 ZAGATO, TOURING AND SEVERAL OTHER COACHBUILDERS DESIGNED AERODYNAMIC BODYWORK, BOTH CONVERTIBLES AND SLEEK COUPES, TO COVER THE POWERFUL CHASSIS OF THE ALFA ROMEOS 8C 2900.

parts left over from Alfa's powerful Grand Prix racing engines, which finally had been overtaken on the track by German racing rivals Mercedes-Benz and Auto Union.

Jano worked at Alfa Romeo until 1937, when Gianni Lancia inherited his father's car company and convinced Jano to become chief engineer. Jano continued to create revolutionary cars, including the D50 racer, which had its engine serve as a stressed part of the chassis, and the Aurelia, a sporty coupe and the first series production car with a V6 engine.

When Lancia withdrew from racing in 1955, Jano rejoined Enzo Ferrari, who now headed his own fairly successful race and road car-making company. Ferrari's young son, Dino, convinced his father to let him work with the veteran engineer on a new engine, a V6 racing engine that one day, posthumously, would bear Dino's name.

70 TOP THE TOPOLINO ENGINE DISPLACED A MERE 567 CUBIC CENTIMETERS, BUT ITS 13 HORSEPOWER WAS ENOUGH TO PROPEL THE LIGHTWEIGHT CAR TO SPEEDS OF MORE THAN 50 MILES PER HOUR.

70-71 OFFICIALLY THE FIAT 500, THE WORLD'S SMALLEST PRODUCTION CAR OF ITS ERA WAS MOST COMMONLY KNOWN AS THE "TOPOLINO," THE ITALIAN NICKNAME FOR CARTOON CHARACTER MICKEY MOUSE.

71 FIAT'S LITTLE CAR WAS BIG ENOUGH TO HOLD TWO TALL PEOPLE AND SOME LUGGAGE, THOUGH MANY PEOPLE FOUND ROOM UNDER THE TOP TO CARRY CHILDREN, PETS AND EVEN CARGO BEHIND THE CAR'S SEATS.

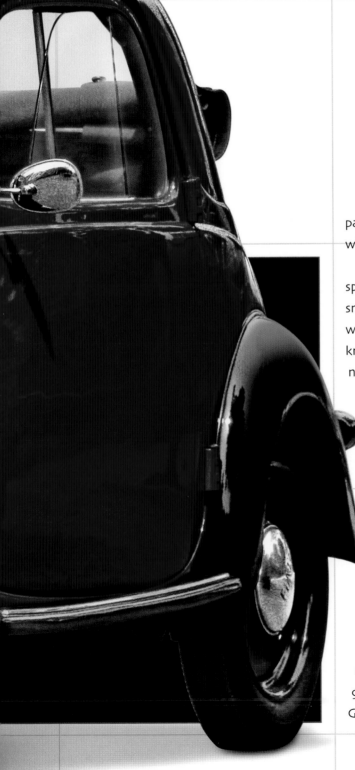

FIAT TOPOLINO

In 1936, Fiat showed that recent advances in automotive aerodynamics could be applied to a small package, even to a "people's car," which is what the Fiat 500 was designed to be.

Styled by engineer Dante Giacosa in response to Giovanni Agnelli's dream of a small, affordable car for all Italians, the 500 was so small that it most commonly was known as the "*Topolino*," the same nickname Italians had given American cartoon character Mickey Mouse.

The Topolino was the smallest production car on the planet.

For example, it's wheelbase stretched a mere 2000 mm (78.7 inches), some 400 mm (nearly 20 inches) shorter than the Volkswagen "Beetle," a car considered very small for its day yet that spanned nearly 4100 mm (160 inches) from front to rear bumper, or more than 75 cm (more than two feet) further than the Fiat. Fiat considered a VW-like design, a car with a rear-mounted, air-collected engine, but when the prototype caught fire, Giacoso's design – with its front-mounted, water-cooled engine and rear-wheel drive architecture — was the obvious choice for production.

The Topolino's 569-cc four-cylinder engine generated only 13 horsepower, but the car weighed less than 600 kilograms (1300 pounds). Despite its unaerodynamic stand-up headlights, a sloped-back grille, raked windshield and smoothly contoured tail section helped the Fiat 500 reach speeds of 85 km/h (in excess of 50 miles per hour) while using only six liters of fuel per 100 kilometers (some 40 miles per gallon).

Priced at less than 10,000 lire. The Topolino still combined a low center of gravity, sprightly engine, synchromesh transmission, sufficient brakes and independent front suspension with an interior roomy enough for two adults to ride in comfort, though people often brought along their children, pets and somehow still found room for cargo in the small area behind the front seats. A canvas top that could easily be opened to the sky helped make the car's interior anything but claustrophobic.

The Topolino was Italy's most popular car.

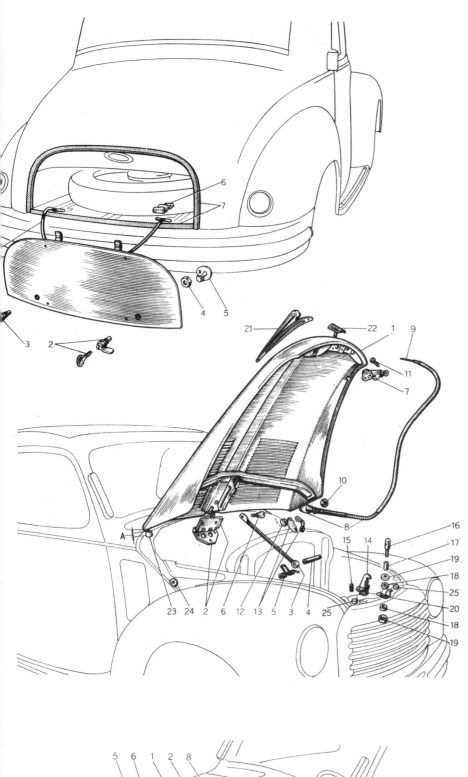

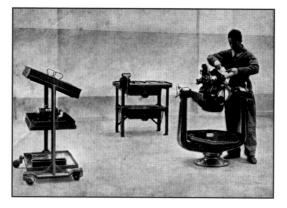

The original 500 remained in production until 1948, with the only significant change being a revision of the rear suspension about halfway through its 12-year production run. In 1948 the 500B launched with a slightly more powerful, overhead-valve engine as well as updated brakes, suspension and electrical components.

Interior styling also was updated in 1948 and a wagon version that could carry four adults joined the lineup.

Finally, in 1949, the 500C evolved with a new nose, an aluminum cylinder head for its engine and a system that used hot air from the radiator to clear the windshield and to heat the passenger compartment.

Production of the 500s ran until 1955, when, after more than half a million of the Topolinos had been built, the new Fiat 600 replaced it.

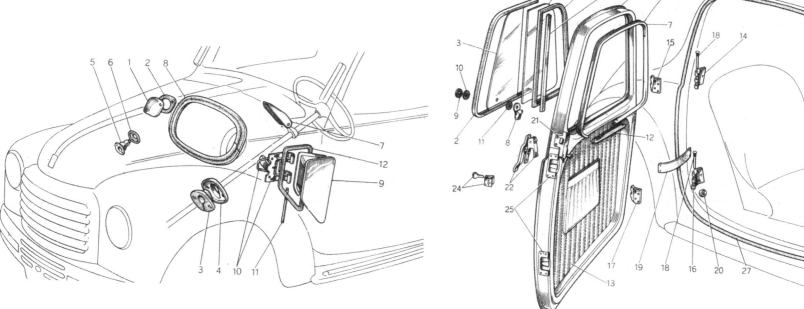

TALBOT LAGO

W hen the Museum of Modern Art staged "8 automobiles: an exhibition concerned with the esthetics of motorcar design" in 1951, one of those eight cars was the Talbot-Lago.

What curator Arthur Drexler referred to as "ornaments on the hood," provided the key to what he called the designer's approach: "points or circles with trailing flow lines, like the tail of a comet, state a theme repeated in the fenders and progressively enlarged to include the entire passenger compartment," Drexler wrote in the exhibition catalog.

"Front and rear fenders, which are connected to each other at the base line, appear to cradle the passenger compartment. This produces a roughly symmetrical balance of oval shapes, so that from all sides a single dominating element is flanked by two smaller ones. The rear wheel is covered to preserve the fender's oval contour, and the clarity of the entire organization is reinforced by color differentiation [the car in the MOMA display had two-tone paint with light fenders and dark hood and passenger compartment]."

Talbot was an Anglo-French company that dated to 1900, when Alexandre Darracq, dissatisfied with both the electric car and the Bollee-designed three-wheeler he drove on the streets of Paris before the turn of the century, built his own car, his powered by a small, single-cylinder engine that drove the rear wheels. Within five years, Darracq was setting speed records – 177.2 kilometers per hour (more than 110 miles per hour) with his own car and its huge 22.5-liter V8 engine.

Darracq's production cars continued with single- or two-cylinder engines until 1911, when he tried an ill-designed rotary engine. On the verge of financial failure, Darracq left the company, which was now run by Owen Clegg, an Englishman who in 1919 merged Talbot with Sunbeam, a British carmaker.

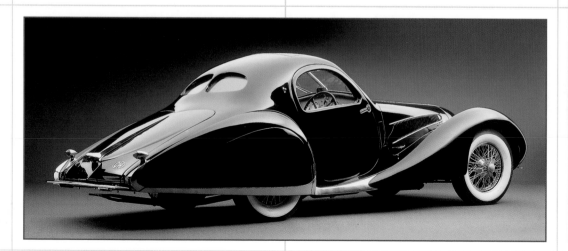

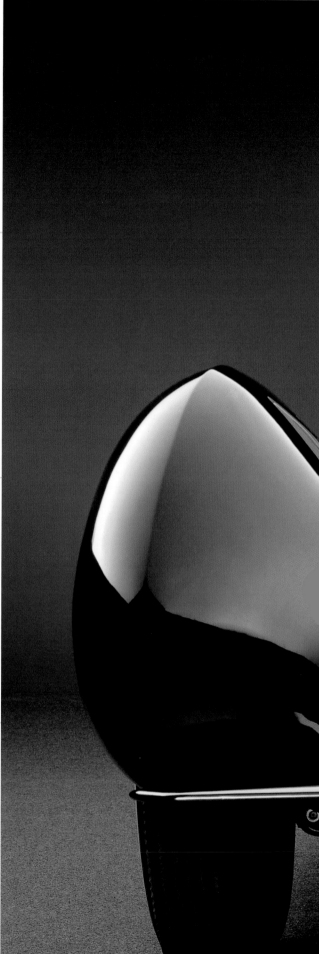

Eventually known as S-T-D (Sunbeam-Talbot-Darracq), the company was sold to the Rootes brothers in 1935. They put a Frenchman, Major Antoine (Antonio) Lago in charge of engineering and management, and a year later he made Talbot his own company, developing his own cars and 2.7- and 3.0-liter six-cylinder engines to power them.

Lago had a history in racing and he specialized in building cars that were suitable not only for motoring, but for motorsports. In 1937 Lago Specials swept the top three positions in the French Grand Prix at Montlhéry.

That same year, Joseph Figoni of French coachbuilder Figoni & Falaschi designed the teardrop bodywork for the Talbot-Lago T150 SS (Speciale Sport) coupe. The car was stunningly beautiful, and its design made it appear larger than it really was. It also was equipped with large brakes, which were useful because the car was powered by Lago's new 4.0-liter, twin-carbureted six-cylinder engine that provided 140 horsepower and a top speed of 100 miles per hour (160 km/h). With its aerodynamically shaped bodywork, the car could cruise comfortably at speeds in the 85-90 miles per hour (140-145 km/h) range. Talbot resumed production in the later part of the 1940s, though in very low volumes. The Talbot Record and Grand Sport were sports cars that were particularly successful in racing. In 1950, they took on the likes of Ferrari, Jaguar, Aston Martin and even Cadillac at Le Mans and finished first and second. A year later they were second and fourth. In 1952 a Talbot held the lead at Le Mans as late as an hour and ten minutes from the finish.

Antonio Lago died in 1960, not long after his ailing company had become part of French automaker Simca.

Henry Ford had an industrialist's heart. His son, Edsel, had the eye of an artist.

In 1919, at the age of 26, Edsel became president of the Ford Motor Company, though his father held tightly to the reins of power. Still, in 1922, Edsel convinced his father to add the bankrupt Lincoln Automobile Company to the Ford portfolio. Henry Ford wasn't happy about the deal, finally agreeing perhaps only because he saw it as a way to extract some revenge against his long-time nemesis Henry Leland.

A skilled engineer, Leland had developed the engine for the Curved-Dash Oldsmobile and was brought in by investors in the original Henry Ford Company, which after Ford quit was renamed Cadillac and won acclaim as the "standard of the world." After Cadillac was folded into General Motors, Leland and his son, Wilfred, founded their own company, Lincoln.

FORD LINCOLN

After Henry Ford bought Lincoln, it became the firm's luxury line, and Edsel knew that luxury cars had to have styling that would appeal to wealthy consumers. Lincoln's first major styling statement was the 1936 Zephyr, which was given a streamlined design by John Tjaarda of Detroit chassis-builder Briggs with finishing touches added by yacht designer Eugene T. "Bob" Gregorie, then a consultant to Edsel (and who, in 1935, at the age of 26, would be appointed chief of Ford design). In 1938 Edsel Ford toured Europe and he came home with the desire to build a very special car, one with would bring "continental" styling to American roads. Basically, he wanted a car that would let him drive in style, and thus he wanted it in time for his annual winter vacation to Florida.

Within an hour, Gregorie had completed preliminary sketches of a car with a long, low hood, a convertible top and with its spare tire not stuck away in the trunk but mounted on the back of the car. Edsel liked what he saw and asked how soon such a car could be built. Quickly, a 20-inch scale model was created, Ford's chief draftsman Martin Regitko produced plans and the craftsmen at the Lincoln plant hand-shaped body panels for Edsel's car, the Continental.

A 1939 Lincoln Zephyr chassis was revised to accommodate a longer and lower hood and the longer front fenders. The car's silhouette was lowered by some three inches compared

CONTINENTAL

to that of the Zephyr. The driver's position moved seven inches (nearly 18 cm farther from the front wheels. The prototype was cobbled together. It weighted more than 5000 lbs, with as much as a fifth of its weight from the solder used to smooth the lines of its body panels. Power came from the Zephyr's 4.8-liter V12 engine, which produced 120 hp and 220 foot-pounds of torque. The car was painted "dove gray" and shipped to Florida. Two weeks later, Edsel called back to Dearborn, said the car was attracting unprecedented attention from winter residents of ritzy Palm Beach and said he could easily sell 1000 such cars.

For production, the car was revised with shorter hood and fenders, with the driver moved forward to provide more room for other passengers, and with a higher trunk. It also was the first Ford with a column-mounted shifter.

Ford built some 2000 Continentals over the course of three years, including some 900 convertibles. But the war effort and Edsel's death in 1943 halted production. But the car more than made up for lack of numbers with its impact on automotive design. In 1951, the Museum of Modern Art included the Lincoln Continental as one of eight vehicles in its special show on significant automotive design.

80-81 LINCOLN CONTINENTALS WERE FAVORITE RIDES FOR HOLLYWOOD STARS, SUCH AS RITA HAYWORTH, SHOWN LEANING AGAINST HER NEW COUPE. FORD BUILT THE CONTINENTAL IN BOTH COUPE AND CONVERTIBLE BODY STYLES.

81 INSTEAD OF LINCOLN'S TRADITIONAL GREYHOUND RADIATOR CAP, THE CONTINENTAL, LIKE THE LINCOLN ZEPHYR, WORE AN ART DECO ORNAMENT ON ITS HOOD.

Accelerating Slowly:
The car companies retool

1945/1954

Just as cars were starting to become artistically interesting, as exciting to see as to drive, vehicle production took a dramatic turn. Instead of cars for families and trucks for the delivery of goods, automakers were building armaments and the means to deliver them and the soldiers who would use them. Plans for sedans and convertibles were swept off the drafting tables, replaced by those for air-

designed for Europeans, where taxes and narrow streets favored small and nimble vehicles, and those for America with its suburban boulevards and vast open spaces.

Historians note that in the United States, cars and highways redistributed people from farms to cities and from cities to suburbs. In *American Cars*, Leon Mandel wrote that the first new suburb – Levittown, Pennsylvania – was built in 1947 by people who had built military housing during the war. A year later

able to focus on "post-war models designed for production in series."

"Excessively refined spring mechanisms, intended to protect passengers from the experience of being in a vehicle moving along a road, also produce that bouncing which rocks us like babes in a crib," Drexler continued. "Sometimes safety precautions are neglected in favor of comfort: a car that does not hold tightly to the road because its center of gravity is too high is technically imperfect, even though its extra height makes it easier for passengers to get in and out. In this case the preoccupation with comfort produces a curious indifference to a demonstrable safety hazard." Drexler's words now seem prophecy, written decades before sports utility vehicles and rollover accidents would become an issue.

Critical of the "glorification of comfort," Drexler added that "if the motorist were to distinguish between the comfort appropriate to his living room couch and the comfort appropriate to a seat suspended between four swiftly moving wheels, he would doubtless resent the padded, sensationless limbo recommended in our advertising as the highest form of motoring pleasure. It is not only the monotony of the superhighway that makes it so difficult for the cross-country motorist to keep awake. A well designed automobile, besides being beautiful, would restore the motorist to the road."

Accelerating Slowly: The car companies retool

planes and jeeps, for tanks and military transporters. After World War II, automakers had to retool. At least those in the United States still had their factories intact. Many European automakers had to rebuild, and even when they did their national economies were slow to recover; for many, a car remained a dream: a motorbike was the reality. Some companies never recovered. Reasons varied to those as bizarre as the quirks of new boundaries that placed them on the wrong side of the Iron Curtain. Meanwhile, Japanese automakers were not allowed to resume production until two years after the fighting ended. When production did resume, there was pent-up demand, but sales would remain slow until national economies also regained their strength.

At first, to get production restarted, the new cars were built with old designs. Quickly, however, trends became evident, particularly in a developing difference between cars

the McDonald's hamburger stand was franchised, and Baskin-Robbins ice cream was as well. Before long there were Howard Johnson's and Kentucky Fried Chicken in seemingly every town. "Henry Ford put us on wheels just before and immediately after World War I," Mandel wrote. "Abraham Levitt, Colonel Harlan Sanders, Ray Kroc, Howard Johnson, Kemmons Wilson, and others lashed us to those wheels in the wake of World War II." And Americans wanted to ride in comfort. "The interiors of American cars are often designed to duplicate in domestic comfort the living room of the driver's home," curator Arthur Drexler wrote in the catalog for the Ten Automobiles exhibit staged in 1953 by the Museum of Modern Art in New York City

Just two years earlier, the museum had held a similar exhibition, but only one of those eight vehicles had been designed since the war ended. By 1953 the museum was

83 CARS ENTERED A NEW GENERATION IN THE LATE 1940S. SO DID CARMAKERS. FERDINAND PORSCHE WAS FAMED FOR HIS WORK ON MANY THINGS, BUT IT FELL TO HIS SON, FERRY, TO PUT THE FAMILY NAME ON A VEHICLE, THE PORSCHE 356.

85 THE ALFA ROMEO GIULETTA SPRINT WAS CREATED BY BERTONE AS A PRIZE FOR THE WINNERS OF A LOTTERY. THE SPRINT BECAME SO POPULAR THAT BERTONE HAD TO BUILD A FACTORY TO MEET DEMAND.

1945/1954

The 1948 Cisitalia 202 may very well have been the seminal statement in modern automotive design.

This was not just a means of transportation. This was sculpture, rolling sculpture, self-propelled sculpture, a mobile masterpiece or such importance as a work of art that it was the first automobile put on permanent display by New York's Museum of Modern Art.

"The automobile's lines must be pure, smooth, essential," said Battista "Pinin" Farina, who not only designed the car but supervised its construction. "We could no longer use the habitual symbols that looks like so much plumbing work. With this car, Dusio and I were playing the poet."

Dusio was soccer player and amateur racer Piero Dusio, who founded the Consorzio Industriale Sportive Italia to produce sports equipment and uniforms. Dusio hired Dante Giacosa, who had created the Fiat Topolino, to design a line of racing cars, and when Giacosa went back to Fiat after the war, he recommended that Giovanni Savonuzzi, head of Fiat's experimental aircraft division, take over.

Using commonplace Fiat components, including the front suspension from the Topolino and the small engine from the Balilla, Savonuzzi created a single-seat, open-wheel racing car that is believed to have been the first with chrome-moly tube frame architecture (he found the structural tubing while wandering through Dusio's bicycle factory).

Three racing spyders also were built, and featured fin-like rear fenders. Italian driving ace Tazio Nuvolari likely would have won the 1947 Mille Miglia with one of the sypders had he not been forced to stop to wait for his magneto to dry after a rain (Nuvolari still finished second, with his teammates third and fourth behind him).

Dusio turned to "Pinin" Farina to complete the design and construction of a Cisitalia coupe and the result was a car with its hood lower than its front fenders, with headlamps integrated into those fenders and with such purity of detail that the wide oval grille featured vertical bars unencumbered by a chrome frame.

Although its four-cylinder, 1090-cc Fiat Barilla engine generated a mere 50 horsepower, the car's sleek shape helped it slice through the air at a top speed in excess of 100 miles per hour.

"The Cisitalia offers one of the most accomplished examples of coachwork conceived as a single shell," the MOMA praised the car more than half a century later. "The hood, body, fenders, and headlights are integral to the continuously flowing surface, rather than added on. Before the Cisitalia, the prevailing approach followed by automobile designers when defining a volume and shaping the shell of an automobile was to treat each part of the body as a separate, distinct element – a box to house the passengers, another for the motor, and headlights as appendages. In the Cisitalia, there are no sharp edges. Swellings and depressions maintain the overall flow and unity, creating a sense of speed."

Some 485 Cisitalia's were built, nearly 200 of them by Pininfarina. The others received coachwork by Vignale, Touring, Frua or Stabilmenti Farina, but none could match the purity of "Pinin" Farina's creation. The clean shapes and wonderful proportions of the Cisitalia 202 sports coupe would serve as inspiration for many vehicles to follow.

Despite the coupe's acclaim, Dusio had other things on his mind. He wanted to go Grand Prix racing and hired Porsche to build racecars and engines to power them. But the cost was more than Dusio could afford. Facing bankruptcy, he moved to Argentina, and started a new company that converted leftover U.S. military Jeeps into civilian vehicles.

CISITALIA 202

88-89 BATTISTA "PININ" FARINA DIDN'T MERELY DESIGN A SPORTS CAR WHEN HE CREATED THE CISITALIA, HE CREATED WHAT HAS BEEN HERALDED EVER SINCE AS ONE OF THE WORLD'S FINEST EXAMPLES OF ROLLING SCULPTURE. "WE COULD NO LONGER USE THE HABITUAL SYMBOLS THAT LOOK LIKE SO MUCH PLUMBING WORK," PININFARINA SAID OF THE CISITALIA'S CLEAN SHAPE. "WITH THIS CAR, [PIERO] DUSIO [OF CISITALIA] AND I WERE PLAYING THE POET."

CITROËN 2CV

At first glance, the Citroën 2CV may appear to 21st-century eyes to be the homeliest car ever designed (well, at least until General Motors unveiled the Pontiac Aztek a few decades later). But there is eternal beauty in this car's simplicity, and there was nothing ugly about the cost-effectiveness of the car designed to bring the typical French farmer into the motoring age.

Just as Ford's Model T, the so-called Tin Lizzie, had put America on wheels, Citroën's "Tin Snail" was for many Frenchmen the first car they would drive. Henry Ford had said people could have their Model T in any color, so long as that color was black. For its first decade in production, the 2CV was available only in gray. But the 2CV made motorized transportation was available, and affordable, priced at 228,000 francs (less than $1000).

The snail-shaped Citroën had one of the most unusual developed mandates ever devised by a car company: It was to be capable of carrying four people, or two people and more than 100 lbs (50 kg.) of farm produce, at speeds of up to 40 mph while averaging more than 50 mpg (20 km on one liter of fuel). It also had to be able to carry a basket with a dozen eggs and carry them unbroken across a plowed field, which is could do even though it had only two springs, one that tied to together the left front and rear axles, the other linking the right front and rear in an amazing self-leveling system. Company founder André Citroën did not live long enough to see the 2CV go into production, though work on the car began before his death in 1936. Styling was done by Italian sculptor Flaminio Bertoni (not to be confused with Nuccio Bertone, the famed Italian coachbuilder). Pierre Boulanger and Henri Lefevre, both of whom had experience with early aircraft design, masterminded the 2CV's lightweight construction.

Minimalist was the theme. Initial prototypes were built from corrugated steel and had a single headlamp mounted on the front fender ahead of the driver. Even in production trim, seats were canvas, suspended from metal frames, and the seats could be easily removed to make more room for produce or other goods. And if those goods were too tall to fit inside the car, the entire roof was made from canvas that could be rolled back and out of the way, creating a huge sunroof and virtually turning the car into a convertible.

WE COULDN'T MAKE IT FASTER.
After all it already exceeds the legal speed limit of 70mph by 1.5mph.

WE COULDN'T MAKE IT ANY ROOMIER.
It will already hold the average family of 3.7 people with room for an additional 0.3 hitchhikers.

WE COULDN'T MAKE IT CHEAPER.
If we made it any more basic there wouldn't be much left.

SO WE PAINTED IT.
How else could we improve it?

THE NEW CITROËN 2CV DOLLY. £2,899.
PRICE CORRECT AT TIME OF GOING TO PRESS AND INCLUDES CAR TAX, VAT AND FRONT SEAT BELTS. DELIVERY AND PLATES EXTRA. SEE YELLOW PAGES FOR NEAREST DEALER. CITROEN CARS LTD., MILL STREET, SLOUGH SL25DE. TEL. SLOUGH 23808.

90 CITROEN HAD USED CORRUGATED STEEL WHEN BUILDING THE PROTOTYPE FOR ITS 2CV AND THIS THEME CARRIED OVER INTO THE HOOD OF THE PRODUCTION VERSION. THE WIDE FLAP AT THE BASE OF THE WINDSHIELD COULD BE OPENED TO PROVIDE VENTILATION FOR THE DRIVER AND PASSENGERS. THE CLOTH TOP ROLLED BACK TO CREATE AN ALMOST CONVERTIBLE LIKE DRIVING EXPERIENCE.

91 CITROEN MADE THE 2CV AVAILABLE ONLY IN A GRAY COLOR FOR ITS FIRST DECADE IN PRODUCTION. WHEN THEY FINALLY OFFERED OTHER COLORS, IT CLEVERLY INTRODUCED THEM BY ALSO POINTING OUT SOME OF THE CAR'S OTHER ATTRIBUTES.

Likewise, the trunk lid also could be removed, so the 2CV could function much like a compact pickup truck. Even the doors, which were hinged not at the front of the car but "suicide" style on the B pillar, could be easily removed, leaving little more than a metal frame and drivetrain.

Power came from a 2-cylinder engine, with its the cylinders horizontally opposed. The engine was air cooled and displaced a mere 375 cc and pumped out only 9 hp to the front wheels. Power would increase gradually through the years, and for a while Citroën made a version of the 2CV with two engines and four-wheel drive. Production lasted until 1990, when the last of more than 5 million of the Tin Snails was built.

92 TOP CITROËN USED PLAYFUL ADVERTISING TO HIGHLIGHT THE PRACTICALITY AND LOW PRICE OF ITS 2CV. WITH ITS SLIDING CANVAS ROOF AND REMOVABLE DOORS AND TRUNK LID, THE CAR COULD CARRY A REMARKABLE AMOUNT OF CARGO.

92-93 FRONT AND REAR DOORS WERE HINGED ON EITHER SIDE OF THE 2CV'S CENTRAL B PILLAR. THOUGH THE CAR HAD A SMALL FOOTPRINT, IT COULD CARRY FOUR PEOPLE, OR TWO PEOPLE AND 100 POUNDS OF PRODUCE, ALONG SMOOTH ROADS OR ACROSS ROUGHLY PLOWED FARM FIELD.

93 TOP CITROËN'S 2CV WAS A FEATURED PLAYER – AT LEAST UNTIL IT WAS TURNED INTO WRECKAGE — IN GERARD OURY'S POPULAR 1964 FRENCH FILM, LE CORNIAUD (THE NITWIT), WHICH STARRED LOUIS DE FUNES AND ANDRE BOURVIL.

JAGUAR XK120

94-95 WHEN THE SEDAN THAT WAS TO CARRY JAGUAR'S NEW INLINE SIX-CYLINDER ENGINE WASN'T READY, THE COMPANY PUT A ROADSTER BODY AROUND THE MOTOR AND A SPORTS CAR CLASSIC WAS BORN. WHILE WAITING FOR THE SEDAN, JAGUAR ANTICIPATED BUILDING 10 DOZEN ITS XK120 MODELS. INSTEAD, IT WOULD BUILD 12,000 OF THE CARS THAT TOOK THEIR NAME FROM THE XK ENGINE FAMILY AND THE CAR'S ANTICIPATED TOP SPEED IN MILES PER HOUR.

Jaguar had planned to launch its XK engine in its new Mk VII four-door sedan, but when it became clear that car wouldn't be ready for the 1948 Earls Court Motor Show, Jaguar crafted a two-seat, aluminum-bodied roadster to showcase its 6-cylinder powerplant.

As long as it went to all the trouble of building what it presented as the Super Sports prototype, Jaguar figured it might as well go ahead and sell ten dozen of them, which it figured it could produce by the time the Mk VII was ready to roll.

That was Jaguar's plan. But like so many plans, it was subject to change, and everything changed when the orders poured in for the stunning XK 120 roadster. The first ten dozen were, indeed, built with aluminum bodies, but for supply to keep up with demand, the next thousand dozen were made from steel.

Not only would Jaguar sell more than 12,000 XK 120s, but the car would beget the XK 140 and XK 150, as well as the C-type race car that would win twice at Le Mans, before giving way to a Jaguar D-type racer that would add three more victories in 1955, 1956 and 1957.

There also would be an XK 120 convertible and well as a coupe, which had teardrop-shaped side windows that gave the car a profile reminiscent of the Bugatti Atlantic

95 TOP AND CENTER BEFORE, DURING AND LONG AFTER PRODUCTION OF THE XK120, JAGUAR BUILT ITS CARS WITH CRAFTSMANSHIP, WHETHER IT WAS MECHANICAL COMPONENTS, THE CUTTING AND SEWING OF LEATHER FOR THE INTERIOR, THE FABRICATION OF WOOD DASHBOARDS OR THE CONSTRUCTION OF THE CAR'S TOP.

95 BOTTOM QUITE NATURALLY, JAGUAR'S EMBLEM WAS AN IMAGE OF THE JUNGLE CAT. "GROWLER" CONTINUES TO BE USED ON THE STEERING WHEEL HUB WHILE "LEAPER" IS THE JAGUAR POUNCING FROM THE HOOD OF MANY OF THE CARS THE COMPANY BUILDS.

The XK 120 took its initials name from Jaguar's new 6-cylinder engine and its number from the fact that Jaguar expected the car to achieve a top speed of 120 mph, which would make it the fastest production car on the road. The car achieved that speed, and then some, exceeding 136 mph in testing.

Jaguar's early history is of interest. William Lyons and William Wamsley founded the Swallow Sidecar Company in 1922 to build motorcycle sidecars from aluminum, and five

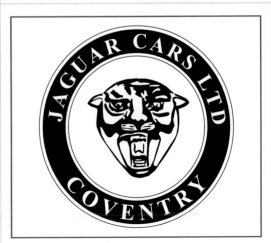

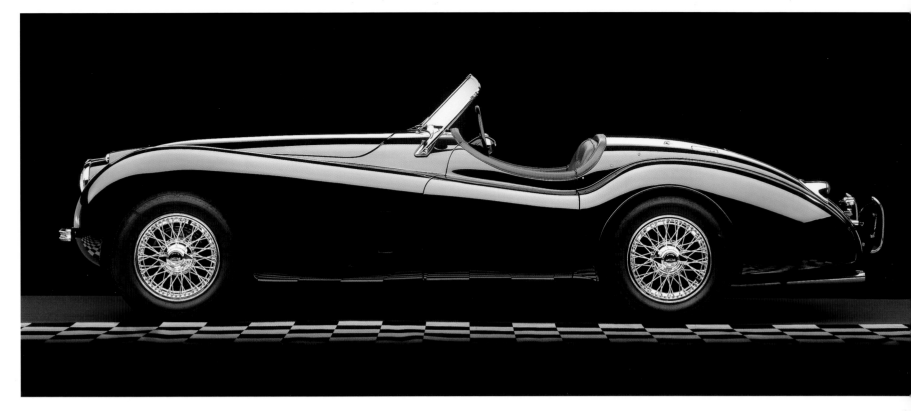

96 TOP MORE THAN 80 PERCENT OF XK120S WERE EXPORTED. THE CAR WAS ESPECIALLY POPULAR WITH AMERICANS, INCLUDING HOLLYWOOD STARS SUCH AS CLARK GABLE.

96-97 THE XK120 WAS ALSO BUILT AS A COUPE WITH TEARDROP-SHAPED SIDE WINDOWS THAT REMINDED MANY OF THOSE IN THE FAMED BUGATTI ATLANTIC.

97 TOP WITH ITS LONG HOOD AND LOVELY, FLOWING CURVES, THE JAGUAR XK120 WAS BEAUTIFUL. BUT IT ALSO WAS FAST, THE FASTEST ROAD CAR OF ITS TIME.

years later were building their own Swallow bodies for the Austin Seven motorcar. Using powertrain and other components from the Britain's Standard car company, they produced their own cars, the SS I and SS II, beginning in 1932. After Wamsley left, Lyons changed the company's name to SS Cars Ltd., which showed a four-door model, the SS Jaguar, at the London show in 1936.

That first "Jaguar" was powered by a Standard engine much modified by William Munger Heynes and Harry Weslake. Heynes led the development of Jaguar's own engine, the XK, a 3.4-liter straight six with dual overhead camshafts that helped it generate 160 hp and 195 pound-feet of torque to propel the car from a standing start to 60 mph in just 10 seconds.

The XK 120 may have had a tiny cockpit, little luggage room, weak headlights and weaker brakes, but it was fast and became the car of choice for daily driving by Hollywood stars and world racing champions. The car was so popular in overseas markets – more than eight out of every ten cars were exported – that it wasn't until 1950 that the car was readily available to British buyers.

1949 FORD

98 FORD'S FOCUS ON AN ALL-NEW CAR FOR 1949 (TOP) MEANT THAT IT DIDN'T PRODUCE A 1948 MODEL; INSTEAD IT CONTINUED PRODUCTION OF THE '47 FORD. BY SKIPPING A MODEL YEAR, FORD WAS ABLE TO LAUNCH THE NEW CAR BY APRIL 1948 (BELOW), GIVING IT A HUGE HEAD START IN THE SALES RACE.

99 LEAK TESTING WAS ONE OF MANY PROCEDURES THE '49 FORD WENT THROUGH DURING ITS DEVELOPMENT. THE CAR WAS ENGINEERED AT FORD, BUT WAS DESIGNED BY OUTSIDE CONSULTANTS. FORD'S INTERNAL DESIGN FOR THE CAR WAS USED FOR THE MORE UPSCALE MERCURY BRAND.

Henry Ford's car company was no healthier than its ailing founder when World War II ended. Founding father Ford died in 1947, outliving his only son, Edsel, by some four years. The car company that bore the family name was bleeding badly, losing some $10 million a month when Ford's wife, Clara, and daughter-in-law, Eleanor, stopped a corporate coup and installed Edsel's 28-year-old son, Henry Ford II, as company president.

Henry "the Deuce," as he would come to be known, recognized the enormity of the task ahead. He brought in auto industry veteran Ernest Breech, who brought with him Harold Youngren to become chief engineer for Ford vehicles. Ford also hired the so-called Whiz Kids, a group of former military officers skilled in modern accounting and business procedures, and started hiring young engineers 50 at a time, right out of college. Still, to keep the company going, Ford would need a blockbuster car to would reinvigorate showroom traffic and cash flow. Henry II's father, Edsel, had gotten stunning designs for the pre-war Lincoln Zephyr and Lincoln Continental from former yacht designer E.T. "Bob"

Gregorie, but when Youngren saw Gregorie's latest designs, he knew they'd be too big and expensive for the sort of mass market Ford needed. The situation was so bleak that Ford basically canceled its plans for a new car for 1948 and instead carried over its 1947 model and put Gregorie and his Ford studio into competition with an outside design team led by Breech's golfing pal, former Nash designer George Walker.

Walker knew Studebaker designer Dick Caleal had just lost his job, and offered him the opportunity to do a proposal for Ford. With help from several designers still working

for the small automaker, Caleal crafted the car that, with just a few modifications, would become the 1949 Ford (Gregorie's proposal became the 1949 Mercury, but he quit Ford after Caleal's car was selected for mainline production). The '49 was the first modern Ford, with smoothed fenders integrated into the body. It also was the first Ford with independent coil-spring front and parallel leaf-spring rear suspension.

Power came from the latest update of Ford's fabled "Flathead Ford" V8 engine. It was lower and shorter than its predecessor, and because Ford had basically skipped the 1948 model year, the '49 was introduced at New York's prestigious Waldorf-Astoria hotel in June 1948, and thus had a huge head start in the sales race against its rivals from Chevrolet and Plymouth. Ford sold more than 800,000 units of the car – sedans, coupes, convertibles and station wagons, nearly equaling all of its sales for the previous two years. Combined with sales of 1949 Mercurys and Lincolns, Ford Motor Company enjoyed its first 1-million-vehicle sales year since the 1930 sand a profit of more than $175 million. Decades later, Mercedes-Benz design chief Bruno Sacco would call the 1949 Ford's envelope body a "trend setting" step in modern automotive design. The '49 Ford also would become popular all over again as hot rodders revitalized aging '49s to produce sleek chopped and channeled cruisers, and then, more than half a century after it went into production, the '49 Ford would again provide inspiration, this time for the stunning Ford Forty-Nine concept car.

100 THE ONE-MILLIONTH 1949 FORD ROLLS OUT OF THE COMPANY'S ROUGE PLANT WITH HENRY FORD II AT THE WHEEL. NEXT TO HIM ARE HIS BROTHERS, BENTON, GENERAL MANAGER OF LINCOLN-MERCURY, AND WILLIAM CLAY, A COMPANY DIRECTOR.

101 THE 1949 FORD LAUNCHED DURING THE 1948 U.S. PRESIDENTIAL RACE BETWEEN HARRY TRUMAN AND THOMAS DEWEY. FORD ADVERTISING DECLARED ITS CAR THE BIG WINNER OF THE FALL CAMPAIGN.

VOLKSWAGEN BEETLE

The creation of the Volkswagen Beetle dates to the 1930s, but production didn't really get underway until 1946, and it wasn't until the 1949 model year that the first Bugs were built in a specification for export to the United States. Even then, only two Beetles made the trip across the Atlantic Ocean that year to the Hoffman Motor Car Company of New York City, but more – so many more – were destined to follow. So many more Beetles would come to the United States and would be sold throughout Europe and the rest of the world that in 1972 the Beetle would surpass the Ford Model T as the best-selling car of all time, a fact that not only underscores the Beetle's popularity and longevity, but shows how important the Model T was to spreading automotive mobility around the planet in the early years of the Twentieth century.

Volkswagen did more than export Beetles to the United States in 1949; it also launched a convertible version of the car as well as a larger, boxy people mover known as the Transporter (and later as the Microbus or Combi or Vanagon, but more commonly as simply the "Van." Other VW models would follow, including one that covered the basic Beetle chassis with a sleek, Italian-designed shell and sold for many years as the fabled Karmann-Ghia.). By the way, Beetle was never really the car's name. Like Bug, Beetle was an affectionate nickname for a car that Volkswagen produced simply as the Type 1.

The Beetle was basic transportation and the basic Beetle was designed in 1932 by Ferdinand Porsche, well known for his work on expensive road and racing cars for big German automakers such as Mercedes-Benz, and his new independent engineering company. Although his family's name would go on a series of sensational sports cars, Porsche wanted to build a car for all people, a car that would be affordable to all people, a people's car, a "volks wagon."

When Adolf Hitler came to power in Germany, he told the country's automakers that he wanted a car that people could buy for one thousand marks that would travel at speeds up to 100 kilometers per hour (62 mph) on the autobahns he would construct, average

102 FERDINAND PORSCHE
AND OTHERS WORKING ON
THE "VOLKS WAGON"
PRESENTED A SCALE MODEL
OF THE CAR TO ADOLF
HITLER ON HIS 49TH
BIRTHDAY IN 1938.

103 TOP FERDINAND PORSCHE (LEFT) SHOWS DESIGN SKETCHES FOR WHAT WOULD GO INTO PRODUCTION AT THE VOLKSWAGEN TYPE 1, A NAME FEW WOULD EVER USE. THE CAR WOULD BE KNOWN AROUND THE WORLD AS THE BEETLE AND WOULD REPLACE THE FORD MODEL T AS THE WORLD'S MOST POPULAR AUTOMOBILE.

103 BOTTOM THOUGH OFFICIALLY THE VOLKSWAGEN TYPE 1, THE BEETLE-SHAPED CAR PEOPLE'S CAR BECAME POPULAR NOT ONLY IN ITS NATIVE GERMANY, BUT AROUND THE WORLD, WITH MORE THAN 21.5 MILLION OF THEM SOLD BETWEEN 1946 AND THE END OF PRODUCTION IN 2003.

more than 30 miles per gallon, be easy to maintain and could carry four or five occupants. He even went so far as to suggest such a car should be shaped like a beetle because of that insect's streamlined shape. Because it was easier to start in cold weather (and few in Germany had garages), an air-cooled engine would be ideal. Project 12 by Porsche's young company, though not quite a streamlined as Hitler's own sketches, was just such a car, and its rear-mounted, air-cooled engine made from aluminum and magnesium helped save weight and cost by eliminating a long and heavy driveshaft.

Prototypes were built and tested, but civilian production at the Wolfsburg plant didn't begin until 1946. Production continued until the summer of 2003, when the final Beetle rolled off the assembly line at a VW plant in Mexico, where the car remained so popular that Phil Patton, author of "Bug," unofficial biography for the original as well as the New Beetle, noted that people had come to know the car affectionately car as the "vocho" or "vochito," Spanish for "navel," because everyone seemed to have one.

Well, maybe not everyone, but between 1946 and 2003, Volkswagen did build more than 21,529,000 of them.

104 TOP CUTAWAY DRAWING SHOWS THE INTERNAL WORKINGS OF THE VOLKSWAGEN'S AIR-COOLED, 1131-CC, HORIZONTALLY OPPOSED FOUR-CYLINDER ENGINE.

104-105 THE 1949 MODEL YEAR MARKED THE END OF THE "SPLIT WINDOW" LOOK AT THE BACK OF THE VOLKSWAGEN.

105 THE ENGINE WAS MADE FROM ALUMINUM AND MAGNESIUM TO KEEP IT AS LIGHT AS POSSIBLE. ITS POSITION AT THE REAR OF THE CAR ELIMINATED THE NEED FOR A LONG AND HEAVY DRIVESHAFT AND ITS WEIGHT ENHANCED WINTER TRACTION OF THE REAR DRIVE WHEELS. AT FIRST, THE ENGINE PRODUCED ONLY 25 HORSEPOWER, BUT MOUNTED IN A LIGHTWEIGHT CHASSIS WITH AN AERODYNAMICALLY BEETLE-SHAPED BODY, COULD PROPEL THE CAR TO SPEEDS OF 100 KM/H (62 MPH) AND AVERAGE SOME 30 MILES PER GALLON OF FUEL (LESS THAN 8 LITERS PER 100 KM).

106 TOP VOLKSWAGEN PRODUCED A CONVERTIBLE VERSION OF ITS BEETLE IN 1949. HOWEVER, UNLIKE THIS PROTOTYPE, THE PRODUCTION VERSION CAME WITH DOORS AND SIDE PANELS TO PROTECT THE REAR SEATS.

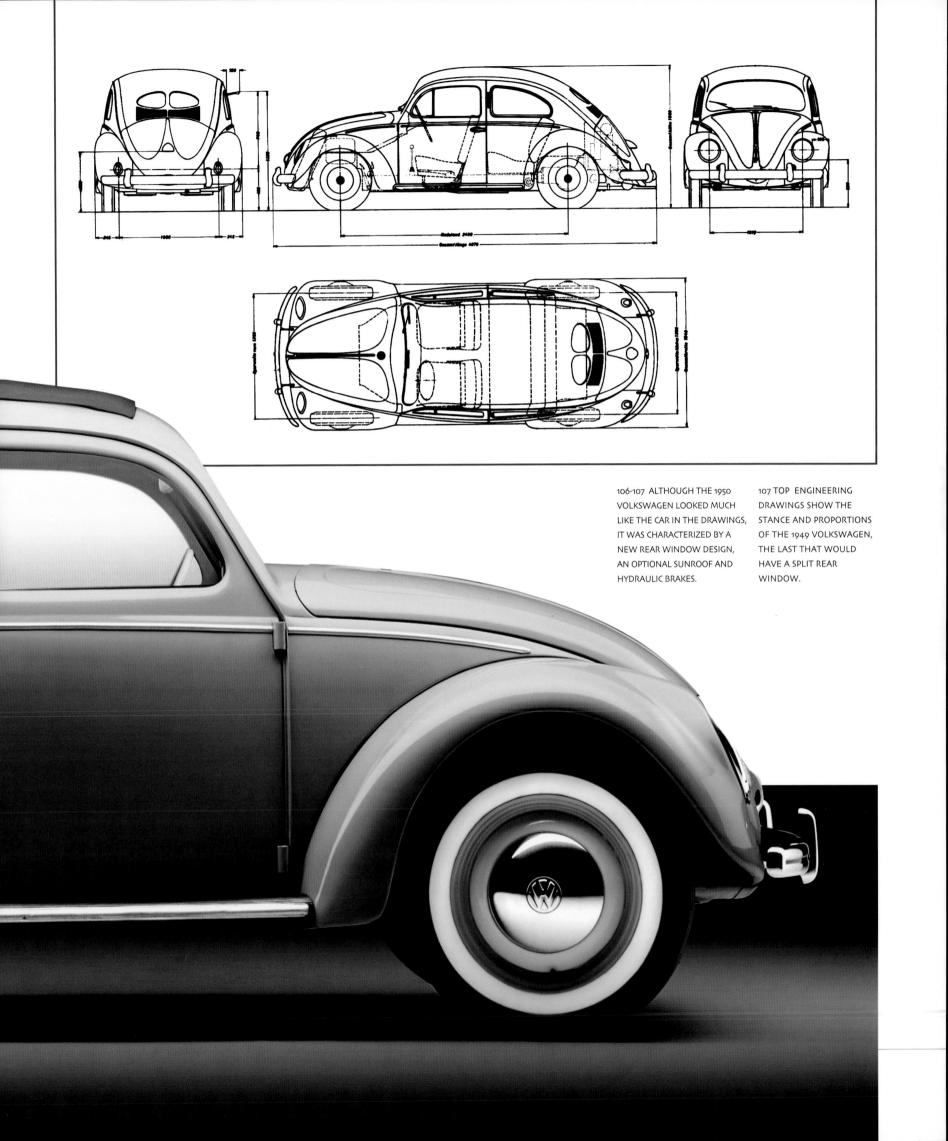

106-107 ALTHOUGH THE 1950
VOLKSWAGEN LOOKED MUCH
LIKE THE CAR IN THE DRAWINGS,
IT WAS CHARACTERIZED BY A
NEW REAR WINDOW DESIGN,
AN OPTIONAL SUNROOF AND
HYDRAULIC BRAKES.

107 TOP ENGINEERING
DRAWINGS SHOW THE
STANCE AND PROPORTIONS
OF THE 1949 VOLKSWAGEN,
THE LAST THAT WOULD
HAVE A SPLIT REAR
WINDOW.

PORSCHE 356

108 TOP KARL RABE (FAR LEFT) AND ERWIN KOMMENDA (CENTER) CONFER WITH FERRY PORSCHE ON THE DESIGN OF THE 356.

108-109 PORSCHE BEGAN PRODUCTION OF ITS 356 WITH A COUPE, BUT IN 1951 IT EXPANDED THE LINEUP TO INCLUDE A CONVERTIBLE.

109 TOP FERRY PORSCHE (FAR RIGHT) AND HIS TEAM INSPECT THE ALUMINUM-BODIED PROTOTYPE OF THEIR NEW SPORTS CAR.

I f the Porsche 356 reminds you of the Volkswagen Type 1 on the preceding pages, it's because these cars are as closely related as a father and a son.

Ferdinand Porsche was the father of the VW "Beetle." He also was the father of Ferdinand "Ferry" Porsche, who was the first to put the family's name on a production car, the Beetle-based Porsche 356. Like many subsequent Porsches, the car took its name because it was the 356th project for the Porsche engineering design company.

Ferry went to work in his father's design and engineering studio in 1931 and later managed development testing for everything from the Auto Union Grand Prix racer to the VW Type 1. In 1945, Ferry re-established the business in a workshop in Gmund, Austria, at first building accessories for farming equipment.

Cisitalia's Piero Dusio commissioned Porsche to develop a radical grand prix racer in 1947, and early in 1948 Porsche produced a prototype for a new sports car. The car was driven to Switzerland and shown to journalists covering the Swiss Grand Prix. They were so impressed they wrote articles praising the car and orders began to arrive. With his father rejoining the business, Ferry built some 52 aluminum-bodied 356s before the Porsche company returned to Germany, where Porsche switched to steel bodies for the 356 and over the course of some 15 years it built more than 75,000 units. While his father's Type 1 was the "people's" car, Ferry's 356, developed with engineer Karl Rabe and body designer Erwin Kommenda, was designed for those very few people who wanted a versatile yet relatively inexpensive sports car that could be driven on the street and raced on the track.

The 356 drew heavily on the Type 1 and its rear-engine architecture, though Volkswagen's 1131-cc horizontally opposed four-cylinder engine was modified to displace just 1086 cc, so it would qualify for the 1100-cc racing class. The VW engine provided only 25 horsepower but Porsche's tweaks, including two carburetors, larger valves and higher compression, pumped out 40 horsepower, enough to propel the aerodynamically bodied car to speed of 135 km/h (nearly 85 miles per hour).

Light and low-slung, and with most of its weight at the rear of the car, the 356 could cor-

ner very quickly, once the driver learned to control and tail-happy car's tendency toward overpowering its VW-based torsion-bar/swing axle rear suspension. But the skilled driver could use the car's superior dynamics and its fuel-efficiency to advantage on the racetrack. The 356 could outmaneuver and outlast larger, much more powerful cars in long-distance endurance races.

The Porsche made its debut at Le Mans in 1951 and scored the first of many victories in its engine-displacement class. Porsche added a special racing version, the 550 Spyder, in 1955 and despite their little 1.5-liter engines, the cars finished fourth, fifth and sixth at Le Mans, trailing only D-type Jaguars and an Aston Martin DB3S/6. Later, more powerful Porsches would post a record number of overall victories in the world's most prestigious round-the-clock competition.

The 356 was built in coupe, convertible and

racy Speedster versions and would go through several updated iterations, such as in 1955 when Porsche introduced the 356A with a 1.6-liter engine and improved suspension and steering.

The 356's development culminated with the Carrera 2, powered by a quad-cam, 2.0-liter four-cylinder engine that produced some 140 horsepower and was stopped by four-wheel disc brakes.

The 356, a son's dream built on his father's legacy, remained in production until late in 1965, when Porsche launched its new model, the 911.

110-111 THE PORSCHE 356 WAS BUILT AS A COUPE, CONVERTIBLE AND IN A SPEEDSTER VERSION WITH A LOW-CUT WINDSHIELD.

111 TOP THE 356 WAS THE FIRST CAR TO BEAR THE NAME OF FERDINAND PORSCHE, ONE OF THE AUTOMOTIVE GENIUS OF THE 20TH CENTURY. THE CAR WAS DEVELOPED USING COMPONENTS FROM FERDINAND PORSCHE'S VOLKSWAGEN.

MG TD

To Europeans, the MG TD was not a milestone in the development of the modern automobile.

It was neither the best and certainly not the most beautiful of British roadsters, but that didn't matter to the many Americans for whom this small two-seater represented their first first-hand experience with a real European sports car. MG takes its name from Morris Garages. Cecil Kimber managed Lord Nuffield's garages and decided to start building sports cars with Morris sedan components. There were the M- and J-type Midgets of the early 1930s and then the T series launched in 1936 with the TA. The TB went into production in 1939, though fewer than 400 would be built before English automakers turned their attention to military production.

MG started building cars again in 1945 and even though its TC roadsters lacked heaters, were stiffly sprung on their rigid axles, had tight cockpits with steering wheels mounted on the right side, used ash wood to join body panels and were powered by ancient, small four-cylinder engines that produced only 54 horsepower, American servicemen stationed in England loved the little MG roadsters. Several thousand of those troops took TCs home with them. In fact, of the nearly ten thousand TCs that MG built between 1945 and 1949, two-thirds of them would find homes on foreign soil.

In the fall of 1949, MG began production of the TD and the fact that some 90 percent of the nearly 30,000 built had left-hand drive had their steering wheels mounted on the left side of the cockpit tells you that this car was designed for American drivers.

The position of the steering wheel wasn't

the only change. Gone was the light on the dashboard that alerted the driver that he was exceeding 48 kilometers per hour (the British town limit of about 30 miles per hour).

While the TD retained the classic "square rigger" MG body design – upright grille, bolted-on headlights, long curving fenders, rear-hinged doors, short rear deck, a flip-down windshield and wood-reinforced body – it was built on a shortened version of the chassis beneath the company's Y-type sedan. Thus the TD went to American buyers with a wider cockpit and independent front suspension and increased rear suspension travel that provided a softer ride (more suitable to American tastes) as well as rack and pinion steering.

The TD also sprouted bumpers. However, instead of the TC's handsome 19-inch wire wheels, the TD rode on sedan-style 15-inch steel discs. But at least MG offered factory-tuning kits to increase the 54-horsepower engine's output. Then, in 1951, MG added a Mk II version, also known as the TDC – C standing for Competition – that provided 60 horsepower and a top speed of more than 80 miles per hour. The TD was succeeded in 1953 by the TF, which had integrated headlamps and bucket seats, and in 1955 MG finally produced its first modern sports car, the MGA. But it was the MG TD that paved the way along American roads for that car and for so many other European sportsters that would follow.

112-113 WITH A WIDER BODY AND SOFTER INDEPENDENT SUSPENSION, THE MG TD WAS DESIGNED WITH THE AMERICAN DRIVER IN MIND. NEARLY 90 PERCENT OF THESE CARS WERE BUILT WITH THEIR STEERING WHEELS ON THE LEFT SIDE. THE LAST OF THE MG TD MODELS WAS THE MK II, WHICH ENDED PRODUCTION IN 1953 AS MG INTRODUCED THE TF.

LANCIA AURELIA B20GT

Lancia was known for trend-setting innovation. Many consider the Italian automaker's 1951 Aurelia B20 coupe to be the first modern grand touring machine.

Vincenzio Lancia had been trained as an accountant, but was still a teenager in 1899, when he went to work as a test driver for F.I.A.T. Almost immediately he was driving for Fiat's racing team and quickly established himself among the most skilled drivers in the world, often as part of Italy's three-man team in the Gordon Bennett Trophy races.

In 1906, while still racing for Fiat, he established his own auto company and within two years was building a series of cars named for the letters in the Greek alphabet.

By the 1920s, Lancia's Lambda sedans were among the first with unit-body construction and independent "sliding pillar" front suspension. In 1937, the year of the founder's death at age 56, Lancia launched the Aprilia, among the first sedans with a streamlined body and all-independent suspension.

Lancia's son, Gianni, brought in Vittorio Jano, the automotive engineer who had been responsible for much of Alfa Romeo's early success in motorsports, and they worked together to create Lancia's first post-war sedan, the Aurelia B10, which debuted in 1950. The cars were the first in series production powered by V6 engines and offered nicely balanced driving dynamics thanks to a rear-mounted transaxle with a four-speed gearbox and the differential and with inboard rear brakes mounted on the final drive assembly.

For 1951 model year, Battista "Pinin" Farina

was assigned to design a coupe version of the car, an open Spyder and a convertible with roll-up side windows would follow in the middle years of the decade. Pinin Farina's design drew on his earlier Cisitalia, but featured Lancia's shield-shaped and vertically barred grille that flowed out of a raised hood. Vignale was among several coachbuilders who produced their own bodywork for the car, but the original design was never challenged for its graceful lines.

The Aurelia GT shared much of its platform with the sedan, though was shorter, by some eight inches in overall length and wheelbase. The car would grow some four inches in its second year.

The car was launched with a larger V6 engine that displaced nearly two liters (1991 cc) and pumped out 75 hp, but over the course

of the car's production, which ran through 1958 and some 4600 units, the engine would grow to displace 2.45 liters and 112 hp, enough to propel the stylish fastback coupe to speeds to around 115 mph. The rear suspension also changed, from trailing arms and coil springs to de Dion tubes and leaf springs.

The cars handled so well that several Grand Prix drivers bought them and several teams, including a Lancia factory crew, used them for racing. Aurelia GTs finished second and fifth in the Mille Miglia in 1951 and one was 12th overall and first in the 1501-2000 cc class in the 24 Hours of Le Mans that year. Aurelias posted a 1-2-3 finish in the Targa Florio in 1952 and a special racing version, the D20, won that race again in 1953 with a D24 Spyder winning it in1954.

114 TOP IT'S NOT DIFFICULT TO SEE HOW PININ FARINA EXPANDED ON THE STYLING CUES HE ESTABLISHED WITH HIS EARLIER CISITALIA WHEN HE DESIGNED THE AURELIA B20GT.

115 TOP FAMED GRAND PRIX RACER LOUIS CHIRON AWAITS THE START OF THE 1953 MONTE CARLO RALLY. CHIRON DROVE A LANCIA AURELIA IN THE EVENT.

114-115 SHORTENING THE CHASSIS AND WHEELBASE OF THE AURELIA SEDAN HELPED GIVE THE TWO-DOOR VERSION A MUCH SPORTIER STANCE. OF 4500 GTS, MORE THAN 3800 WERE BUILT AS COUPES.

116 AND 117 PININ FARINA, EXTENDING STYLING THEMES HE ESTABLISHED WITH HIS EARLIER CISITALIA, ALSO DESIGNED A SPYDER VERSION OF THE AURELIA.

BENTLEY R-TYPE

The car company founded by W.O. Bentley had made its name with fast cars, cars that were so fast and reliable that the famed "Bentley Boys" won the 24 Hours of Le Mans marathon race five times, first in 1924 and then four years running from 1927-30. A 4.5-liter Bentley won the Brooklands 500 race in England in 1927 at an average speed of 106 mph (170 km/h).

The Depression proved devastating to Bentley, which became a subsidiary of Rolls-Royce in 1931 and for many years Bentley's were basically Rolls' with a different grille and "winged B" emblem. Soon after World War II, Ivan Everden, director of Bentley's Experimental Department, went to work on a special car, codenamed Corniche II, designed to recapture Bentley's earlier glory. While the "mule" for the pro-

gram was a reworked Bentley Mk VI known as "Olga," such a special car would have to have a glorious body, so Everden used Rolls-Royce's wind tunnel and its design chief John Blatchley to sculpt a wind-cheating, fastback shape that featured curving tail fins to help stabilize the car at high speeds.

The car's design may have borrowed much from American automaker Cadillac, both its 1948 Series 62 coupe and its Berlina concept by Pinin Farina, who also was retained to sculpt a Bentley concept that was shown at Paris in 1948 and resembled a larger-scale Cisitalia. But regardless of the inspiration, the

CONTINENTAL

118-119 THE BENTLEY R-TYPE CONTINENTAL WAS A LARGE AND STUNNING FASTBACK COUPE AND THE FASTEST FOUR-SEATER IN THE WORLD WHEN IT WAS INTRODUCED IN 1954.

Bentley R-Type Continental was not only the fastest four-passenger car and most expensive production passenger vehicle on the road when it was introduced, but also was among the world's most beautiful motorcars.

The R-Type Continental was a luxury car designed for the owner who wanted to drive, not ride in the back seat. To trim weight, body panels were made from aluminum, and while the interior remained plush, the usual over-stuffed seats were replaced with bucket seats built on alloy frames, and the full-width wood instrument panel was given an extensive set of gauges, including a tachometer and oil temperature reader.

Drivers kept an eye on the tach and they manipulated a four-speed manual transmission to keep the 4566-cc inline 6-cylinder engine in the heart of its power band. The engine was the standard R-Type motor with overhead intake and side exhaust valves, but operated at a higher compression ratio and with a larger diameter exhaust to produce some 175 hp, enough to propel the car from a standing start to 60 mph in 13.5 seconds on the way to a top speed of 120 mph. In addition to being fast, the Bentley R-Type Continental was expensive, priced in the

United States at $17,330, some four times as much as the top of the line Cadillac coupe. In fact, only 208 of the expensive Bentley R-Type Continental coupes were built. Of those, 193 had bodywork by H.J. Mulliner, 100 were sold outside England and only 43 had left-hand drive.

Bentley offered a new R-Type Continental in 1955, but this one was built on a longer and heavier S Series platform and came with an automatic transmission. Bentley revived the spirit of the original in 1991 with the Continental R, a turbocharged V8-powered car that was the first Bentley in 40 years that didn't share its body shell with a Rolls-Royce model. Then, for 2005, Bentley launched the Continental GT and this twin-turbocharged, 12-cylinder coupe brought the title of world's fastest four-seater back to the "Bentley Boys."

120-121 BENTLEY'S NEW R-TYPE WAS AVAILABLE AS A STANDARD SEDAN FROM THE FACTORY IN CREWE, AS A CUSTOM-BODIED COUPE OR SEDAN FROM VARIOUS COACHBUILDERS (THIS 1954 VERSION IS BY FREESTONE & WEBB) OR AS THE CONTINENTAL COUPE, DESIGNED NOT FOR RIDING IN THE BACKSEAT BUT FOR THE ENJOYMENT OF THE DRIVER.

CHEVROLET CORVETTE

By 1949, General Motors design director Harley Earl had decided that America needed a sports car of its very own. American drivers were enjoying the MG TCs, Jaguar XK120s, Porsche 356s and other roadsters that were trickling in from across the Atlantic. Earl saw an opportunity to go the imports one better. His goal: Build an American sports car that would be both low-priced and high-powered. When General Motors staged its first Motorama auto show in January, 1953 in the ballroom of the New York's famed Waldorf-Astoria Hotel, the magnet that drew the crowds was Earl's sports car dream machine, codenamed EX-122 during its development but introduced to the public as the Chevrolet Corvette.

Earl's Corvette had classic front-engine, rear-drive, two-seat roadster architecture wrapped by a sleek body with low and smooth contours. A handsome grille comprising 13 vertical chrome bars ran across the front of the car between pontoon-style fenders with inset headlamps protected by racing-style mesh covers. A wrap-around windshield protected the driver and passenger. Behind the hard tonneau that covered the convertible top, the rear deck plunged between rounded rear quarter panels topped by distinctive cylindrical extensions that extended the car's shoulder line and housed afterburner-style tail lamps. GM

thought it could sell as many as 10,000 Corvette a year, and set Earl, engineering chief Ed Cole and their staffs to work to get production started as quickly as possible. Earl's original prospectus for the car called for its engine to provide 150 horsepower and for the car to be priced at less than $2,000, in other words it would match Jaguar on performance and MG on price. The power target was tough but achievable. The pricing target was unrealistic. In an attempt to reach it, GM had to cut corners, us-

ing an engine, transmission, suspension components and brakes out of the Chevrolet sedan parts bin and making the car's body from fiberglass instead of steel. The engine was a 3.8-liter inline six designed back in the mid-1930s. Cole's crew did a lot of hot-rodding – new camshaft and valve gear, lighter pistons, higher compression and triple carburetors – and finally got it up to 150 horsepower, a remarkable feat considering the stock engine was rated at 115.

But they still had to use GM's two-speed

122-123 THE CHEVROLET CORVETTE BEGAN PRODUCTION AS A 1953 MODEL (THE 1954 MODEL SHOWN WAS VIRTUALLY IDENTICAL).

123 TOP THE CORVETTE WAS RESTYLED FOR 1956. A YEAR LATER (THAT'S A 1957 'VETTE BELOW), A FUEL-INJECTED V8 PROVIDED 250 HORSEPOWER AND THE CORVETTE WAS TRULY UP AND RUNNING.

Powerglide automatic transmission instead of the manual gearbox that sports car enthusiasts demanded.

Production began on June 30, 1953. Americans weren't eager for a car that had side curtains instead of roll down windows, and the Corvette didn't match the Jaguar on performance or the MG on price. In fact, at $3,250, the car's price tag was twice that of a typical Chevrolet sedan.

GM would build only 300 Corvettes in 1953 and it would take four years and a second-generation body style change before the company would build the 10,000 roadsters it thought it would sell each and every year. The car likely would have died an early and quiet death had it not been for three things: The arrival of a young engineer named Zora Arkus-Duntov, who had been among those who saw the Corvette at the Motorama and who won a job at GM by convincing the company that he could make the car even better, by GM rival Ford's announcement that it would build it own sports car, the Thunderbird, for the 1955 model year, and by GM's development of a new V8 engine that, with a three-speed manual transmission, finally would make the Corvette not only the car Earl and Arkus-Duntov wanted all along, but now and truly America's sports car.

124 FRENCH ACTRESS,
MODEL AND IN 1958 THE
WORLD PARACHUTE
RECORD HOLDER COLETTE
DUVAL — WITH A
SUCCESSFUL JUMP FROM

40,700 FEET (12.410
METERS) — POSES ON A
"GULLWING" MERCEDES-
BENZ 300 SL IN FRONT OF
PARIS' NOTRE DAME
CATHEDRAL.

MERCEDES-BENZ 300 SL

Late in spring 2004, Britain's CAR magazine bedecked its cover with a Ferrari Enzo, the original Bullitt Mustang and James Bonds' very own Aston Martin to tout "The 100 Coolest Cars" of all time. But inside, as readers worked their way through the list, Steve McQueen's Ford rated only No. 10. Sean Connery's DB5 made it only to 6th place. The Enzo was no better than runner-up.

And what did the editors consider to be the coolest car ever? Why, the Mercedes-Benz 300SL, the famed Gullwing, of course. This car, they noted, was "not so much ahead of its time as completely, glorious out of step with the known universe."

"Isolate the three main constituents of cool and you get there: authenticity; innovation; and unique style. Aside from these, the race-bred Mercedes-Benz 300 SL has almost no other moving parts…"

Authenticity: This car was created for the racetrack long before anyone thought about unleashing it on the road. When it finally did reach regular streets, it was the fastest car in the world, with an even more powerful engine than it had when it won the 24 Hours of Le Mans or the Carrera Panamericana race up the spine of Mexico.

Innovation: A space frame chassis, fuel injection – the first in a production car – instead of carburetors, plus dry sump oil lubri-

124-125 THOUGH OFFICIALLY THE 300 SL COUPE (A SOFT-TOP CONVERTIBLE VERSION ALSO WAS AVAILABLE), THIS CAR WILL FOREVER BE KNOWN AS THE "GULLWING" BECAUSE OF THE WAY ITS DOORS OPEN WITH HINGES MOUNTED IN THE ROOF.

126 SO TIGHT WAS THE COCKPIT THAT THE STEERING WHEEL WAS DESIGNED TO PIVOT DOWN SO THE DRIVER HAD ROOM TO ENTER OR EXIT.

126-127 BENEATH ITS LONG HOOD WAS THE FIRST PRODUCTION CAR ENGINE WITH FUEL INJECTORS INSTEAD OF CARBURETORS. THE INLINE SIX-CYLINDER ENGINE WAS TIPPED SLIGHTLY TOWARD ITS SIDE SO THE HOOD COULD BE LOWER AND THE CAR'S LINES MORE AERODYNAMIC.

cation for an inline 6-cylinder engine tipped toward its side so the hood could be lower and thus reduce aerodynamic drag.

Unique style: The 300SL's doors pivot open from near the centerline of the car's roof and incorporate roof panels, side window and door in a single stair-stepped unit that achieves both form and function, because such doors were needed to add structural integrity to the car's space frame chassis architecture. Mercedes-Benz developed the 300SL as the vehicle for its return to international motorsports competition and it recorded 1-2 finishes at both Le Mans and in Mexico in its inaugural season.

That and a few other victories might have been all there was for the remarkable car had New York auto importer Max Hoffman not placed an order for road-going versions of the car. Hoffman was persuasive; he also convinced Porsche to develop a Speedster and BMW to build the 507. The SL stood for "sport light" and the car was both sporty and lightweight.

The engine, based on the 115-hp, 3.0-liter 6-cylinder unit in Mercedes' 300 series sedans, pumped out 240 hp (by American horsepower ratings) in its fuel-injected form, propelling the 2600-lb coupe from a standing start to 60 mph in only 8.8 seconds. Top speed was nearly 150

mph, a rate unmatched by any other production car on the road. However, driving this car was not a simple thing, because its swing-arm rear axle had a tendency toward oversteer, and civilian buyers quickly had an appreciation for the skills of racers such as Rudolf Caracciola, Hermann Lang, Karl Kling and John Fitch. But get things right and, well, a British magazine reported that being in the car felt as though you were being "rocketed through space" as the car accelerated toward its top speed. Mercedes-Benz produced 1400 of the "Gullwing" coupes between 1954 and 1957, and then added 1858 300SL roadsters between 1957 and 1963.

ALFA ROMEO GIULIETTA SPRINT AND SPIDER

128-129 PININ FARINA DESIGNED THE GIULIETTA SPIDER, WHICH WAS BUILT ON A WHEELBASE SHORTENED BY SEVEN INCHES FROM THE SPRINT COUPE. THE CHANGE ENHANCED THE CAR'S OPEN-TOP STANCE. THE LITTLE ROADSTER WAS LIGHTWEIGHT, HAD ROLL-UP WINDOWS AND A TOP THAT WAS EASY TO OPEN OR CLOSE, BUT WERE MORE EXPENSIVE THAN THE JAGUAR XK 150 OR AC ACE THAT WERE IN PRODUCTION AT THE SAME TIME.

When Alfa Romeo resumed automobile production in 1946, it did so with an updated pre-war sports car design. By 1951, and with the help of Italy's broad array of coach-builders, it began production of the 1900 line of sedans, which featured unit-body architecture and perky little double overhead-cam engines.

Then, in 1952, Italy's Institute for Industrial Reconstruction decided that Alfa Romeo should add another line of even smaller sedans and a lottery was organized to raise funds to underwrite the car's development, with several of the cars being awarded as prizes. But a problem arose when it became clear that the car would not be ready in time. Alfa Romeo turned again to the coach-builders, to Bertone and "Pinin" Farina. Bertone put Franco Scaglione to work on a coupe and Pinin Farina concentrated on a convertible. The results were the Alfa Romeo Giulietta Sprint and Spider, which were introduced nearly a year before the sedan was in production.

Scaglione had designed the jet-like Abarth coupe concept car and was working on his stunning, bat-winged Berlina Aerodinamica Technica (B.A.T.) series of concepts, but as British design professor Penny Sparke writes in *A Century of Car Design*, "he was equally capable of holding back from such extravagances and achieving very simple, unostentatious forms that depended for their impact on their attention to visual detail. Nowhere, perhaps was this more evident than in his design for the Giulietta Sprint of 1954."

The Sprint was rushed into production to serve as the prize for the Alfa lottery, and it was such a wonderful prize that those who didn't win one still wanted one and Bertone had to build a new factory to keep up with demand.

The Giulietta, given its Shakespearian name by Italian poet Leonardo Sinisgalli, was powered by a smaller version of the 1900's 4-cylinder engine, but now with an aluminum block as well as dual overhead camshafts. While the 1290-cc Giulietta engines were rated at only 53 hp, those used in the Sprints pumped out 80 hp, thanks to two-barrel carburetors and higher compression ratios, and drivers could put that power to its best uses thanks to the car's well-engineered chassis and suspension.

In 1956 Alfa and Bertone launched the Veloce (speed) version with dual carburetors and 90 hp. Later, they added an exotically bodied, 100-hp Sprint Speciale and coach-builder Zagato used the same engine in a smaller and lighter SZ variation. The higher-performance Sprints were popular as race and rally cars, but the Spider was the car of choice for cruising the boulevards.

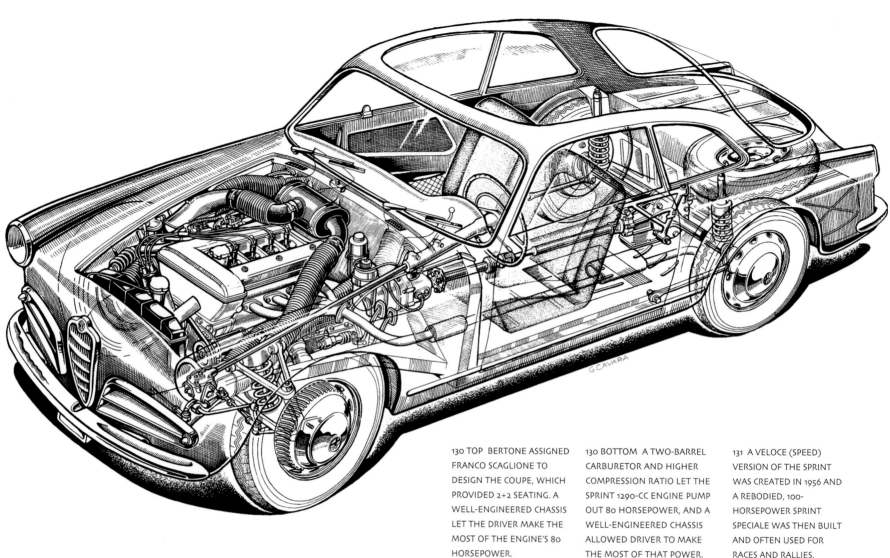

130 TOP BERTONE ASSIGNED FRANCO SCAGLIONE TO DESIGN THE COUPE, WHICH PROVIDED 2+2 SEATING. A WELL-ENGINEERED CHASSIS LET THE DRIVER MAKE THE MOST OF THE ENGINE'S 80 HORSEPOWER.

130 BOTTOM A TWO-BARREL CARBURETOR AND HIGHER COMPRESSION RATIO LET THE SPRINT 1290-CC ENGINE PUMP OUT 80 HORSEPOWER, AND A WELL-ENGINEERED CHASSIS ALLOWED DRIVER TO MAKE THE MOST OF THAT POWER.

131 A VELOCE (SPEED) VERSION OF THE SPRINT WAS CREATED IN 1956 AND A REBODIED, 100-HORSEPOWER SPRINT SPECIALE WAS THEN BUILT AND OFTEN USED FOR RACES AND RALLIES.

Pinin Farina shortened the Giulietta and Sprint's wheelbase base some seven inches and shortened overall length by four inches to achieve the right proportions for the convertible, which featured roll-up windows, a top that was easy to put up or down and a surprisingly roomy passenger area, yet was even lighter in weight than the coupe.

As with the coupe, there would be a Veloce version, with a discreetly wide but thin hood scoop poised above the badge-shaped Alfa grille that split the chromed front bumper to give the convertible a face distinct from the coupe's, which had a full-width front bumper.

Both Sprint and Spider were distinctly different from the sedan, but their halo effect helped keep the Giulietta popular and in production for nearly a decade.

Style and Speed:
The pace increases

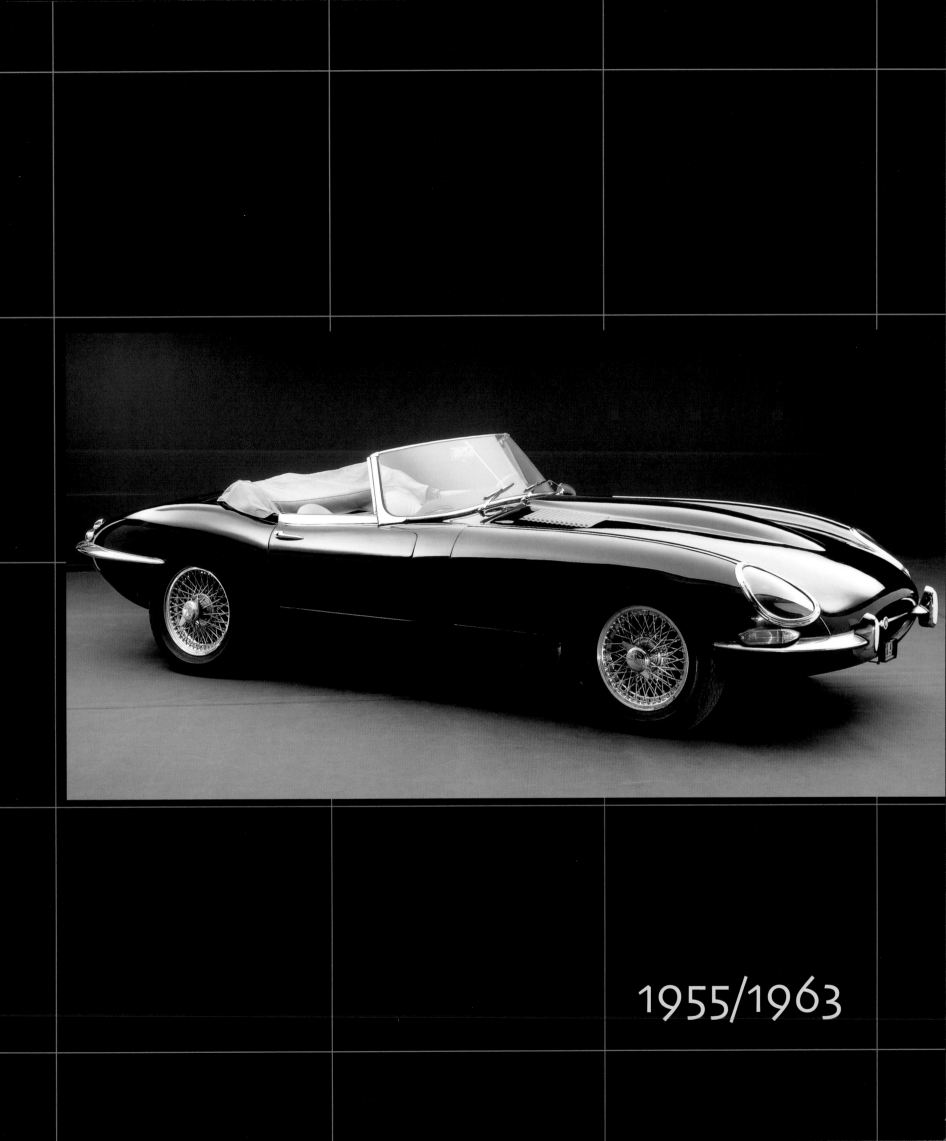

1955/1963

After all, the entire world was changing, on the roads and in the sky. It was October 4, 1957 that the Union of Soviet Socialist Republics launched Sputnik, a basketball-sized, 183-pound (83-kilogram) artificial satellite into orbit around the Earth. The Space Race was on. As a result, new technologies were coming that would affect every aspect of life on the planet, from new foods

duction to yet another new body shape in the form of the 1958 Austin A40. A rare British car styled by an Italian designer, Battista "Pinin" Farina created a new "two-box" design that was a precursor to the hatchback styling that would become so popular throughout Europe in the ensuing decades.

Meanwhile, in the United States, the optimistic confidence of the post-war boom was showing up on the highways in

road-building frenzy. Whether they were called autoroutes or motorways, autostradas or autobahns, expressways or Interstates, these new highways were designed to increase the flow of transportation.

Thus whether they were British and proud of being able to build cars that were fast and nimble in the tight corners of a city or while blasting around on narrow country lanes, or Italians finally trading two wheels for four, or Frenchmen proud of their nation's technological advances, or Germans unbound on their autobahns, or Americans portraying their success in chrome and fins, people wanted to travel quickly.

Style and Speed: The pace increases

In seemingly every country, motorists could drive many miles of these new superhighways just about as fast as their cars could carry them. In many areas, speed was governed more by the capabilities of their cars than by a government-imposed legal speed limit.

to new materials and microprocessors.

But long before any of those things would move from the sky to the pavement, this era would spawn a succession of vehicles that would go from the little Fiat 500 and aptly named British Mini to the sleek Jaguar E-type and racy Chevrolet Corvette Stingray all the way the fast Ferrari 250 GT and the awesome AC Shelby Cobra.

It also was an era in which an upstart Japanese motorcycle maker named Soichiro Honda rebelled when told that his country had enough automobile manufacturers and went ahead with production of the S500, his first car, but certainly not his last.

Eager for any kind of four-wheeled transportation, some Europeans opted for the new "bubble cars," little more than enclosed capsules powered by motorcycle engines. Others were getting their intro-

the form of chrome-laden cars that underwent complete styling changes on an annual basis. Bigger was better, and that applied not only to the cars themselves but especially to the wing-like appendages – the fins — rising above their rear quarter panels. In an era of Sputnik, these cars looked more like rocket ships than automobiles.

The world knew America as the land of wide-open spaces. Route 66 may have been the "Mother Road" that carried the migration to Los Angeles and the promised land of Southern California, but it was the country's new superhighway system, the Interstates, that was paving the way for America's love affair with speed and style.

As President of the United States in the 1940s, Eisenhower would push for an expansive network of superhighways, and the United States was not alone in its

But people also wanted to travel in style, in cars that expressed both personal and national personalities. Sometimes, this combination of speed and style were carried to excess. But with delightful frequency, speed and style were hallmarks of an era of automotive engineering and design.

133 FEW CARS HAVE EVER CAPTURED THE ESSENCE OF STYLE AND SPEED QUITE LIKE THE JAGUAR XK-E, A CAR DESIGNED BY AERODYNAMICIST MALCOLM SAYER AND A LOT OF HELP FROM THE WIND ON THE MULSANNE STRAIGHT AT LE MANS.

135 THIS CUSTOM-BODIED CADILLAC EPITOMIZES A DIFFERENT PART OF THE SPEED AND STYLE EQUATION. ITS HEAVILY CHROMED CHARACTER WAS DESIGNED NOT FOR EUROPEAN ROADS AND TASTES, BUT FOR AMERICA'S WIDE-OPEN SPACES.

1955/1963

C ars 1930-2000: The Birth of the Modern Car is a technically oriented book by three authors who consume more than 700 pages with text and illustrations that trace the development of what we know as the contemporary automobile. The authors note that cars were pretty much the same for some two decades, from the mid-1930s into the early 1950s. The "next phase of innovation," they write, coincided with the introduction of Citroën's DS19 in the fall of 1955.

Citroën's Dérivation Spécial rode not on conventional metal springs but on a height-adjustable hydropneumatic suspension – and on Michelin's new radial tires. Should one of those tires suffer a puncture, the suspension system could raise the car so the flat tire could be changed without the need of a jack. The DS had power steering. It had front – and inboard – disc brakes. It had a clutchless gear

CITROËN DS

shifting. It had a chassis with front and rear "crumple zones" and body panels that could easily be unbolted and replaced in the event of an accident. The car's remarkable construction may have helped save the life of French president Charles de Gaulle, who drove away from a 1962 assassination attempt in a DS that had two flat tires and a bullet-riddled body.

With front-wheel drive, there was no driveshaft tunnel protruding into the passenger compartment, there was overstuffed-seating comfort for five people.

The car's curving rear glass stayed dry even in the rain. Midway through this remarkable car's 20-year production run it featured headlamps that moved along with the car's single-spoke steering wheel to illuminate the road around a curve.

The French called the car the Déesse, the goddess. French philosopher Roland Barthes said the car's body appeared "as if it has fallen from the sky." Actually, the shark-shaped body with only a slit of a grille was designed by Flaminio Bertoni, the Italian sculptor who also had designed the Citroën 2CV. Bertoni collaborated with Pierre Franchiset and worked in clay rather than at a drafting table to sculpt an aerodynamic body around a chassis that had a rear track that was some eight inches narrower than the front wheels.

In addition to Citroën's sedan and Safari Estate wagon versions, French coachbuilders

produced stretched limousines of the DS and Henri Chapron crafted a sleek Croisette cabriolet. Art museums in Milan, London and New York would put the DS on display, but this goddess more than a heavenly body, she seemed to float above the road as if on a magic carpet.

Citroën's hydropneumatic system used non-compressible liquid (mineral oil) and a compressible gas (nitrogen) to maintain a smooth ride and to allow the driver to use a knob on the dashboard to adjust the car's height above the road from 6.5 inches to a full 12 inches. Although its aerodynamic body helped provide a top speed of 90 mph, the DS was underpowered, in part because its aging, 1.9-liter, 4-cylinder engine provided power not only to the front wheels but to the complex hydraulic systems, but the engine in the original DS19 could generate only 75 hp. Later versions – DS20, DS21 and fuel-injected DS23 with more than 140 hp – took their name from slightly larger and more powerful engines

In many ways, the Citroën DS was years ahead of its time when it was launched in 1955, and that statement remained true when production ended two years later.

In 2004, when Britain's CAR magazine selected the 50 "coolest" cars of all-time, the DS ranked fourth, ahead of all Porsches, the AC Cobra and even the Jaguar XK-E.

138 AND 139 BOTTOM ITALIAN SCULPTOR FLAMINIO BERTONI AND CITROËN BODY ENGINEER AND DESIGNER PIERRE FRANCHISET STYLED THE DS FROM CLAY RATHER THAN ON A DRAFTING TABLE. PHILOSOPHER ROLAND BARTHES SAID THE CAR'S BODY APPEARED HEAVENLY. OTHERS SIMPLY CALLED THIS CITROËN THE *DEESSE*, THE GODDESS.

139 TOP SPEAKING OF GODDESSES, ITALIAN ACTRESS GINA LOLLOBRIGIDA SHOWS JUST HOW MUCH LUGGAGE CAN BE SWALLOWED BY THE DS'S TRUNK. IN ADDITION TO ITS VAST INTERIOR, THE CAR HAD A NARROW SLOT RATHER THAN A TALL FRONT GRILLE AND ITS CURVED REAR GLASS WAS DESIGNED TO STAY DRY EVEN IN THE RAIN.

ROLLS-ROYCE SILVER CLOUD

140 THE SILVER CLOUD WAS THE FIRST ROLLS-ROYCE SENT TO CUSTOMERS WITH "STANDARD" RATHER THAN CUSTOM COACH-BUILT BODYWORK. THE CAR WAS DESIGNED TO APPEAL TO OWNERS WHO WOULD RATHER DRIVE THAN SIT IN THE BACK SEAT WHILE A CHAUFFEUR TOOK THE WHEEL.

141 MOST COMMONLY KNOWN AS "THE FLYING LADY," THE ROLLS ROYCE SYMBOL WAS DESIGNED IN 1911 BY ARTIST CHARLES SYKES, WHO USED A SECRETARY, ELEANOR THORNTON, AS HIS MODEL FOR WHAT ORIGINALLY WAS "THE SPIRIT OF SPEED" AND LATER WAS OFFICIALLY DESIGNATED "THE SPIRIT OF ECSTASY."

Charles Stewart Rolls and Frederick Henry Royce seemed to have nothing in common – except their interest in a better automobile. Rolls was born to wealth. His Peugeot was reported to be the first motorcar to grace the campus of Cambridge University and soon he was considered among England's best drivers. By 1903, he'd set the world land-speed record at 93 miles per hour in an 80-horsepower, French-built Mors. Instead of applying his degree in engineering, he opened a car dealership but wasn't satisfied with the cars he was importing. He wanted something better and that's how he met his unlikely partner.

Royce was born to a working-class family and had gone to work himself at age 10. By day he worked – selling newspapers, then as an apprentice in a locomotive works, then at machine tool and electric light companies. But by night he went to school at night and, still in his early twenties, he opened his own company to manufacture electrical cranes.

About the time Rolls was setting speed records, Royce was buying his first car, a second-hand car. He tired to having to make constant repairs and decided to build his own car and had a pair of them on the stand at the Paris auto show in 1904.

Soon Rolls-Royce was established, though instead of building entire cars, the firm focused on developing smooth, powerful and quiet engines and the rolling chassis on which custom coachbuilders could craft bodies for the rich and famous.

But that changed with the introduction in 1955 of the Silver Cloud, which was designed to go to customers with its "standard steel" body intact rather than with coach-built bodywork. For the first time, Rolls-Royce was primarily in the business of building cars that

customers would drive rather than be seated in the back while a chauffeur did the steering.

The Silver Ghost took its name from one of the earliest Rolls-Royce cars, which had first appeared as a prototype with a polished aluminum body that gave off a ghostly appearance.

Design of the modern Silver Ghost was done by John Blatchley, who formerly had worked for coachbuilder Gurney Nutting and he sought to build a "flying drawing room," though many considered the lush walnut, leather and thickly carpeted interior to be more of a throne room on wheels so quiet that the loudest sound heard in the passenger compartment was the ticking of the car's clock.

This may come as a shock to modern luxury car buyers, but until 1958 you could buy a Silver Cloud with a four-speed manual transmission, though only a few were ordered; most came with the four-speed automatic developed by

General Motors and built under license in England.

Until 1959, Silver Clouds were powered by an inline 4.9-liter six-cylinder engine. It as beneath Rolls-Royce dignity to provide something as common as a horsepower figure; "sufficient" was how the company described the output of its engines. Still, to give its car more appeal to wealthy American buyers, in 1959 Rolls-Royce finally introduced its first V8 engine, a 6.2-liter unit that could propel the more than two tons of wood, leather, wool and metal at speeds of some 120 miles per hour (190-plus km/h).

The Silver Cloud began its third and final generation in 1962 when it was equipped with dual-quad headlamps, designed again to increase appeal to American buyers. Though not positively received at first in England, the dual-quad headlamps would become a Rolls-Royce design signature.

142 AND 143 BOTTOM THE THIRD AND FINAL GENERATION OF THE SILVER CLOUD WAS INTRODUCED IN 1962 AND WAS EQUIPPED WITH DUAL-QUAD HEADLAMPS DESIGNED TO INCREASE THE CAR'S APPEAL TO WEALTHY AMERICAN CUSTOMERS.

143 TOP AUDREY HEPBURN PLAYED THE CHAUFFEUR'S DAUGHTER IN BILLY WILDER'S MOVIE *SABRINA*, WHICH ALSO STARRED HUMPHREY BOGART, WILLIAM HOLDEN AND A CLASSIC ROLLS ROYCE.

MGA

The MGA was the sports car that brought MG into the modern era. It also was the first MG to sell more than 100,000 units. So one wonders why MG's owner, the British Motor Corporation, waited so long to put the popular roadster into production.

For decades, MG had been building small but boxy and upright T-series roadsters, including the TC and TD that introduced thousands of Americans to the phenomenon of the European sports car, and in 1954 introduced yet another version, the TF. Yet as early as 1951, MG's Syd Enever had crafted a sleek, integrated and aerodynamic body to cover the MG TF chassis that George Philipps and Alan Rippon would race at Le Mans. Entered as the MG TF "Mark II," the car ran for eight hours before its engine expired.

145 TOP AFTER A LONG SUCCESSION OF BOXY MG ROADSTERS, SYD ENEVER DESIGNED AN INTEGRATED AND AERODYNAMIC BODY, SHOWN FIRST AS A RACING SPECIAL FOR LE MANS. IN 1955 AN UPDATED VERSION BECAME MG'S FIRST MODERN SPORTS CAR, THE MGA, SHOWN GOING THROUGH AERODYNAMIC EFFICIENCY TESTING IN A WIND TUNNEL (ABOVE).

144 TOP A YEAR AFTER THE MGA LAUNCHED AS A ROADSTER, A COUPE VERSION WAS OFFERED WITH A FIXED HARDTOP, EXTERIOR DOOR HANDLES AND ROLL-UP WINDOWS INSTEAD OF REMOVABLE SIDE CURTAINS.

144-145 THE MGA, LAUNCHED IN THE FALL OF 1955 AND SHOWN HERE IN ITS 1958 MODEL YEAR GUISE, WAS AN ALL-NEW CAR WITH A NEW CHASSIS, ENGINE AND TRANSMISSION AS WELL AS A MUCH MORE AERODYNAMIC BODY.

Enever's design was little changed when it was presented to an apparently unmoved BMW management board in 1952 at the EX175 prototype. It re-emerged again a few years later in the form of the EX182, a trio of racecars that served as the MG factory team in 1955 at Le Mans, where one of the cars crashed after six hours but the other two went on to finish 12th and 17th overall. Finally, years after Enever had designed its body, MG unveiled its first modern sports car, the MGA, at the London Motor Show in the fall of 1955, and put some public relations effort

behind the launch with a 100-mph run by the car on the high-speed Montlhéry oval track in France. Despite its sleek new body, with rear-hinged hood and doors, the MGA still was saddled with a heavy, T-series style boxed frame, but its lower center of gravity enhanced its handling and its aerodynamic body gave it better top-speed potential. Power came from a drivetrain borrowed from BMC's Austin A50 sedan, and even in stock form the 72-hp, 1489-cc B Series engine could propel the MGA to speeds of 95 mph. Making the MGA even more attractive

to buyers was pricing that made it less expensive than the rival Triumph TR3 or BMC's own Austin Healey 100. MG sold 13,000 MGAs in the car's first full year of production. Of the 101,081 built from 1955 to 1962, more than 81,000 were exported to the United States.

In 1956, a year after the roadster's launch, MG added a "fixed-head" coupe version with a wrap around windshield and roll-up windows. The roadster had no exterior door-handles; a person had to reach inside and pull a cable to open its doors. However, the roadster could be

equipped with an optional heater. In 1959, MG introduced a twin-cam version of the car that benefited from Harry Weslake's engine tweaks, four-wheel disc brakes and Dunlop center-lock steel wheels. Only 2000 copies of this model, which could run at speeds up to 115 mph, were built. A year later, in 1960, MG replaced the MGA's 1.5-liter engine with a 1.6-liter unit, basically an 80-hp, pushrod version of the twin-cam motor. The MGA 1600 also had front disc brakes, helpful for slowing a car that could hit speeds in excess of 100 mph.

146-147 SHOWN HERE AS A 1958 MODEL ROADSTER, THE MGA REMAINED IN PRODUCTION UNTIL 1962 AS BECAME THE FIRST MG MODEL TO SELL MORE THAN 100,000 UNITS, WITH MORE THAN 80,000 OF THEM EXPORTED TO THE UNITED STATES.

AUSTIN HEALEY 100

ritish automaker Austin designed its A90 Atlantic with Americans in mind. It even used the Indianapolis Motor Speedway to set a series of stock car speed records; over the course of seven days and nights and despite inclement weather, the Atlantic covered nearly 12,000 miles (more than 19,000 kilometers) around the famous Brickyard at an average speed of more than 70 miles per hour (112 km/h).

The Austin Atlantic went on sale as a 1949 model, first as a convertible and later as a sedan. Americans bought them, though not in the sort of numbers Austin had anticipated, so the automaker asked several British specialists to see what they could do with the A90's mechanical components to create a product more suited to American tastes.

Donald Healey had been among Europe's top rally racers and then became technical director at Triumph. After World War II, he started his own car-building company and built more than 600 Healey touring cars and Silverstone sports cars in the late 1940s and early '50s.

Healey's designer Gerry Coker created a two-seat sports car that Healey packaged around Atlantic components. The project drew considerable attention when Healey took his car to Belgium, ran it at speeds of up to 117 miles per hour (188 km/h) and then immediately displayed it on his stand at the 1952 London Motor Show, where the car was presented as the Healey 100. Austin merged with Morris in 1952 to form the British Motor Company and BMC's Sir Leonard Lord was so impressed with Healey's car that he put it into production as the Austin Healey 100.

Healey had recognized a gap in the fledgling American sports car market between MG's T series roadsters and Jaguar's XK120, both in terms of price and performance. The Austin Healey 100 sold for just less than $3,000 (U.S.), about a thousand dollars more than an MG and a thousand less than the Jaguar.

To demonstrate the car's potential, Healey himself drove a modified Austin Healey 100 to speeds of more than 142 miles per hour (nearly 230 km/h) in October 1953 at the Bonneville Salt Flats. Even in stock trim, the car could exceed 100 miles per hour (160 km/h) and accelerate from a standing start to 60 miles per hour (96 km/h) in slightly more than 10 seconds.

Stock trim for the Austin Healey 100 included a 90-horsepower, 2.6-liter Austin A90 four-cylinder engine, double-wishbone front suspension and a life rear axle with leaf springs. The car sat almost too low to the ground, and exhaust routing made things hot in the cockpit, but the body was beautiful, the windshield would fold flat and the car set standards for a relatively inexpensive roadster. In the first year of production, half of all Austin Healey 100s were sold in the United States. Over the course of some six years of production, thousands more would cross the Atlantic.

Austin Healey introduced the 100M in 1956; this car drew power from a 110-horsepower engine and came with a two-tone paint scheme.

The company also produced slightly more than 50 100S versions, designed for motorsports competition, with aluminum bodies, 132 horsepower and was the first production car to wear Dunlop disc brakes inside all four of its wheels.

In 1957, the car grew heavier and longer, with a 2.6-liter six-cylinder engine, a back seat and an available detachable hardtop.

Austin Healey introduced its back-to-basics Sprite roadster model in 1958 and a year later 100 production ended when the company introduced the Austin Healey 3000.

148 TOP THOUGH BUILT AS A ROADSTER, A REMOVABLE HARDTOP WAS AVAILABLE FOR THE AUSTIN HEALEY 100.

148-149 DONALD HEALEY MADE THE 100 DURABLE AND FAST, ABLE TO EXCEED 100 MILES PER HOUR EVEN IN STOCK TRIM.

Ford executives were at the Paris Motor Show in 1951 when they realized they, too, should be working on a two-seat roadster like those the Europeans were building. They sent a message back to Dearborn, where preliminary design and engineering work began.

By the following summer, sketches had been made and a clay model was under construction, although it would not be until the 1954 Detroit auto show that a mock-up of the new vehicle would be shown to an American public that had been so excited by the Chevrolet Corvette unveiled at General Motors' 1953 Motorama spectacular. Frank Hershey and W.P. "Bill" Boyer designed the two-seat Ford and chief engineer Bill Burnett and his team used a lot of pieces from the company parts bin in the car's construction. Although this new Ford looked like a European-style roadster, its suspension was shared with a big Ford station wagon and the car drew its power not from a small four-cylinder engine, or even a straight six like the Corvette, but from a 193-horsepower, 4.8-liter V8.

Though fast, this new car was much more a boulevard cruiser than a sports car, and was designed more for the executive than for the enthusiast. With its big engine and steel body, the new Ford weighed hundreds of pounds more than the Corvette, and offered the options of power windows and driver's seat, and could be equipped with either a hard fiberglass or a soft and folding convertible top.

Ford considered names such as Beverly, Debonnaire, Playboy, Tropicale and even Hep Cat for the car, but finally agreed to a name suggested by design staffer Alder Gilbertson, who created the turquoise-colored emblem and suggested the name, Thunderbird, considered a sacred spirit by the Native American peoples of the South-

FORD THUNDERBIRD

western United States where Gilbertson had grown up.

Ford's Thunderbird took wing immediately. The company received four thousand orders on the first day the car was available. Sales of the initial 1955 model totaled more than 16,000 compared to only 700 for the more expensive but not nearly as luxurious Corvette.

For 1956, the Thunderbird's spare tire was moved to the back of the vehicle via a Continental kit, creating more room in the trunk but adding a lot of weight well behind the rear axle. The rear bumper and exhaust were changed and the car also got vent windows alongside its wrap-around windshield.

The car was restyled for 1957 with the spare moved inside an enlarged trunk and more noticeable tailfins, but retained its stylish continental flair.

By 1958, a change in leadership at Ford caused the Thunderbird to become a different car, a larger and heavier car with a back seat, though still available as a convertible or coupe, and with much more angular styling. Although sports car enthusiasts weren't happy, this new "Squarebird" was well accepted by the car-buying public, with sales doubling immediately, and reaching more than 90,000 units by 1960.

In 1964, Ford introduced the sporty Mustang and soon Thunderbird evolved again, with a four-door version offered in 1967, then by the start of the next decade into an even larger and heavier car.

Although this larger Thunderbird would carry Ford's banner in American stock car racing, sales declined until production halted in 1997. But the Thunderbird was reborn in 2001 as a retro roadster with styling cues brought forward from the original 1955 model.

But this new 'bird was expensive and after an initial sales flurry, was scheduled to conclude production by the end of the 2006 model year.

150-151 FORD LAUNCHED THE THUNDERBIRD IN 1955. THOUGH MORE A BOULEVARD CRUISER THAN A TRUE SPORTS CAR, THE THUNDERBIRD WAS POWERED BY V8 ENGINE AND OUTSOLD CHEVROLET'S CORVETTE BY MORE THAN A 20:1 RATIO THAT FIRST YEAR.

FERRARI 250 GT

Enzo Ferrari made his marque in motorsports, but he made his money, money that paid for those blood-red racing cars, by selling sports cars for the road as well as for the track.

It was almost with reluctance that Ferrari built road cars, but in the days before corporate sponsorship brought money to underwrite the cost of racing, Ferrari had little choice but to put his Prancing Horse emblem on real cars as well as racecars.

According to Ferrari: Design of a Legend, the company's official history and catalog, Ferrari's first true "production" model was the 1958 250 GT, which was designed and produced by Pininfarina in its new facilities at Grugliasco, a western suburb of Turin, Italy.

As early as 1953, Ferrari and various coachbuilders had done the 250 "Europa" model intended for the road rather than the track, but only around 20 had been built before Ferrari turned to Pininfarina, which would produce some 2400 of the 250 models in various forms through the early years of the 1960s.

The 250 would come in many versions – GT, GT SWB, GT Spider, GT California, GT Berlinetta, GT 2+2, GTO – and not all were designed within Pininfarina's studio. But all were constructed around tube-frame chassis and all shared a key common component, though there was nothing very "common"

152 TOP AND 152-153 PININFARINA DESIGNED AND BUILT THE 250 GT, AROUND A TUBE-FRAME CHASSIS AND FERRARI'S "COLOMBO" V12 ENGINE. MOST OF THE 250 GT SERIES, INCLUDING THE 1959 MODEL, WERE POWERED BY 250-HORSEPOWER V12S, THOUGH THE 250 TESTA ROSSA AND 250 GTO COUNTED ON 300-HP MOTORS.

153 TOP PHOTOGRAPHED AT MODENA, ITALY IN 1956, ENZO FERRARI MADE HIS REPUTATION IN MOTORSPORTS, FIRST AS A DRIVER, THEN AS A TEAM MANAGER AND CAR CONSTRUCTOR. TO FINANCE HIS RACECARS, FERRARI FINALLY BEGAN "SERIES" PRODUCTION OF ROAD-GOING SPORTS CARS.

about the "Colombo" V12 engine that was created by Gioacchino Colombo and was first used in the 1952 Ferrari 166 MM (Mille Miglia) racer.

At first, the engine generated some 220 hp, but before 250 series production ended, that figure had grown to 300 hp for the 250 Testa Rossa, a Pininfarina-designed, open-cockpit racing car that took its name (red head) from the red valve covers on its engine, and the 250 GTO, the famed Gran Turismo Omologato berlinetta (coupe) racecar, conceived by Ferrari engineer Giotto Bizzarrini and designed by Franco Scaglietti, who also had created the famed B.A.T. concept cars.

TRs and GTOs were dominant in international motorsports and were largely responsible for Ferrari's seven overall victories in eight years in the 24 Hours of Le Mans and the 250s contributed to winning of 10 world GT championships in an 12-year period.

But the focus here is on the Ferraris built primarily for the road, not the track, and the dashboards of some of these cars actually were designed so the dealer could install a radio for those rare occasions when the wonderful sounds emitting from the 12-cylinder engine weren't enough music to the ears.

The best seller among the 250 series, with more than 900 produced, though many others in the series had production runs only in the dozens, was the 250 GTE 2+2, a four-seat though still two-door Ferrari. Second in production numbers but perhaps first in the hearts of

Ferrari faithful was the 250 GT SWB. Built from 1959 until 1962, the "short-wheelbase" car benefited in so far as shortening its chassis also made it stiffer. The car also was the first Ferrari equipped with four-wheel disc brakes to slow the speed of the Borrani wire wheels. Even with a steel body (Ferrari also offered aluminum-bodied *competizione* specials), the car could sprint from a standing start to 60 mph (100 km/h) around 6.5 seconds and didn't top out until moving at nearly 150 mph (just short of 240 km/h). The 250 GT SWB was gorgeous. Shortening the wheelbase by some eight inches eliminated the room for a second side window and allowed Pininfarina to create a fastback shape with more rounded corners. The bodies were crafted by Scaglietti's shop and the result was a sports car with marvelous proportion and stance. Even Enzo Ferrari seemed to like this one, because its owners could use the car on the road on weekdays and – in Ferrari's favored environment – on the racetrack on weekends.

154 FRANCO SCAGLIETTI, WHO HAD DESIGNED THE FAMOUS TRIO OF BAT-WINGED BERLINETTA AERODYNAMICA TECNICA CONCEPT CARS AT BERTONE, WAS RESPONSIBLE FOR THE STYLING OF THE FERRARI'S 250 GT CALIFORNIA SPYDER LAUNCHED IN 1958.

155 FERRARI'S FAMOUS 250 SERIES OF SPORTS CARS WOULD REMAIN IN PRODUCTION UNTIL 1964, WITH MORE THAN OF THEM 2500 BUILT IN A VARIETY OF BODY STYLES. THE BEST-SELLING MODEL WAS THE 250 GT 2+2, THE FIRST FERRARI DESIGNED WITH SEATING FOR FOUR.

TRIUMPH TR3A

Triumph dates to 1845, when Siegfried Bettmann, a German who worked for the White Sewing Machine Company, started importing bicycles into England, though it wasn't until 1886 that Bettmann replaced his name on those bicycles with "Triumph."

Not long after, Bettmann started building bicycles, then motorcycles but his desire was to join those building the new motorcars, and production of the first Triumph car started in 1923 in the aftermath of World War I.

But the company floundered, finally being bought out of receivership by John Black of the Standard Motor Company, who saw an opportunity to use the Triumph brand as a competitor for Jaguar's sports cars.

Triumph introduced its Standard Vanguard-engined 2000 roadster in 1946, and then at the 1952 London Motor Show unveiled the Triumph Sports, or TR1, though soon its test driver would be calling it "a bloody death-trap."

By the 1952 Geneva Show, the car had been thoroughly re-engineered, with a new and re-inforced ladder frame and a longer and re-designed body by Walter Belgrove. With twin carburetors on its 2.0-liter engine, this TR2 could accelerate to 60 miles per hour (96 km/h) in less than 12 seconds and could achieve a top speed of slightly more than 100 miles per hour (162 km/h).

The car and its engine both were strong and durable. They won races and rallies and be-

156-157 AFTER PRODUCING SOME 8000 TR2 AND 13,000 TR3 MODELS, TRIUMPH FOUND A MUCH WIDER MARKET FOR ITS TR3A, BUILDING MORE THAN 58,000 OF THEM OVER A FOUR-YEAR PERIOD.

157 TOP THE TR3A WAS DISTINGUISHED BY ITS FULL-WIDTH GRILLE AND THE ADDITION OF HANDLES ON ITS CUT-DOWN DOORS, A FEATURE THAT WOULD CHANGE ON SUBSEQUENT TRIUMPH SPORTS CARS, WHICH WERE DESIGNED IN ITALY, NOT IN BRITAIN.

came popular with Americans, who liked the idea of a British sports car that could hit 100 but cost only $2500.

By 1953, to compete with the new MGA, the Triumph got a new grille, a little more power and was designated the TR3. In 1956 the TR3 became the first "mass-produced" car with standard front disc brakes. By 1957 Triumph had intended to have a new model ready, but it wasn't so the company introduced what was supposedly an interim version, the TR3A.

Interim became extraordinary and sales soared. People especially liked the car's new front end, with its "wide-mouth" full-width grille. The interior also was updated, the trunk enlarged a little and exterior handles were added to what would be the last of Triumph's traditional cut-down doors.

The TR3A remained in production until 1961, with more than 58,000 built.

Finally, it was replaced by the larger TR4, but this car's Italian-designed body was not popular with buyers, at least not in the United States, so Triumph extended production of the earlier model, now dubbed the TR3B for American distribution.

The TR4, designed by Giovanni Michelotti, was wider and had a taller and more squared-off profile. It also had traditional style doors and was the first Triumph roadster with wind-up windows.

While the TR4 was not a success in all markets, Triumph didn't suffer because in 1962 it also introduced another Michelotti design. This one was a new, smaller and less expensive roadster, the Spitfire, and it outsold MG's Midget and Austin Healey's Sprite combined.

MINI

Not everybody will have heard of the Austin Se7en, but this car born of crisis became an international cultural icon. Austin Se7en was the official name given to the tiny (on the outside) yet roomy (on the inside) car created in response to the 1956 Suez Crisis and a blockade of the canal that demonstrated the West's vulnerability to interruptions in the flow of oil from the Middle East.

Though the crisis soon quieted, the British Motor Corporation issued a call for a new, fuel-efficient car that would be only 4 feet wide, 4 feet tall, 10 feet long and yet comfortably hold

158 TOP AND 159 TOP ACTOR PETER SELLERS (LEFT) OWNED A MINI AND ALSO DROVE IT IN HIS FILM ROLES. AN EARLY ADVERTISEMENT (RIGHT) FOR THE MORRIS MINI-MINOR.

158-159 THE BRITISH MOTOR CORPORATION CHALLENGED ENGINEERS TO CREATE A CAR JUST FOUR FEET WIDE, FOUR FEET TALL, 10 FEET LONG YET CAPABLE OF CARRYING FOUR PEOPLE AND THEIR LUGGAGE.

four people and their luggage. Soon after World War II, Britain's Morris Motors had developed the Morris Minor, its answer to the Volkswagen Beetle and Fiat Topolino. Architect of the Minor was Alex Issigonis, who was educated as an engineer but spent much of his career as a designer. Issigonis had quit Morris in 1952 after its merger with Austin created BMC, but the Turkish-born son of a Greek father and Bavarian mother was persuaded to return to create a new and even smaller car than the Minor.

Though officially launched as the Austin Se7en, that car would forever after be known simply as the "Mini."

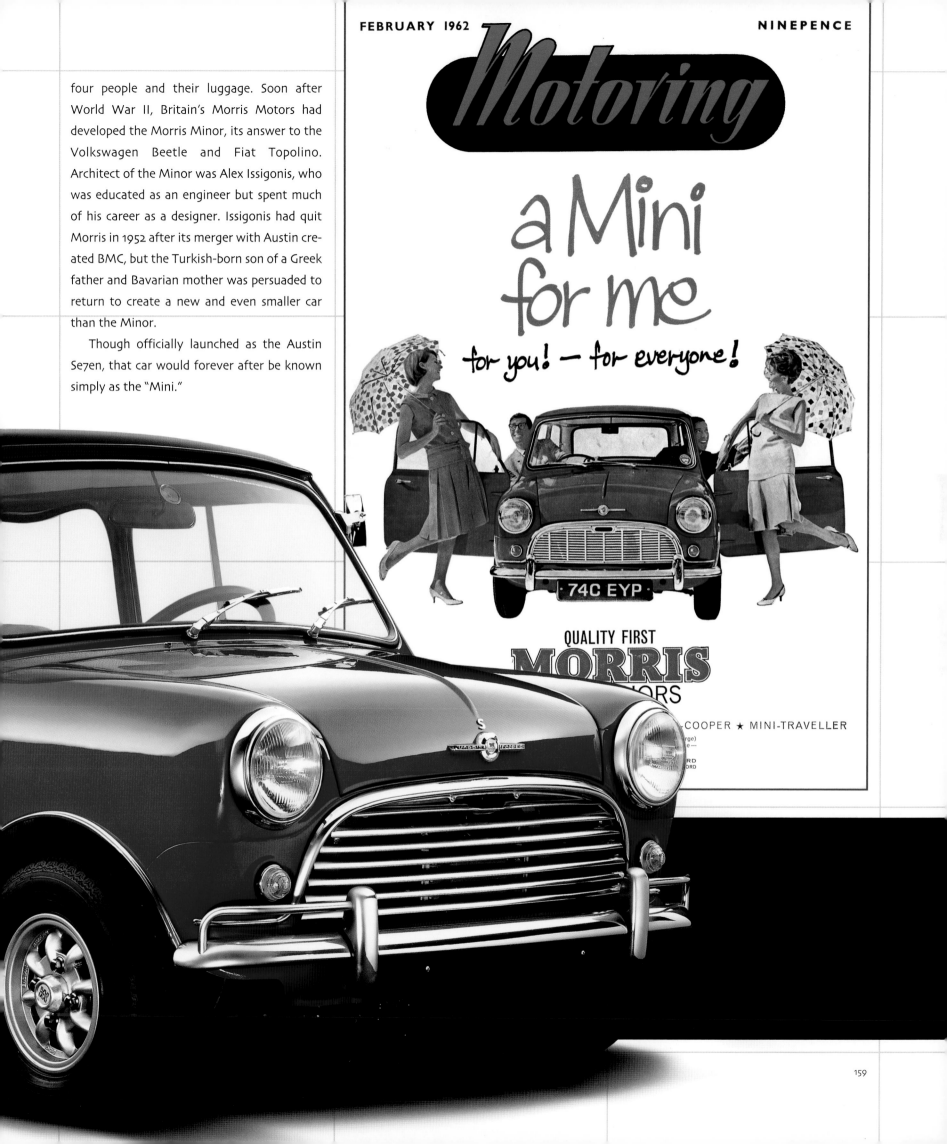

Motoring

a Mini for me

for you! — for everyone!

74C EYP

QUALITY FIRST
MORRIS

-COOPER ★ MINI-TRAVELLER

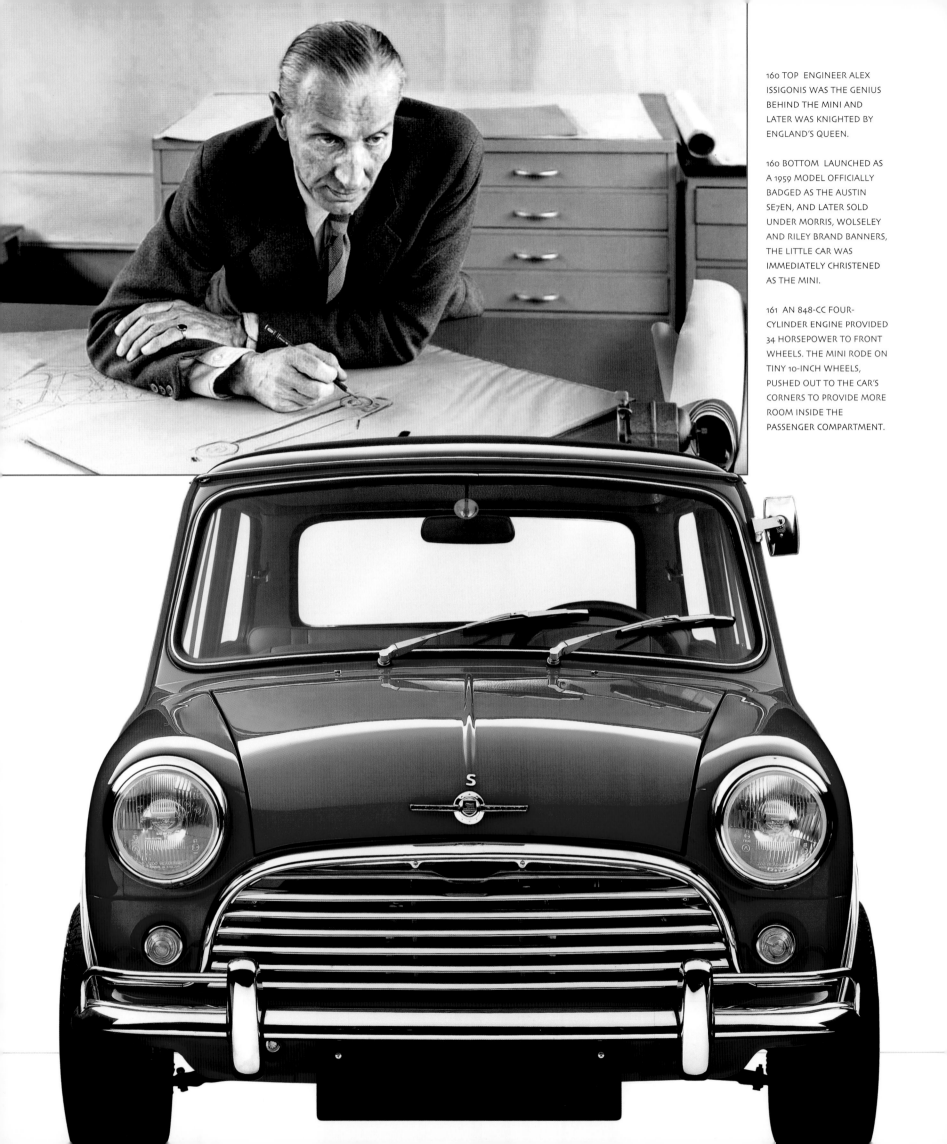

160 TOP ENGINEER ALEX ISSIGONIS WAS THE GENIUS BEHIND THE MINI AND LATER WAS KNIGHTED BY ENGLAND'S QUEEN.

160 BOTTOM LAUNCHED AS A 1959 MODEL OFFICIALLY BADGED AS THE AUSTIN SE7EN, AND LATER SOLD UNDER MORRIS, WOLSELEY AND RILEY BRAND BANNERS, THE LITTLE CAR WAS IMMEDIATELY CHRISTENED AS THE MINI.

161 AN 848-CC FOUR-CYLINDER ENGINE PROVIDED 34 HORSEPOWER TO FRONT WHEELS. THE MINI RODE ON TINY 10-INCH WHEELS, PUSHED OUT TO THE CAR'S CORNERS TO PROVIDE MORE ROOM INSIDE THE PASSENGER COMPARTMENT.

At first glance, the car almost appears to be an unstyled box with exterior welds and door hinges, designed to provide the bare minimum needed for covered transportation. But it was a brilliant basic solution and the original coupe spawned vans, wagons, trucklets, convertibles, even luxury editions and the Jeep-like Mini Moke, and in addition to original Austin, those various versions wore Morris, Wolseley and Riley badges. The Mini remained in production for more than 40 years – with more than 5.3 million units produced. Then, after a brief hiatus, the car was reborn (as Issigonis had been born) to a Bavarian mother – BMW, the Bavarian Motor Works, which acquired Britain's Rover Group in 1997.

Like Issigonis' Morris Minor, the Mini had a front-mounted and transversely positioned 4-cylinder engine and front-wheel drive. But to maximize interior room, Issigonis put the car on tiny 10-inch wheels and pushed those wheels out to the far corners of the chassis. This produced a car with an amazingly spacious passenger compartment and, as a bonus, a low center of gravity and incredible dynamic capabilities. The Mini's handling was so outstanding that famed Grand Prix racing team constructor John Cooper made some modifications that turned the minimalist Mini – which was launched with a 34-hp engine – into an overachieving champion in international rally racing.

The little Mini Coopers outscored Ford's specially built V8-powered Falcons to win the 1964 Monte Carlo Rally, and the Minis dominated again in 1965, 1966 (although the 1966 1-2-3 victory sweep was denied on a technicality) and in 1967. The little car also was a big hit with celebrities. Beatles (the mop-haired singers, not to be confused with the Volkswagen car) and Twiggy were among the many famous Mini owners.

In many ways the little cars also overshadowed actors such as Michael Caine and Noel Coward for the role they played in the 1969 movie "The Italian Job." Even the mini skirt, created by Mini owner Mary Quant, took its name from the Mini machine.

JAGUAR MK II

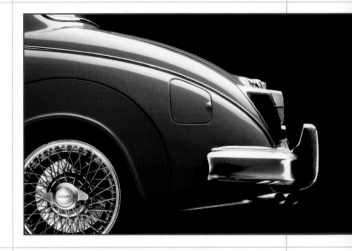

Part luxury sedan, part sports car, Jaguar's Mk II was among the first of a new breed, the sports sedan.

Though founded to build sidecars for motorcycles, the company that would become Jaguar made its name building large luxury cars and smaller, racier models wearing SS and later XK labels.

In 1951 Jaguar moved into an old military plant at Browns Lane, Coventry and the new facilities provided an opportunity to expand the company's vehicle range.

In 1954 Jaguar introduced its first unibody car, the Mk I 2.4. The car was powered by a 2.4-liter version of Jaguar's 3.4-liter inline six-cylinder XK engine. Unlike the larger Jaguars, this sedan featured integrated fenders. Emphasizing its more streamlined shape were cov-

ers over the rear wheels, which were set less than 51 inches (127 centimeters) apart. A year later, the 3.4-liter engine with its full 190 horsepower was available and the car could achieve speeds of around 120 miles per hour.

By 1959, Jaguar was in position to launch a new model, based on the Mk I but featuring a four-door body that was beautiful both in its lines and its proportion, and such mechanical improvements as a widened (to 54.1 inches, or more than 137 centimeters) rear tread with a standard limited-slip differential helping to provide better traction and control, which this car needed with its new-generation, 3.8-liter XK engine pumping out 220 horsepower. The car also had four-wheel disc brakes to slow it from speeds in excess of 125 miles per hour, the top limit on the new motorways that had just opened in Britain. To help keep those brakes cool, the car's rear wheels were exposed.

Jaguar had learned much about unibody architecture and was able to design an elegant yet athletic structure for the Mk II, with larger windows and smaller pillars to support the roof. The result was a seemingly timeless automotive design.

Inside, the car was pure Jaguar, with leather seats, wood dashboard with switchgear like that found on airplanes, deep-pile carpeting and wood picnic trays for those sitting in the rear seats. The speedometer and tachometer were moved to directly in front of the driver and were better positioned for the sort of aggressively dynamic driving this car

was fully capable of achieving – on the road or track.

Though it was a luxury sedan, the Mk II weighed less than 3150 pounds (1420 kilograms) and could sprint from a standing start to 60 miles per hour (100 km/h) in less than eight and a half seconds. In the hands of drivers such accomplished drivers as Stirling Moss, Graham Hill, John Surtees and many others, the Jaguar Mk II won many touring car and "saloon" races on road circuits throughout Britain and on the Continent.

The car was not only a favorite of racers, but also of British outlaws, who made use of the Mk II's speed and agility as a getaway vehicle from their crime scenes so often that British police had get their own Jaguars just so they could give chase.

Jaguar kept up Mk II production until 1968, when its parent, British Motor Holdings, merged with Leyland Motors to create British Leyland. After producing nearly 84,000 of its beautiful Mk II sports sedans, Jaguar switched its sedan production to the new, larger and more sedate XJ series.

162 AND 163 WITH ITS 3.8-LITER XJ ENGINE PUMPING OUT 220 HORSEPOWER, THE JAGUAR MK II COULD REACH SPEEDS OF 125 MILES PER HOUR ON BRITAIN'S MOTORWAY, AND REAR WHEELS WERE EXPOSED TO HELP KEEP BIG DISC BRAKES COOL.

164-165 JAGUAR'S MK II WAS ELEGANT AND ATHLETIC AT THE SAME TIME. ALTHOUGH TECHNICALLY A LUXURY SEDAN, THE CAR WON MANY TOURING CAR RACES AND CAME A FAVORITE FOR USE AS A GETAWAY CAR BY BRITISH CRIMINALS.

CADILLAC ELDORADO BIARRITZ

Harley Earl certainly went out in style.

In 1926 General Motors recruited 34-year-old Harley Earl, who had been designing custom cars for Hollywood stars, and installed him as head of the automaker's new Art and Color Section, the initial name of the company's styling department. Earl's 1927 LaSalle is considered the first series production car consciously designed rather than simply engineered. In 1938 Earl introduced the first true concept or "dream" car in the form of the Buick Y-Job.

Earl also created the Chevrolet Corvette, oversaw the futuristic Firebird concept cars and convinced General Motors to stage the Motorama, a traveling extravaganza that provided a Broadway show-style setting for the debut of the company's new concepts and production models.

Earl's reign over the GM design studios would last until his retirement in 1959. That historic tenure culminated with the 1959 Cadillac Eldorado Biarritz, the most outrageous example of America's chrome and fin era. "Depending on your taste, the most outlandish or magnificent of all tailfinned Detroiters," write the editors of *The Complete Book of Collectible Cars*. "No single automotive design better characterizes the [American] industry's late-1950s flamboyance than the 1959 Cadillac," adds the encyclopedic reference book, *Standard Catalog of American Cars*. How's this for flamboyant?

The Biarritz is a convertible with large, dual-quad headlight clusters that bracket a nearly six-foot wide chrome grille. Some 20 feet (more than 5.7 meters) toward the rear of this massive 5060-lb (2295 kg) machine are twin tail fins, each rising 42 inches (nearly 107 cm) above the pavement, and each punctuated by a pair of red, rocket-style tail lamps. As at the front, there is a wide and chromed rear grille, this one stretching between back-up lights set into huge chromed bezels that resemble the afterburners on jet engines.

The car's interior had full-width leather-covered seats (available in more than half a dozen colors) providing plush comfort for six people and a dashboard that might easily have been transplanted from the control panel of a jukebox. Standard features included a six-way power front seat, power windows – including the vent windows – a power lifting hood, power door locks, a heater and more. The options list included air conditioning, cruise control, Twilight Sentinel headlamps that came on automatically in the dark and Automatic Eye controls that dimmed the

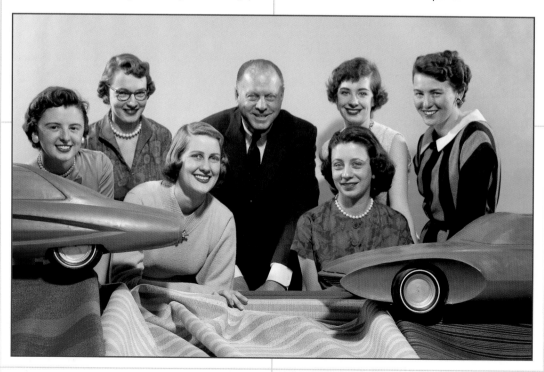

166 BOTTOM IN THE 1950S, GM STYLING CHIEF HARLEY EARL'S STAFF INCLUDED THE "DAMSELS OF DESIGN." THEY WERE (FROM LEFT) SUE VANDERBILT, RUTH GLENNIE, MARGORY FORD POHLMAN, SANDRA LONGYEAR, JEANETTE LINDER AND PEGGY SAUER.

167 THE 1959 CADILLAC ELDORADO BIARRITZ WAS THE MOST EXTREME EXAMPLE OF AMERICA'S LOVE AFFAIR IN THE LATE 1950S WITH HUGE CARS WITH TALL TAIL FINS AND TAILLIGHTS MODELED AFTER ROCKETS AND JET-PLANE AFTERBURNERS.

bright lights whenever there was oncoming traffic. The Biarritz was named for the resort town on the French coast. It was a two-door convertible and part of a special 6400 subset of Cadillac's famed Series 62 model line. The two-door hardtop version was called the Eldorado Seville while Cadillac commissioned Pininfarina of Italy to hand build the Eldorado Brougham four-door sedan. Of all '59 Eldorados, the Biarritz was the most popular, with 1320 of them produced.

The Eldorados were powered by Cadillac's new 390-cubic inch (6.3-liter) V8 engine that provided 345 hp while slurping fuel at the rate of around a gallon per every 8 miles. The huge and heavy cars rode on air suspension and were slowed – though not immediately – by drum brakes. After Earl's retirement, General Motors quickly reduced the size of its cars' tailfins. Just a year later, the new Cadillac's fins reached just 36 inches (91 cm) above the road and by 1965 they were reduced to mere creases along the top edge of the rear fenders.

168 TOP ACTOR PAUL NEWMAN LEANS AGAINST THE BACK END OF A 1958 CADILLAC DURING THE FILMING OF THE 1963 MOVIE *HUD*.

168-169 THE 1959 CADILLAC ELDORADO CONVERTIBLE WORE JUST SLIGHTLY LESS JEWELRY THAN DID THE SPECIAL ELDORADO BIARRITZ VERSION.

169 TOP BY 1960, EVEN THE ELDORADO BIARRITZ'S TAILFINS HAD BEEN TRIMMED DOWN AND LOST THE GAUDY ORNAMENTATION OF THEIR TWIN, ROCKET-STYLED TAIL LAMPS.

JAGUAR XK-E (E-TYPE)

Sculpted as much by the wind along the Mulsanne Straight as by designer Malcolm Sayer, the Jaguar E-type, or XK-E as it was known in the United States, remains one of the most sensual shapes ever to grace a paved surface.

"Because of the E-type's beauty and sculptural quality, its functionality and its seminal impact on overall car design, it perfectly suits the criteria of a landmark design object," the chief curator of the Museum of Modern Art in New York City declared in the spring of 1996 – nearly four decades after the car's launch – when a dark blue 1963 E-type roadster became only the third motor vehicle in the museum's permanent collection.

"Rarely has a car inspired the kind of passion in both car enthusiasts and the general public that the E-type has," added his assistant, who termed the car 'an icon." Jaguar unveiled its sensational new sports car at the Geneva Motor Show early in 1961, but auto enthusiasts who had been paying attention had seen the car nearly a year earlier, driving on public roads in France and carrying the colors of American Briggs Cunningham's racing team.

Jaguar's C-type racing car won the 24 Hours of Le Mans in 1951 and 1953 and was

succeeded by the D-type, which posted victories in 1955, 1956 and a 1-2-3-4 sweep in 1957, the same year Jaguar began development on a production car based on the historic racers.

The first prototype – E1A – used the basic D-type monocoque chassis, aluminum bodywork, Jaguar's XK engine and an independent rear suspension setup. An updated second prototype – E2A – was built with racing in mind, again with lightweight aluminum body-

170-171 THE JAGUAR E-TYPE MADE ITS DEBUT AT THE GENEVA MOTOR SHOW IN 1961. WORK ON THE CAR HAD BEGUN IN 1957 AND WAS BASED ON THE ACCLAIMED D-TYPE RACING CAR.

171 TOP LEFT THE E-TYPE, OR XK-E AS IT WAS KNOWN IN SOME MARKETS, WAS INTRODUCED IN BOTH COUPE AND CONVERTIBLE BODY STYLES.

171 TOP RIGHT JAGUAR'S 3.8-LITER, INLINE SIX-CYLINDER XK ENGINE PROPELLED THE LIGHTWEIGHT CAR TO SPEEDS IN EXCESS OF 140 MILES PER HOUR.

work and a fuel-injected engine. The car was turned over to Cunningham to race at Le Mans, where it set fast lap before its engine blew a head gasket after 10 hours.

The production car – launched in both coupe and convertible forms – was powered by the same engine 265-horsepower, 3.8-liter inline six that had propelled the Jaguar XK-150S that the E-type replaced. But the sleek new sports car was some 400 pounds lighter and much more aerodynamic and, even with a tall and non-synchronized first gear in its four-speed manual transmission, could sprint from a standing start to 60 miles per hour in 7.0 seconds and on to a top speed in excess of 140 miles per hour (more than 230 km/h). The car also featured disc brakes for each wheel and the independent rear

suspension that Jaguar developed for the Mk X sedan it would introduce in 1962.

The E-type was updated in 1965 with an improved gearbox, upgraded brakes and a 4.2-liter engine that produced more torque. A year later the wheelbase was extended nine inches to produce a new 2+2 coupe that could be equipped with an automatic transmission.

In 1968 the car's beauty began to erode. American safety regulations forced the installation of new bumpers and headlamps.

Then, for 1971, Jaguar responded to new American emission rules by putting a 5.3-liter V12 under the E-type's bonnet, though weight and pollution controls pretty much offset the added power the larger engine provided. Jaguar built some 72,000 E-types; two-thirds of them

were exported. Production ended with the 1975 model, but instead of replacing the XK-E with a sexy new F-type sports car, Jaguar introduced "a new breed of cat," but the sedan-based XJ-S was a touring car, a purring kitten rather than a leaping cap. Still, cats do have many lives; early in 2000 Jaguar had an E-type concept car on its stand at the Detroit Auto Show.

172-173 EVEN WITH ITS HIGH SPEED AND GORGEOUS STYLING, THE JAGUAR E-TYPE COSTS LESS THAN HALF AS MUCH AS A COMPARABLE FERRARI OR ASTON MARTIN MODEL. IN 1996, AN ORIGINAL JAGUAR E-TYPE BECAME ONLY THE THIRD VEHICLE ADDED TO THE PERMANENT COLLECTION OF THE MUSEUM OF MODERN ART IN NEW YORK CITY.

173 DIABOLIK, WHO
UNDERWENT A
TRANSFORMATION FROM A
1960S ITALIAN COMIC BOOK
CRIMINAL TO BECOME A
NATIONAL SUPERHERO,
DROVE A JAGUAR E-TYPE ON
HIS MANY ADVENTURES.

SHELBY AC COBRA

Carroll Shelby may have been a bib-wearing chicken farmer from Texas, but he was a good enough racecar driver to be able to turn down an offer to become part of Enzo Ferrari's factory team.

Shelby declined Ferrari's offer because he would be driving only when the mood struck *il Commendatore,* and that was not an arrangement the tall Texan could live with. Shelby remembers telling Ferrari that he'd have his revenge. He did, two years later, in 1959, when he and Roy Salvadori took the measure of Ferrari's best by winning the 24 Hours of Le Mans for Aston Martin.

A heart condition prematurely ended Shelby's career as a racecar driver, so he decided to become a racing team owner. But to race he'd need a car, and figured the quickest and most economical way to do it was to get cars from AC Cars, a struggling British sports car maker,

but to power them with big American V8 engines. Auto-Carriers was founded in England in 1908 and had been owned by the Hurlock brothers since 1930. The company built sports cars in low volumes, most recently the Ace, which combined a body that looked a lot like a Ferrari 166 with a chassis like the one developed by British racecar constructor John Cooper. With power supplied by Bristol's inline six-cylinder engine, AC's Ace had acquitted itself well in sports car racing, even finishing seventh overall and winning the GT class at Le Mans in 1959, the year Shelby and Salvadori were winning in the Aston Martin.

Shelby recognized potential opportunities when he saw them and realized that inserting a little American ingenuity in the form of a big V8 engine and adding a proper, professional racing team would be a way to win races, lots of races. But he needed a supply of V8 engines. Chevrolet already was winning with its

Corvette, so Shelby turned to Ford, Chevy's rival, which offered a couple of its 221-cubic-inch) V8s so Shelby could see if his idea would work. It did. A supply of 260-cubic-inch Ford engines got Shelby started. In 1963, things really accelerated with Ford's new 289 c.i.d. V8, which provided 271 horsepower in street trim and more when tuned for racing. Like Ferrari, Shelby needed to fund his racing program, and selling sports cars was the solution.

The Shelby Cobras, as the cars were known, were fast but brutal. All that horsepower in such a small package could be difficult to handle. The cockpit was cramped. The suspension was stiff. But the cars were oh so fast, on the road as well as on the racetrack.

The Shelby American team's Cobras won the U.S. Road Racing Championship series in 1963 (and again in 1964 and 1965), and in 1964 he took his team to Europe to take on Ferrari in the GT class of the World Manufacturers Championship. A new Daytona Coupe version of the Shelby Cobra was fourth overall and

won the GT category competition at Le Mans that year, then in 1965 Shelby's Cobras won nine manufacturers' series races and made Ford the first American marque to claim the world GT championship.

Ford recruited Shelby to help with the company's GT40 prototype racing effort and his cars were first and second as GT40 Mk. IIs posted a 1-2-3 sweep at Le Mans in 1966. Ford built a new GT40, the Mk. IV, for 1967 and a Shelby team car won Le Mans again, again beating Ferrari's newest prototypes.

The GT40 Mk IV was powered by Ford's big 427 c.i.d. (7.0-liter) NASCAR stock car racing motor and Shelby offered the big motor in the Cobras he was building and selling through select Ford dealerships.

Shelby would build nearly 1,000 of his Cobras before moving on to other projects, including heart transplant surgery. AC also produced V8-powered versions of its Ace and several companies continue to offer Cobra kits and replicas.

174 TOP BEFORE THE FAMED DAYTONA COUPE WAS READY TO RACE, SOME COBRAS COMPETED WITH SPECIAL HARDTOPS ADDED TO ENHANCE HIGH-SPEED AERODYANMICS. AMONG THEM WAS THE NO. 4 CAR THAT WAS PRIVATELY ENTERED AT LE MANS IN 1963.

174-175 AFTER CREATING HIS COBRA BY WEDGING FORD'S 260 AND THEN 289 CUBIC-INCH ENGINES INTO A BRITISH SPORTS CAR CHASSIS CARROLL SHELBY LAUNCHED THE 427 COBRA IN 1965 WITH A LARGER FORD V8. THE CAR ALSO GOT FLARED FENDERS OVER ITS WIDENED TRACK, LOUVERS IN ITS FRONT QUARTER PANELS AND A SINGLE-BAR GRILLE.

ASTON MARTIN DB5

I t's been called the world's most famous car, the Silver Birch-colored Aston Martin DB5 that Bond, James Bond drove, first in Goldfinger, then in Thunderball.

Equipped by Q with such non-factory options as an ejection seat, retractable machine guns, bulletproof rear shield, oil slick sprayer and tire-shredding wheel extensions, the car became a star in its own right, so

famous that sixteen years after shuttling actor Sean Connery through his various adventures, it came out of retirement for a cameo appearance in yet another movie, "The Cannonball Run."

Aston Martin launched the DB5 in 1963 as the mildly updated successor to the seven-year-old DB4, which had been the first all-new model the company produced after it was purchased in 1947 by David Brown. Brown gave his initials to the company's cars

176-177 THE DB4'S DESIGN WAS DONE IN ITALY BY TOURING, WHICH ALSO BUILT THE BODIES FOR THE CAR, WHICH WAS AVAILABLE AS EITHER A FIXED-HEAD COUPE OR A CONVERTIBLE WITH AN OPTIONAL REMOVABLE STEEL HARDTOP.

177 TOP SOME THINK SEAN CONNERY WAS THE STAR OF THE JAMES BOND MOVIE, *GOLDFINGER*, BUT MANY SAY THE MOVIE'S CLASS ACT WAS THE "SPECIALLY EQUIPPED" ASTON MARTIN DB5.

JAMES
BOND
IST
WIEDER
IN
AKTION

"GOLDFINGER"

TECHNICOLOR

United Artists 1985

177

after he added Aston Martin to industrial holdings that included tractor and transmission manufacturers as well as the Lagonda car works. Robert Bamford and Lionel Martin were early car enthusiasts who in 1913 put a Coventry Simplex engine into a Bugatti-designed Isotta Franchini chassis. They won their first outing with the vehicle, the Aston Clinton hill climb. They incorporated the event's name into their own and soon started building cars under the Aston Martin banner.

But the company built very few cars, and while they had success in racing, there were not substantial profits for ownership to be sustained. Aston Martin when through a succession of hands until purchased by Brown, who owned the company until 1972, after which it again went through a succession of owners until being added to the Ford Motor Company portfolio in 1987. Brown's first Aston Martin was the DB1, a 1948 model based on a pre-war chassis, though it carried a new body designed by Frank Feeley, formerly of Lagonda. By 1950, the car was updated as the DB2, now powered by a new six-cylinder engine that W.O. Bentley had designed at Lagonda.

Success in motorsports continued. In 1951 an Aston was third overall, with teammates placing fifth and seventh, and won its class in the 24 Hours of Le Mans. Astons also won their class in the Mille Miglia in 1951 and again in 1952.

By 1958 the company had developed its first all-new vehicle under Brown's ownership. The DB4 rode on a new platform and was powered by a new, racing-inspired inline six-cylinder engine designed by Tadek Marek. The motor

pumped out 224 horsepower and could carry the car's new Touring-designed aluminum body to speeds of more than 140 miles per hour (more than 226 km/h). The company also produced the lighter but even more powerful DB4GT, and Italian coachbuilder Zagato added its interpretation with the stunning DB4 Zagato. After finished second at Le Mans three times in the previous four years, Aston Martins finished 1-2 in the 24-hour even in 1959, Carroll Shelby and Roy Salvadori driving the winning car with Paul Frere and Maurice Trintignant in the runner-up. By 1963, the DB4 had evolved to the point of earning a new model designation: DB5, which had such luxurious features as exceptionally fine leather and electric windows (and a price tag twice that of the Jaguar E-type). The powertrain also had evolved, now displacing 4.0 liters and generating 282 horsepower. The DB5 was available as a 2+2 coupe or Volante convertible. Brown even had a dozen special "shooting-brake" station wagons built for wealthy friends. And, of course, Q built a very special DB5 for secret agent 007.

178-179 WHEN THE DB5 WAS LAUNCHED IN 1963, CUSTOMERS COULD CHOOSE AMONG FOUR TRANSMISSIONS: FOUR-SPEED MANUAL, FOUR-SPEED WITH OVERDRIVE, FIVE-SPEED MANUAL OR AUTOMATIC.

CHEVROLET CORVETTE STING RAY

n 1963 Chevrolet had as much as 360 horsepower available for the Corvette and the all-new Sting Ray was ready to put that power to its proper use.

Until 1963, all Corvettes had been convertibles, but in 1963 the Sting Ray also was available as a coupe. Hidden headlights allowed a knife's-edge nose that cut through the air and the fastback roof style, with its signature split-window rear backlight, helped make the Corvette look fast even when sitting still, which had been part of General Motors' newly promoted design director Bill Mitchell's assignment to a team led by Larry Shinoda. Shinoda and the staff actually began working on the car years before it would go into production, in the guise of the Corvette SS race car owned by Mitchell, who later used it as his daily driver after the car was retired from active competition after the 1960 season. Beneath Mitchell's

shark-styled body and around the Corvette's new twin-cowl passenger compartment, Arkus Duntov built a new chassis, with a wheelbase that was 4 inches (10 cm) shorter than the '62 model, but now featured independent suspension front and rear, although it would take until 1965 for disc brakes to be installed. Options for 1963 included 300-, 340- and 360-hp engine upgrades, as well as a very special Zo6 package that included aluminum wheels with knock-off hubs, a "positraction" rear axle, "finned" brake drums, heavy-duty suspension stabilizer bars with stronger shocks and stiffer springs, four-speed manual gearbox, 360 hp engine and even a larger fuel tank better suited for long-distance endurance racing.

"Suitably equipped and set up, the new Corvette promises a potential that is hard to equal or surpass by even the world's costliest cars," Arkus Duntov noted in a statement that was true then and has continued to be a Corvette hallmark.

Corvette sales soared with Chevrolet selling not only more than 10,000 convertibles – and thus meeting its initial sales target – but also more than 10,000 split-window coupes.

180-181 CHEVROLET PUT A PERMANENT ROOF ON ITS CORVETTE FOR THE FIRST TIME IN 1963, WHEN THE REDESIGNED CAR ADDED THE STING RAY MONIKER.

181 TOP THOUGH THE HARDTOP VERSION WOULD REMAIN PART OF CORVETTE PRODUCTION IN THE FUTURE, ONLY THE 1963 MODEL FEATURED A SPLIT-WINDOW REAR DESIGN.

height of steering wheel from ground... approximately 10½ inches

height of seat from ground... approximately 8 inches

overall length approximately 22 inches

steering wheel shaft hooks over front axle

corvette
STINGRAY

A PRESENTATION OF REPUBLIC TOOL & DIE CORPORATION

FOR THE **CHEVROLET**

PARTS MERCHANDISING DEPARTMENT

182 TOP THE CORVETTE CONVERTIBLE SHOWED OFF THE MUSCULAR BULGES AND CRISP CREASES THAT HIGHLIGHTED THE CAR'S FIBERGLASS BODYWORK.

182-183 CONCEALED HEADLAMPS ENHANCED THE 1963 CORVETTE'S AERODYNAMICS AND WOULD REMAIN A CORVETTE STYLING CUE UNTIL THE LAUNCH OF THE 2005 MODEL.

183 TOP THE STING RAY UNDERWENT SOME DESIGN AND MECHANICAL CHANGES IN 1965, INCLUDING VERTICAL LOUVERS IN ITS FRONT FENDERS, A NEW CONVERTIBLE TOP AND STANDARD SEAT BELTS.

Flexing Their Muscles:
Horsepower rules

1964/1974

*I*n the late 1930s, Delmar Roos, chief engineer for American automaker Willys-Overland, declared that, "the object of an automobile is to transport a given number of people with reasonable comfort, with the least consumption of gasoline, oil, and rubber, and for the slightest operating cost and prime price."

That certainly seemed a reasonable proposition at the time. Even today, Roos' automotive thesis fulfills the needs of the vast majority of mainstream motor vehicle buyers. For the most part, people want what might be termed an automotive appliance, one with the same dependability found in a refrigerator, stove or washing machine. Turn the key, put it in gear and go to your destination with neither excitement nor worry.

But in the late 1960s and early 1970s, Roos' words were drowned out by the fuel-consuming, tire-burning, rumbling and roaring wail generated by engines as large and as powerful as someone could wedge into the space beneath a car's hood.

Just a few pages ago encountered a small British sports car into which an American from Texas, naturally, had inserted first a 260-horsepower V8 engine but soon would find a way to jam in a gigantic, 7.0-liter monster motor.

And it wasn't only Texans from the Wild West who were doing such things. In Italy, Maserati was putting its racing engines into a four-door sedan to create the Quattroporte, which could then be driven at speeds approaching 150 miles per hour (230 km/h).

And these were just the preliminary acts.

Soon, mainstream American family cars would be turned into all-out "muscle" machines. The American muscle car phenomenon began at Pontiac, where executives found a way around corporate rules by putting the largest V8 engines they could find into family sedans designed for smaller powerplants.

As if their action wasn't brash enough, they named their new car after the most famous of all Ferraris, the fabled GTO, and they expanded on the legend with a song that became a hit on the popular music charts.

Soon all of Detroit's automakers added their own muscle to the momentum. Oldsmobile quickly rolled out its 4-4-2, Chevrolet showcased its Chevelle SS, Dodge added two more stripes to the pavement with its Charger. The race was on.

Even Porsche would replace its venerable 356 with a new model, the 911, which would quickly escalate from 140 horsepower to 180 to 200. Even that wasn't enough to feed the horsepower frenzy, so the engine was turbocharged to boost its output to the point that it needed a large whale-tail rear spoiler to help keep it stable at high speeds.

In 1966 Lamborghini upped the ante again by building what was acclaimed not just a sports car but at last, a super car. Propelled by a 350-horsepower V12 engine, the Miura was the fastest thing yet to be legally unleashed on public roads.

Sports car. Muscle car. Super car. We're not finished yet.

Before this need for speed would be brought back to some semblance of reality, first Lamborghini, and others afterward, would give us the exotic car.

Lamborghini's Countach took its name from the dialect expression a man utters when an especially beautiful woman enters his view. The Countach was especially beautiful, exotic in the way it was designed with doors that opened like a beetle's wings (or maybe it more like an exotic dancer's fans), and also in the way it ran, at speeds approaching — and before long exceeding — 300 kilometers per hour (180 mph).

But storm clouds were gathering on the horizon. While speed was king of the road, concern was growing about the impact these fast cars – and all cars — were having in terms of safety, or lack thereof, and in the emissions that were pouring out of their twin tailpipes.

Suddenly, the supply of the oil needed to produce gasoline would become an international issue. Greatly restricted speed limits would slam the brakes on the horsepower race.

Nonetheless, the decade from the mid-1960s to the mid-1970s provided a wild ride. It was fun while it lasted.

Flexing Their Muscles: Horsepower rules

185 THE V6 ENGINE IN FERRARI'S DINO 206 GT PRODUCED ONLY 180 HORSEPOWER, BUT THE CAR NAMED FOR ENZO FERRARI'S LATE SON MADE UP IN DESIGN FOR ANYTHING THAT IT MIGHT HAVE LACKED IN ABSOLUTE PERFORMANCE.

187 LIKE THE DINO, PORSCHE'S 911 DREW POWER FROM ONLY SIX CYLINDERS, BUT THE SUCCESSOR TO PORSCHE'S 356 ESTABLISHED NEW BENCHMARKS IN HANDLING AND DURABILITY, ON THE ROAD AND THE RACETRACK.

1964/1974

FORD MUSTANG

THOUGH BUILT
WITH ECONOMY CAR
COMPONENTS, THE FORD
MUSTANG OFFERED SPORTS
CAR STYLING THAT
APPEALED TO A HUGE
SEGMENT OF THE CAR-
BUYING PUBLIC.

As general manager of the Ford Division, Lee Iacocca wanted the cars he sold to be youthful and exciting, and when he invited Henry Ford II to compare their company's offerings with those of rival Chevrolet, there was an obvious gap in the Ford lineup. Ford offered nothing to compete with Chevy's Corvair, a compact, Euro-styled, rear-engine car available as a coupe or convertible.

Ford wasn't eager to launch any new vehicle so soon after the Edsel debacle, but reluctantly he gave Iacocca approval to develop a car that would appeal to youthful buyers. To keep costs down and to speed development, Iacocca's product team would have to draw so heavily on components from Ford's compact Falcon sedan that Iacocca's new car was known within Ford by the nondescript nickname Falcon Special.

The development team was led by Don Frey and Hal Sperlich (later in his career, Sperlich would create yet another new market segment, the minivan). Disguising the Mustang's humble Falcon underpinnings was a sleek body with a long hood, short rear deck lid and room inside for four. Design involved a team – Joe Oros, Gail Halderman and David Ash – led by Gene Bordinat, who also was responsible for the rear-engine 1963 Mustang concept car that inspired the Ford GT40 racecar. Their work earned the Tiffany Award of

Excellence in American Design, the first time an automobile had won such an honor.

This new Mustang was indeed truly special. Though approved as a car to compete with the Corvair, the Mustang created an entirely new automotive segment, the "pony car," a name that came from the wild horse galloping across the emblem on the Mustang's grille.

The Chevrolet Camaro, Pontiac Firebird, Mercury Cougar, Plymouth Barracuda, Dodge Challenger, American Motors Javelin and even the Toyota Celica would follow in the Mustang's tracks.

But none of them would be launched with cover stories on both national newsweekly magazines or with a nationally televised (by all three major networks!) unveiling at the New York World's Fair. And anyone who might have missed the launch in April likely saw the Mustang, introduced as a 1964 1/2 model, when it paced the Indianapolis 500 a few weeks later, or in 1966 when the car played a leading role in the Oscar-winning movie, "A Man and A Woman," which would be one of many movies – "Bullitt," "Gone in Sixty Seconds" in which the car would star (and don't forget the hit song, "Mustang Sally").

According to automotive trade publication Automotive News, no car ever before or since would so quickly achieve sales of one million units, which the Mustang did within two and a half years.

The Mustang launched with both coupe and convertible models, and for 1965 there was a third version, with a fastback roofline. Buyers of the first Mustangs could choose between an inline six and two V8s offering more than 270 hp. Higher-performance "Mach 1" and "Boss" models followed and racer Carroll Shelby helped take the car to extremes with his GT350 and GT500.

The Mustang survived downsizing in the mid-1970s, galloped back into full pony car splendor, survived through tough financial times when Ford considered switching to a front-drive platform, and outlived all its competitors. With sales of more than eight million units, the Mustang celebrated its 40th anniversary in 2004 with an all-new generation of pony cars ready to roll out of the Ford factory for the 2005 model year.

PORSCHE 911

192-193 FOR PORSCHE'S 911, FORM FOLLOWED FUNCTION, NOT FASHION. THE BASIC SILHOUETTE OF THE REAR-ENGINE SPORTS CAR HAS UNDERGONE ONLY SUBTLE CHANGES THROUGH MORE THAN 40 YEARS OF PRODUCTION.

193 TOP FERDINAND ALEXANDER "BUTZI" PORSCHE SCULPTS A CLAY MODEL OF THE 911. AFTER DESIGNING RACECARS AND THE 911 SPORTS CAR, BUTZI FOUNDED HIS OWN FIRM, PORSCHE DESIGN, IN 1972.

After nearly two decades on roads and racetracks, it was time for Porsche to replace the 356; its venerable, 4-cylinder, two-seat sports car as well as the racers developed from the same basic architecture.

F.A. "Butzi" Porsche, son of VW Beetle designer Ferdinand Porsche and cousin of Porsche 356 creator Ferry Porsche, studied design, joined the family firm and crafted the low-slung, fiberglass-bodied, mid-engine 904 racing car, which won the 1964 Targa Florio road race, was runner-up in the snowy Monte Carlo Rally and nimble enough to ran competitively at Le Mans against a huge power advantage enjoyed by the 12-cylinder Ferraris and Ford V8-powered Shelby Daytona Coupes. "Butzi" also crafted Porsche's new sports car, which was presented at the 1963 Frankfurt Auto Show as the 901.

By the time the car entered production as a 1965 model, it had been renamed the 911 (Peugeot had registered the use of three-digit car names with zero as the middle number) and was powered by Porsche's new 6-cylinder, horizontally opposed and air-cooled "boxer" engine. At just 1991 cc, the 6-cylinder had slightly less displacement than 1996-cc 4-cylinder that powered Porsche's racy 356 Carrera 2, but the new six generated nearly 140 hp and that figure grew to 180 for the 911S version in 1967, then hit 200 when the engine expanded to 2.2 liters in 1970.

The car also featured a five-speed manual transmission, new MacPherson front suspension with trailing arms at the rear, sharp ZF steering and four-wheel disc brakes.

Compared to the 356, the 911

rode on a wheelbase nearly 4.5 inches (more than 11 cm) longer and was 8 inches (more than 20 cm) longer overall. Slightly shorter and narrower overall than the 356, the 911 had a wider track. Large headlamps were set at the front of prominent fenders. The car's hood sloped sharply down from base of the windshield to a thin front bumper. A fastback roofline covered the passenger compartment, which now included a small rear seat, as well as the still rear-mounted engine.

To provide an open-air driving experience, Porsche introduced the Targa top for 1967. It would not be until 1983 that Porsche produced the 911 in a true convertible version. Instead, the large, front portion of the roof panel lifted off the car. The center section of the roof served as an integrated roll bar and a large rear window wrapped around the back portion of the passenger compartment.

While maintaining the same basic architecture, Porsche added new versions. In 1972 it planned to build 500 Carrera 2.7 RS models to homologate the car for international racing, but there was such demand that Porsche had to produce three times that number. In 1974, the firm introduced the 911 Turbo, its now 3.0-liter flat six turbocharged to generate 260 hp and with a so-called whale tail spoiler used to enhance high-speed aerodynamics.

In the 1980s Porsche built a 911-based 959 "supercar" with twin turbochargers boosting engine output to 450 hp and with four-wheel drive to help keep that power under control at speeds of around 200 mph on the road, and also providing traction to win the Paris-Dakar rally across the sands of the African desert. Soon, twin turbos and four-wheel drive were available on the 911. Through many generations since the 911's launch, Porsche has maintained the car's

basic silhouette, focusing instead of improving rather than recreating.

As a senior engineer for a rival automaker explained it, while others have spent time making their sports cars look different from generation to generation, Porsche has focused on the details, enhancing engines, aerodynamics and the like, getting closer and closer in the pursuit of perfection.

194-195 AND 195 TOP PORSCHE DIDN'T OFFER A CONVERTIBLE VERSION OF ITS 911 UNTIL THE 1980S. BUT IN 1966 IT BEGAN PRODUCTION OF A "TARGA" STYLE ROOF. INSTEAD OF A FOLDING CLOTH TOP, PORSCHE'S TARGA FEATURED A REMOVABLE ROOF PANEL THAT LOCKED BETWEEN THE WINDSHIELD HEADER AND A BUILT-IN ROLLOVER BAR. THE REAR WINDOW WAS MADE OF GLASS IN A WRAPAROUND DESIGN. IN 1975, PORSCHE OFFERED A TURBOCHARGED ENGINE IN THE 911 WITH A HUGE "WHALE TAIL" REAL SPOILER.

PONTIAC GTO

196 TOP PONTIAC'S GTO WENT FROM OPTION PACKAGE TO BECOME A SEPARATE SERIES WHEN THE TEMPEST GOT NEW BODY STYLING IN 1966. A YEAR LATER THE GRILLE UNDERWENT SUBTLE CHANGES AND THE BODY SIDE WAS CLEANED UP WITH THE ELIMINATION OF A BADGE BEHIND THE FRONT WHEEL WELL.

196-197 THE 1967 GTO COULD BE EQUIPPED WITH A 360-HORSPOEWR, RAM-AIR V8 ENGINE. WHAT APPEARS TO BE A SMALL AND REVERSED HOOD SCOOP ON THE GTO IS ACTUALLY A HOUSING FOR THE TACHOMETER, POSITIONED ON THE HOOD SO THE DRIVER COULD WATCH RPM AND THE ROADWAY.

It was typical hot-rodders' stuff: Take a car, lighten the body by stripping it of air conditioning condensers and other items that added unwanted weight, stuff in the biggest, most powerful engine that will fit under the hood, beef up the suspension and add just enough dressing, maybe a hood scoop or two, to hint that something special is coming down the road.

Typical stuff. Nothing unusual. Only this time, the hot-rodders didn't work in a garage out behind the house. These guys worked for a car company, although just like outlaw hot-rodders, the company didn't know what they were doing. In fact, the company had a strict policy against such activity.

But by the time the company discovered what they were doing it was too late. If you were paying attention, you could order a 1964 Pontiac Tempest Le Mans, check the right box on the options list and instead of an ordinary

the GTO as a separate model beginning in 1966, when sales of the car, officially the Tempest GTO but more popularly known by its nickname, the "Goat," reached nearly 100,000 units.

The story of Pontiac's GTO begins in the mid-1950s, when Semon "Bunkie" Knudsen became the division's general manager, with Pete Estes and chief engineer and John Z. DeLorean as Estes' assistant. They needed a new image for a division that seemed to be building little more than higher-priced Chevrolets and found it through motorsports and a "Wide Track" design theme. It worked so well that Knudsen was promoted to Chevrolet. Estes moved up to run Pontiac with DeLorean as chief engineer, and all as Detroit was having serious second thoughts about a horsepower race. GM established a rule about limiting the use of its largest V8 engines to its largest cars just as the guys at Pontiac discovered that it was possible to "intermediate" sized American car with a mundane 6-cylinder engine you took delivery of a gto, the first official, made-in-Detroit, mighty American iron "muscle" car.

After seeing how popular the option package proved to be – more than 32,000 customers checked the right box in 1964 and that number more than doubled the following model year – and how eager their competitors were to build muscle cars of their own, General Motors had no choice but to approve shoehorn the Bonneville's 389 cubic inch (6.37 liter) V8 into the engine bay of the smaller, lighter Pontiac Tempest, which for 1964 was moving up from the compact class to Detroit's new "intermediate" family sedan category.

Check the right option package and for less than $300 instead of a 140-hp inline 6-cylinder engine you got 325 hp, a three-speed manual shifter mounted on the floor, stiffer suspension, upgraded steering and tires, dual exhaust and a hood with twin air scoops as well as GTO badges. Since Ferrari hadn't trademarked the name of its famous GTO racing car, Pontiac borrowed it for its car, which could sprint from a standing start to 60 mph (99 km/h) in a mere but tire-smoking 6.2 seconds. Car & Driver magazine's March 1964 cover proclaimed "GTO vs GTO" and included images of the new Pontiac and the famous Ferrrari. Inside, however, there was no head-to-head test, though based on its road test of the Pontiac the magazine promised the American muscle car would beat the Ferrari in a drag race. To further jump-start interest in the GTO, Jim Wangers of Pontiac's advertising agency created a band, Ronnie and the Daytonas, to record a song, "Little GTO," With a catchy tune and lines such as "turn it on, wind it up, blow it out GTO," the song – basically a commercial for Pontiac's new car – became one of the top hits on the pop music charts.

LAMBORGHINI MIURA

Italian tractor manufacturer Ferruccio Lamborghini wasn't happy with the Ferrari he bought in the early 1960s, but when he complained to Enzo Ferrari, he was told the problem was with the driver, not the car. Angry as a fighting bull, Lamborghini vowed to build a better car.

So Lamborghini acquired a factory at Sant' Agata, not far from Ferrari's own facility at Modena, hired former Ferrari engineer Giotto Bizzarrini to build him a 12-cylinder engine and added such talented chassis specialists as Paolo Stanzani, Gianpaolo Dallara and New Zealander Bob Wallace.

Lamborghini's talented team built his first car, the front-engine 350GT, in 1964. Then, at the Geneva auto show in early 1966, he displayed the rolling chassis for a new car, this one with its engine behind the cockpit, as in the Ford GT40 Le Mans racing car, but turned

198 TOP LAMBORGHINI'S MIURA TOOK ITS NAME FROM A FAMOUS BREED OF SPANISH FIGHTING BULLS. THE BULL ALSO WAS THE ZODIAC SIGN UNDER WHICH FERRUCCIO LAMBORGHINI WAS BORN AND SERVED AS HIS CORPORATE LOGO.

198-199 MARCELLO GANDINI, SON OF AN ORCHESTRA CONDUCTOR, WAS ONLY 25 YEARS OLD WHEN HE WAS ASSIGNED DESIGN OF THE MIURA. THE CAR'S ROOFLINE IS LITTLE MORE THAN A METER FROM THE PAVEMENT. IN KEEPING WITH THE LOW PROFILE, EXPOSED HEADLAMPS POP UP TO ILLUMINATE THE ROADWAY AFTER DARK.

90 degrees, as in the little Austin Mini. The thought was that by turning the engine sideways and casting its crankcase, the gearbox and final drive into a single piece, enough room might be spared so the driver and passenger could be relatively comfortable while traveling at very fast speeds.

Remarkably, each member of Lamborghini's engineering trio was still in his 20s, and so was the designer who would create the proper body to surround this amazing chassis. That designer was 25-year-old Marcello Gandini, and this would be his first assignment for the Bertone studio. Rarely has anyone made such a spectacular debut.

Born under the zodiac sign of the bull, Lamborghini named the car Miura, after Spain's famous breed of matador-mauling fighting bulls. Lamborghini had no interest in racing, but his Miura was the fastest car on the street, the first mid-engine "supercar," and

it would be seven years before Ferrari would catch up with his own mid-engine, 12-cylinder Boxer.

With four cams and four carburetors, the four-liter V12 generated 350 horsepower. To keep its load as light as possible, Dallara found a way to cut away holes in the steel monocoque chassis without losing structural integrity. With racing-style double-wishbone suspension, rack and pinion steering and large disc brakes, the Miura provided outstanding driving dynamics, except for some front-end lift at very high speeds.

And the Miura was capable of very high speeds. Gandini's body was sleek from its knife-edge nose to its close-cropped tail. Air vents were subtly sculpted into the door panels just behind the windows and into rocker panels just ahead of the rear wheels. Even the headlights were designed with airflow in mind; they set flush into the steeply raked

front fenders, then popped-up into position for driving at night. The car could accelerate from a standing start to 60 miles per hour (96 km/h) in less than seven seconds and its top speed exceeded 170 mph (277 km/h), making it the fastest car on public roads.

Lamborghini anticipated selling maybe 25 of the cars a year. Demand far exceeded his expectations. Between 1966 and 1972 nearly 900 Miuras were built.

In 1970, the Miura S arrived with another 20 horsepower and an even stiffer chassis, wider tires and ventilated brakes to deal with the increased power. The car also offered power windows and optional air conditioning.

Then, in 1972, came the Miura SV with another 15 horsepower, changes within the engine to improve oil flow under high lateral acceleration, and a body enhanced to reduce high-speed lift – a good thing in a car that could exceed 180 miles per hour.

ALFA ROMEO DUETTO

To the string-back gloved sports car aficionado, the Alfa Romeo Duetto was revered as Battista "Pinin" Farina's last automotive design.

Even though its deeply scalloped body sides weren't highly praised when the car was unveiled at the Geneva Motor Show in 1966, and while its Jaguar E-type price tag might have put off many potential customers, the Alfa roadster nonetheless remained in production for a remarkable 27 years.

One reason for this Alfa's long run was the joy it brought its drivers, but another factor was its status as a popular culture icon. The Duetto was car that, along with haunting music from Simon and Garfunkel carried Dustin Hoffman in the 1967 movie "The Graduate," as he pursued Mrs. Robinson's daughter, Elaine.

"…and here's to you, Mrs. Robinson…"

British auto authorities tend to be particularly critical of vehicles not built in the United Kingdom, but in their "encyclopedia of the world's most fabulous automobiles," Martin Buckley and Chris Rees note that the Duetto, "with smooth steering, slick gearchange and fine disc brakes, offered driver involvement and satisfaction that few cars could equal.

"It was a civilized car, too," they add, "with a good ride and a watertight hood [convertible top] that could be raised with one hand."

The Duetto succeeded the Giulietta Spyder in Alfa Romeo's lineup.

Alfa held a contest to name its new sports car. More than 140,000 entries were delivered. Suggested names included the Lollobridgida, the Bardot, even the Panther and the Sputnik. The winning name was selected because it captured both the style of car's twin-cam engine and the roadster's two-seat architecture.

Pininfarina not only designed the car, but his compa-

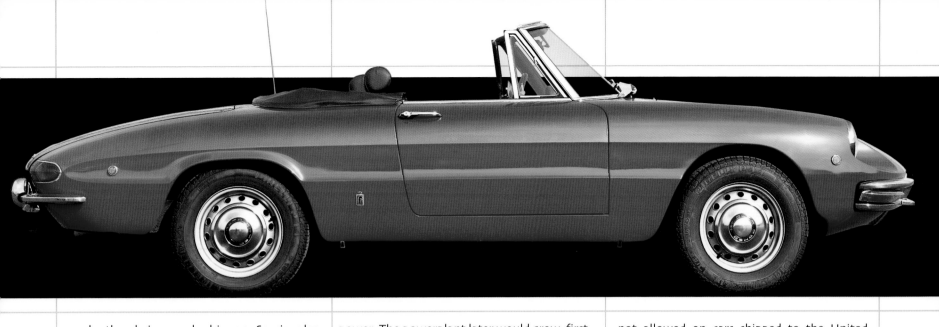

ny, by then being run by his son, Sergio, also handled production, with some 100,000 Duettos built during the car's long life span.

At first, a 1.6-liter inline four-cylinder engine provided slightly more than 100 horse-power. The powerplant later would grow, first to 1.8 and then to 2.0 liters.

Pininfarina's original design had simple but beautifully rounded lines, including boat-tail style rear end, and a large trunk for a two-seat roadster. In 1970 the tail was clipped into a Kamm-style rear.

Headlamps were recessed into the front fenders. In Europe they wore aerodynamic covers that were not allowed on cars shipped to the United States. In 1985, Alfa created renewed interest in what was then known as the Spyder Veloce by paying homage to the movie that had made the car so popular in so many parts of the world. Alfa began offering a lower-price version of the car. This Spyder Graduate wore stripes along its sides and special Graduate insignia.

"…where have you gone, Joe DiMaggio?…"

FERRARI DINO 206 GT

It has been said that Enzo Ferrari only acted once with his heart instead of his head. Ferrari's focus was firmly on winning. He could be especially cold and calculating when it came to managing his racing teams, and everything else in his life was secondary. Well, almost everything else. Even Ferrari had a heart, and it was broken when his son, Alfredino, died of kidney disease in 1956. Before his death, "Dino" Ferrari had convinced his father to let him work with engineer Vittorio Jano on a new V6 racing engine, although Dino died two years before a version of that engine powered Mike Hawthorn to the World Driving Championship in 1958.

Ferrari mourned for his son for several years and finally turned to Pininfarina for a very special tribute. The Dino Berlinetta Speciale was on display at the Paris auto show in 1965 as a concept car and the following year it came alive at the Turin show with its namesake's V6 engine mounted transversely behind just behind its cockpit. The Dino would go into production as Ferrari's first mid-engine sports car designed for the road rather than for the racetrack. It also would go into production without any Ferrari badging (though some owners would add it later). Instead of the Prancing Horse on a shield-shaped emblem, the new car had a rectangular yellow emblem with a script "Dino" written in blue.

But before it could go into production, the engines would have to be produced, and since the 65-degree motor was designed for racing, it would be eligible for Formula Two competition provided at least 500 were built.

Ferrari liked the idea of producing the Dino, not only in memory of his son but also as a separate model line that would be positioned to compete against Porsche and other small displace-

202-203 AND 203 TOP THE BEAUTY OF THE DINO'S DESIGN WAS AS MUCH IN ITS EXQUISITE DETAILS AS IT WAS IN THE CAR'S SMOOTH LINES AND OVERALL BALANCE. FLYING BUTTRESSES EXTENDED THE CAR'S ROOFLINE AND FRAMED AN ENGINE COMPARTMENT POSITIONED BEHIND THE CAR'S SEATS. AIR SCOOPS IN THE DOORS WERE BOTH FUNCTIONAL AND AESTHETIC. HEADLAMPS SET WELL BACK INTO THE FRONT FENDERS DIDN'T DETRACT FROM THE CAR'S LOW FRONT PROFILE.

ment sports cars. But 500 engines was more than Ferrari figured to need on its own, so he struck a deal with Fiat to manufacture the motors. Fiat would use its supply in its own Dino tribute: a front-engine spider designed by Pininfarina and a front-engine coupe by Bertone. The Fiats would be powered by Dino engines tuned to produce 160 hp.

For the Dino from Ferrari, the engines would have 180 hp, though within two years displacement was enlarged to 2.4 liters to provide nearly 200 hp and there was such demand that some 4000 of the Dinos – 246 GT coupes and 246 GTS Targa-topped spyders – were built by 1973, when the Dino engine went into the Lancia Stratos and, now tuned to 300 hp in an all-out competition version, would add three World Rally Championships to its resume.

To create a body worthy of a car to carry the name of Ferrari's own son, Pininfarina turned to young designer Leonardo Fioravanti, who would go on to style a record eight Ferrari models and, after 24 years at Pininfarina, would be hired by Ferrari himself.

For the Dino, Fioravanti created a masterpiece in mid-engine architecture.

The hood swept back from just above the road surface between prominent front fenders, with a single headlamp mounted in an upright position with a pocket scooped out into each of those fenders. The windshield was dramatically raked back. Air inlets that started midway back on the door panels added an element both sculptural and functional.

Flying buttress-styled panels flowed from the roofline to provide bookends around the engine compartment and a close-cropped tail section featured four round lamps.

FERRARI 365 DAYTONA

206 AND 207 "I MADE THE FIRST SKETCHES AND THE SURFACE DRAWING WORKING NIGHT AND DAY FOR A WEEK, SLEEPING ONLY A FEW HOURS EVERY NIGHT," HE REMEMBERS. "THE DAYTONA DESIGN PROCESS IS A VERY SPECIAL MEMORY." FIORAVANTI'S VERSION OF THE CAR WAS UNVEILED TO THE PUBLIC AT THE PARIS SHOW IN 1968. "IT IS ONE OF THE MOST BEAUTIFUL CARS EVER BUILT AND ITS NAME CELEBRATES ONE OF THE GREATEST VICTORIES FERRARI EVER ACHIEVED," PROCLAIMS *FERRARI, DESIGN OF A LEGEND*," THE COMPANY'S OFFICIAL HISTORY AND CATALOG PUBLISHED IN 1990.

With Lamborghini introducing the first true "supercar" in the sensual form of its mid-engine Miura model, there was considerable anticipation to see how Ferrari would trump the tractor-maker turned upstart sports car manufacturer.

Thus there was no small degree of disappointment when the 275 GTB/4 was unveiled at the Paris auto show in 1967. The news wasn't that Ferrari had revised the car's architecture and positioned its 12-cylinder engine behind the driver as it did in its sports-racing prototypes and has Lamborghini had done in the Miura. This was really just a carryover model, although the first Ferrari road car equipped with double overhead camshafts on its still front-mounted V12 engine and, as a result, would make 300 hp available to its driver.

Among those with other ideas was Pininfarina's young designer Leonardo Fioravanti, whose first major assignment had been the sensational styling for the Dino 206 GT, the car named in memory of Ferrari's own son. Working day and night, with only a few hours of sleep in any one stretch, Fioravanti consumed a week making sketches and surface drawings for a new Ferrari, still with front-engine architecture, but taking Pininfarina's "Superfast" design cues to a new plateau. The result was the Ferrari 365 GTB/4, the so-called "Daytona" model, unveiled at Paris in 1968. No

one was disappointed by this car. Even Mike Lawrence, whose *A-Z of Sports Cars Since 1945* is full of critical comments about cars many other have praised, says that calling the Daytona merely the successor to 275GTB/4 is like calling the cathedral at Chartres just another building. "The last, greatest, and most popular of the front-engine, two-seat production Ferraris," add the authors of *The Complete Book of Collectible Cars.* "Arguably the prettiest, too."

BBC commentator Quentin Wilson, in his *The Ultimate Classic Car Book*, describes the Daytona as "a poem in steel."

Instead of voluptuous bulges, Fioravanti's design was smooth and clean. The body seemed to flow from a sharp front edge, over headlights either protected behind clear plastic covers or hidden behind revolving doors, back over a long hood and compact passenger compartment to a short rear deck lid and tightly cropped tail.

Though technically the 365 GTB/4 – the numbers generated by the displacement of each cylinder, 365 cc, and the engine's four-cam architecture – the car was immediately dubbed the Daytona in

honor of Ferrari's 1-2-3 victory sweep – ahead of two Porsches and three Ford GT40s – in the 24 Hours of Daytona endurance race of 1967.

Powering the Ferrari "Daytona" was a 4.4-liter "Colombo" V12 breathing through six carburetors and pumping out 352 hp and 365 pound-feet of torque. The car accelerated from a standing start to 60 mph (96 km/h) in less than 6 sec-

onds, though in this case the more meaningful figure was its 0-100 mph (161 km/h) sprint time of just 12.8 seconds. With the engine set back in the chassis and with the transmission at the rear of the vehicle, the Daytona had amazing dynamic balance and its aerodynamic shape helped it achieve a top speed of 175 mph, faster even than Lamborghini's Miura "supercar."

208-209 OF SOME 1400 DAYTONAS PRODUCED AND DISTRIBUTED BY FERRARI, FEWER THAN 130 WERE THE CONVERTIBLE-TOPPED SPYDER VERSION, WHICH MADE ITS DEBUT AT THE FRANKFURT AUTO SHOW IN 1969.

MASERATI GHIBLI

210-211 AND 211 TOP GHIBLI IS THE HOT WIND THAT BLOWS FROM THE SOUTH ACROSS THE SAHARA DESERT. IT ALSO IS A "HOT" CAR THAT CREATES ITS OWN WIND AS IT SIZZLES ALONG THE HIGHWAY AT SPEEDS OF MORE THAN 160 MILES PER HOUR.

212-213 GIORGETTO GIUGIARO'S DESIGN FOR MASERATI'S LATE 1960S SUPERCAR HAS WIND-CHEATING SURFACES THAT ARE LONG AND LOW AND EXTREMELY SMOOTH SIDES. EVEN THE HEADLIGHTS ARE HIDDEN UNTIL NEEDED.

G iorgetto Giugiaro made both a spectacular and prolific debut as head of design and prototype building at Ghia in December 1965. Within a year, Giugiaro had five new concepts on the stands of the world's major international auto shows. They included a four-seat coupe for Japan's Izusu, the Fiat 850 Vanessa, a car designed for women, especially those, such as Giugiaro's wife, who had a new child, and the Rowan elettrica, an electric-powered mini. There also was the De Tomaso Mangusta.

But none of Giugiaro's early works for Ghia and its clients was quite as spectacular – or as long lasting – as the Maserati Ghibli, a car that still looks fresh and contemporary some four decades later.

Like its designer, the Ghibli has aged very well. It is still considered the most beautiful of all Maserati road cars and outsold both of its contemporary rivals, the Ferrari Daytona and the Lamborghini Miura, even though both had more modern mechanicals.

The Ghibli was built on a shortened version of the chassis used for the Maserati Quattroporte sedan and the notch-backed, four-seat Mexico coupe.

Thus the Ghibli had a tubular chassis, a relatively heavy steel body and a live rear-axle with leaf-spring rear suspension. It also had Maserati's racing-bred, four-cam, 4.7-liter V8, mounted ahead of the driver. The engine drank in large quantities of fuel and air through a quartet of carburetors and used it good result, pumping out 330 horsepower.

Then, in 1970, Maserati enlarged the motor to 4.7 liters, adding only a little horsepower but greatly increasing torque.

But what truly set the Ghibli apart and made it capable to achieving speeds in excess of 160 miles per hour (nearly 260 km/h) was its sleek body with its low and long hood and its even longer fastback roofline. Hidden, pop-up headlamps and a tightly cropped tail helped make Giugiaro's design even more aerodynamic.

Maserati had been founded in the early decades of the 20th century. At first, Bindo, Ettore and Ernesto joined their brother Alfieri in his shop in 1914. A dozen years later, the brothers launched a company under the family name, selecting Neptune's Trident, symbol of their native Bologna, as the emblem to place on their racing cars.

Racing made Maserati famous, and was the basis of the company's work until it left motorsports in the late 1950s to concentrate on the development of road cars.

The brothers sold out to industrialist Adolfo Orsi in 1938, but agreed to stay with the company for a decade. Together they built the cars that won the Indianapolis 500 in 1939 and 1940.

After their commitment to Orsi was fulfilled, the brothers formed another successful racecar-building company, O.S.C.A., which they sold in 1963 to the maker of Agusta motorcycles. Thus they were not part of the effort behind the Maserati in which Juan Fangio won the 1957 Grand Prix championship or the exotic road-going sports cars that bore their name after the company left racing, cars such as the 3500GT, Mistral, Ghibli and Bora.

The Ghibli remained in production until 1973 with some 1150 coupes and 125 convertible Spyders built.

Giugiaro stayed with Ghia only until early in 1968, when he left to found his design firm, Italdesign.

DE TOMASO PANTERA

Alejandro De Tomaso was born in Argentina, raced OSCAs for the Maserati brothers, and married Isabel Haskell, accomplished sports car racer and well-off granddaughter of the founder of General Motors.

De Tomaso Automobili was founded to build racing and then road cars. De Tomaso launched his first sports car, the Vallelunga. in 1963. The car was powered by a mid-mounted, four-cylinder engine from a Ford Cortina and carried a body designed at Ghia by Giorgetto Giugiaro. But there were underlying mechanical problems and only a few dozen of the cars were built.

However, that same year, Henry Ford II thought he had done a deal to buy Enzo Ferrari's racing team and sports car company. When the deal fell, Ford commissioned the famed GT40 racecar and then, with encouragement from his executive vice president Lee Iacocca, offered to help De Tomaso improve his sports car operation, which was located in Modena just like Ferrari's.

Ford and Carroll Shelby, racer and building of the Cobra sports cars, commissioned a pro-

totype for a possible Cobra replacement, but when Shelby was dissatisfied with the car's dynamic capabilities, the project was offered to De Tomaso, who again had Giugiaro do a body for what De Tomaso called the Mangusta. A Ford V8 provided power, but only a few hundred of the cars were built over a four-year period. In 1970, Ford took an equity stake in De Tomaso and Ghia and they announced plans to develop and produce niche vehicles. Thus the Pantera, powered by Ford's 351 "Cleveland" V8, wearing an exotic body with curves and creases by Ghia's Tom Tjaarda, and sold in the United States by selected Lincoln-Mercury dealers. The Pantera was the "poor-man's" exotic, with 310 horsepower, sprinting to 60 miles per hour (96 km/h) in just 5.5 seconds and on to a top speed that approached 150 miles per hour (nearly 235 km/h), and for price of only $9995, less than half of what Maserati wanted for its Ghibli and around a third of the price of a Ferrari Daytona.

Again, there were some underlying problems, and they would only be exacerbated by trying to deal with the United States' new safety and emissions laws.

Import into the U.S. stopped after the 1974 model year, though De Tomaso continued to build cars in Italy – around 10,000 total – some of which were federalized for the U.S. market in the 1980s, when De Tomaso had emerged as Italy's fifth-largest auto producer.

In 1981, America's Popular Mechanics magazine staged a 16-car comparison test of exotic sports cars. The field included a BMW M1, Porsche 928, Lamborghini Countach, three Ferraris, a Maserati, Lotus, Jaguar, Aston Martin and Mercedes-Benz, and the winner was a Pantera GTS, a later version with a body modified by Marcello Gandini and power from an Australian-built Ford V8.

LAMBORGHINI COUNTACH

How sexy was the Lamborghini Countach? Sexy enough that across the United States, and likely in countries all around the world, teen-age boys took down their pictures of Charlie's Angel Farrah Fawcett, the one with her posing in a red swim suit against a stripped background, and replaced them with posters of the Countach, frequently in bright yellow, sometimes in stunning red or bright white, and, on occasion, in sinister black.

The story goes that one day a Lamborghini employee got his first glimpse of the prototype for Project 112 and all he could say was "Countach!" a dialect expression men reserve for the entrance of a particularly beautiful woman.

Lamborghini's Miura may have been the original supercar, but its successor was the original supermodel, the exotic of exotics, especially when its doors opened like a beetle's

wings on scissors-style hinges.

Those doors and several of the Countach's other design cues had been introduced at the 1968 Paris auto show on a wedge-shaped concept car, the Carabo, which Bertone built around the chassis of the Alfa Romeo Type 33 sports racing car. Carabo is Italian for beetle and the car, designed by the automotive artistic genius Marcello Gandini, was displayed in an iridescent beetle-green color.

Three years later, at the Geneva show, the Carabo had evolved into the Countach LP500 concept. Instead of Alfa's 2.0-liter V8, the car carried a 5.0-liter version of the 3.9-liter V12 engine that Giotto Bizzarrini had designed for Lamborghini. In the Miura, the engine sat

latitudinally behind the passenger compartment, but for the new car – LP stood for "longitudinale posteriore" – the powerplant was turned 90 degrees and the five-speed transmission extended forward, toward the cockpit, where the driver had access to a direct shift lever.

While the setup didn't leave a lot of space in the cockpit, it gave Gandini the latitude he needed to compose a dramatic blend of lines and angles, creases and wedges, and to create his masterpiece.

But Gandini's canvas would be altered in

the two years it took to take the Countach from LP500 concept to LP400 production car.

Where the concept had cleanly creased sides with small louvers behind the B pillar to guide airflow to the engine, the production car needed a large NACA duct ahead of each rear wheel, plus big scoops over the rear fenders to help keep components cool. Still, the Countach was a hot number, with six carburetors feeding 12 cylinders that displaced 4.0 liters and pumped out 375 horsepower, shooting the car down the road at speeds approaching 300 kilometers per hour (some 180 miles per hour).

Another feature of Gandini's design were the distinct trapezoidal cuts around the wheel openings. But before long, those, too, would have to be changed, with bulging blisters to cover the foot-wide rear wheels, new tires and revised rear suspension on the LP400S in 1978.

The Countach evolved some again in 1982 with the LP500S getting a 4.8-liter V12 to help make up for power lost to new emission regulations. Some of these cars also featured a delta-wing spoiler that stood well above the rear deck lid.

Another update came in 1985 in the form of the LP500S QV with new four-valve (Quattro Valvole) cylinder heads helping to boost output to 455 horsepower and top speed to better than 190 miles per hour.

Finally, to celebrate Lamborghini's 25th anniversary and the end of Countach production (as well as the coming of the Diablo), a final anniversary edition featured extensively revised bodywork by Lamborghini's young Argentine industrial designer Horatio Pagani.

Rough Road Ahead:
The gasoline and
other crises

1975/1984

If the ten-year period that ended in the mid-1970s was marked by the speed at which cars could travel, the ensuing decade would be marked by the speed at which things changed for those who built and sold and for those who bought and drove automobiles.

Instead of how fast, the questions became how safe, how clean and how fuel-efficient could cars become.

Rough Road Ahead: The gasoline and other crises

In 1964, the American Congress had set safety standards for vehicles purchased by the federal government. The following year Congressional advisor Ralph Nader published a widely publicized book, Unsafe at Any Speed, *an indictment of the state of automobile safety and especially inherent dangers facing those who drove the Chevrolet Corvair and the reluctance of General Motors to remedy the problem (at the cost of some $15 per vehicle).*

In 1966, Congress passed the National Traffic and Motor Vehicle Safety Act, which applied those 1964 – as well as additional safety regulations — to all cars sold in the country. Since the United States had recently begun importing more cars than it exported, these rules affected automakers around the world.

Soon safety regulations, some even more stringent than the American standards, were being established in Europe and

Japan as well. For example, the United States required cars to be equipped with safety belts that could restrain vehicle occupants in a collision. In many countries, though ironically not in the United States, drivers were actually required to use those belts. To save American drivers from themselves, rules would be drafted in 1984 requiring automakers to equip vehicles with "passive restraints," safety features such as airbags that automatically inflated in a

crash to provide a protective barrier between a driver and the steering wheel and a front-seat passenger and the instrument panel and windshield.

Meanwhile, in Southern California, known for its sunshine and beaches, for its suntanned surfers, too often the sun's ultraviolet radiation mixed with industrial and automotive emissions to create a hazardous air pollution condition known as "smog." In 1963, California passed legislation to mandate a reduction in exhaust emissions from motor vehicles.

These standards were applied throughout the United States in 1965 and those in California were made even more stringent, as were those across the country after the 1970 updating of the Clean Air Act.

Other countries drafted their own air quality rules in the early years of the 1970s, with Europe, which already had more fuel-efficient vehicles, turning to diesel engines

as a way to reduce so-called greenhouse gases such as carbon dioxide. In ensuing years, vehicle emission regulations around the world have become increasingly stringent. As if new safety and pollution laws weren't enough of a challenge for automakers, in 1973, in the aftermath of an Arab-Israeli conflict, the Organization of Arab Petroleum Exporting Countries staged an oil embargo that hit particularly hard in the United States and some parts of Europe. The flow of petroleum slowed again in 1979 after the overthrow of the Shah of Iran.

To save fuel, speed limits were greatly reduced – to a mere 55 miles per hour on American Interstate routes. Then, in 1975, a new Energy Policy and Conservation Act required American automakers to drastically improve the fuel economy of their vehicles. Three years later, a "gas guzzler" tax was placed on all cars sold in the United States that didn't meet minimum fuel-economy standards.

Such rules stimulated the sale of cars made in Japan and Europe, where taxes made gasoline much more expensive than it was in the United States and had encouraged the production and sales of more fuel-efficient vehicles.

219 THE TESTAROSSA WAS THE MOST AUDACIOUS DESIGN OF ITS ERA, THANKS TO A LONG AND WEDGE-SHAPED BODY THAT FEATURED BOLD AND STRIKING DUCTWORK THAT DIRECTED COOLING AIR INTO RADIATORS MOUNTED ON ITS REAR FLANKS.

221 A PEUGEOT SAFETY ENGINEER USES MOVABLE RODS TO DETERMINE THE RANGE OF MOTION BY A DUMMY WEARING SEAT BELTS IN A CRASH SIMULATION.

1975/1984

BMW M1

222 DESIGNER GIORGETTO
GIUGIARO EXPLORED NEW
IDEAS IN FRONT AND REAR
CRASH PROTECTION IN
DRAWINGS HE MADE IN
1978 FOR THE BMW M1.

223 THE DESIGN OF THE
BMW M1 INCORPORATED
THE COMPANY'S

CHARACTERISTIC TWIN-
KIDNEY GRILLE INTO THE
THIN NOSE OF A WEDGE-
SHAPED BODY THAT
FEATURED GULL WING
DOORS. THE CAR WAS THE
ONLY BMW PRODUCTION
VEHICLE BUILT AROUND
MID-ENGINE
ARCHITECTURE.

In celebration of the 1972 Olympic Games hosted by its headquarters hometown of Munich, Germany, BMW had its design director Paul Bracq create a special concept car. The gull-winged BMW Turbo was presented it as an experimental safety vehicle, although its wedge-shaped and low-slung body looked more like an exotic sports car than something designed with safety in mind.

The Olympic concept car was notable for many reasons. It took its name from the turbocharging of its 4-cylinder engine, which a year later would provide power to the highest-performance version of the company's heralded sports coupe, the 2002. The Olympic car also was the first BMW with mid-engine architecture.

Fast-forward to 1975 and to recently revised international racing rules and BMW's desire to maintain its competitiveness in international endurance racing. With BMW's 3.0CSi showing its age, a new car would be needed for racing in the Group 4 category of the World Manufacturers Championship. With Bracq having returned to his native France to work for Peugeot, BMW turned to Giorgetto Giugiaro to design a body based on the '72 Olympic Turbo concept.

BMW contracted Italian sports car maker Lamborghini to do development engineering for the tube-frame chassis and to build the

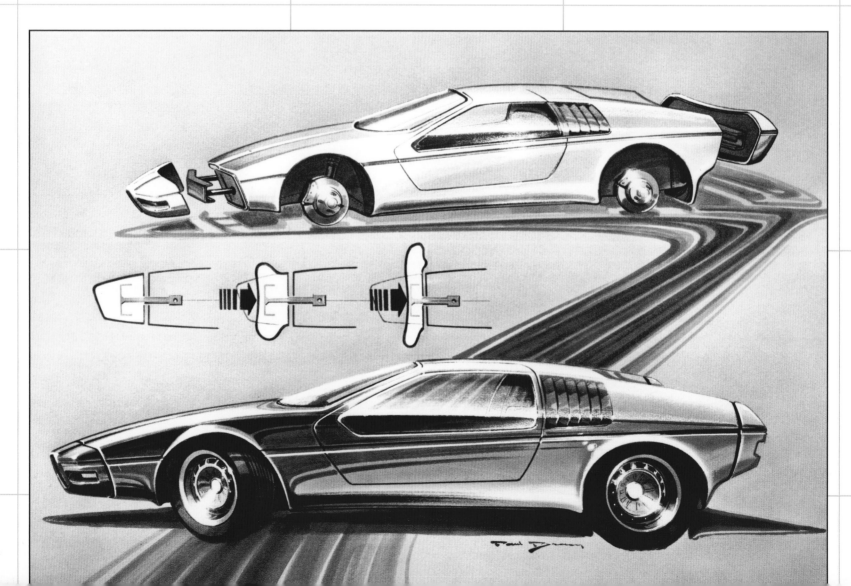

400 vehicles needed to meet Group 4 homologation requirements.

Power for this new car, the BMW M1, would come not from a 4-cylinder turbo but from a specially created version of BMW's inline 6-cylinder engine.

While the new engine shared its basic architecture with the 3.5-liter powerplant in BMW's beautiful 635CSi coupe, BMW Motorsport GmbH, the corporate racing department, would custom-build these motors, installing special components, including 24-valve, double-overhead cam valve gear.

The result would be a more than competitive 470 - 500 hp in racing trim. Even road-going versions of the car would produce in excess of 270 hp, enough to propel the M1 from a standing start to 60 mph (96 km/h) in less than 5.5 seconds and on to speeds in excess of 160 mph (257 km/h) on the autobahn. But results would be slow in coming. Financial problems at Lamborghini delayed construction and BMW had to turn again to Giugiaro and Italdesign not only for design but to manage production, which they did, with final assembly subcontracted to German coachbuilder Baur.

At last, the cars were built, and the BMW M1 was officially unveiled at the 1978 Paris Auto Show. But there was another problem: racing's rules now required that instead of just constructing 400 cars, they actually had to be sold. At 100,000 German marks (around $55,000 in U.S. dollars), the BMW M1 was as expensive as it was exotic. Even with car enthusiasts eager to own and drive such an exotic BMW, it wasn't until 1980 that sales were sufficient for the cars to be eligible to race.

One of them, driven by Hans Stuck and Nelson Piquet, won the prestigious 1000 km at

the Nürburgring that year, but the rules of racing had evolved yet again and the M1 already was becoming outdated.

But it also was being acclaimed. BMW and the Formula One Constructors Association created the Procar series to entertain spectators at Grand Prix events and many of the world's best drivers were able to showcase their talents at the M1's wheel.

But the M1's real success was on public roads, where the mid-engine BMW was fast and sleek – and a rare treat for those who caught a glimpse as one sped past.

224-225 THE M1 REFLECTS ITS ITALIAN HERITAGE. PRELIMINARY ENGINEERING WAS DONE BY LAMBORGHINI. FINAL DESIGN WAS BY GIORGETTO GUIGIARO.

225 TOP THE USE OF MID-ENGINE ARCHITECTURE GAVE THE M1 A PROFILE UNLIKE ANYTHING BMW HAD PRODUCED FOR THE ROAD.

August Horch worked for Carl Benz in the infancy of the motorcar. In 1899 Horch started a car company under his own name but 10 years later he quit again and started over. No longer holding the commercial rights to his own name, Horch named his new company Audi.

"Horchen" is the German word for "listen" and Horch used the Latin translation, Audi, for his new company, and people did listen as Horch's Audis won the Alpine Rally so often that the company took permanent possession of the rally's championship trophy – and provided a foreshadowing of things to come. Based in Berlin, Audi barely survived the 1940s, relocating to Ingolstadt in southern Germany and rebuilding under the umbrella of Daimler-Benz. Volkswagen took controlling interest in 1964. In 1972, Ferdinand Porsche's grandson, Ferdinand Piech, arrived to run Audi's technical development. Piech had been deeply involved in Porsche's renowned racing programs and was eager to establish a competitive edge for Audi.

Audi engineer Jorg Bensinger found that edge while doing winter testing of the Iltis, a Jeep-like vehicle Audi was developing for its parent company. Piech saw potential in putting an Iltis-style four-wheel-drive system under an Audi car platform. Development started in 1977. In January 1978, prototypes were hustling up Europe's steepest mountain pass on summer tires and that spring they displayed the fair-weather advantages of all-wheel grip by running around the Hockenheim race track posting times competitive with Porsche's 911.

The Audi Quattro was unveiled at the 1980 Geneva Auto Show. To save weight versus a truck-style 4-wheel-drive system with its heavy transfer box, Audi used an elegant but simple, full-time system with a hollow drive shaft to deliver equal power to front and rear axles. To save time and money, this full-time 4WD system was installed beneath the body of an Audi 80 coupe. But for power to make things exciting, the 80s 4-cylinder engine was displaced by the turbocharged, 2.1-liter 5-cylinder engine from the Audi 200.

With all four tires providing propulsion and with 177 hp – soon to grow to 200 for the road and to 300 in the short-wheelbase Sport Quattro version for Group B international rally competition – the Audi Quattro was quick and sure-footed. The car made its unofficial competitive debut in fall 1980, where, despite serving only as a service vehicle, it beat the Portuguese Rally winner to the finish line by a half an hour.

A year later, in 1981, with the car now in official competition, people were indeed listening as Audi Quattros won four world rally events. The victory at San Remo by French driver Michelle Mouton and navigator Fabrizia Pons was the first for an all-female team; Mouton was runner-up in the driver's championship in 1982. Audi drivers won the championship the next two years and Mouton, American Indy car racer Bobby Unser and Walter Rohrl brought international attention to the car by winning the Pikes Peak Hill Climb three times between 1984 and 1987.

"The Audi Quattro was one of the major cars of the 1980s," write the authors of Cars, 1930-2000, an encyclopedic technical history of the modern car. "Some," they add, "would say the most important."

Even more important than the racing victories on gravel and forest roads was how the Audi Quattro paved the way for proving the viability of all-wheel-drive technology to increase safety and security in cars for ensuing decades.

226-227 AUDI ESTABLISHED THE CAPABILITIES OF ITS QUATTRO SYSTEM THROUGH RALLY RACING AND IN HILL CLIMBS WHERE TRACTION WAS CRUCIAL TO SUCCESS.

227 TOP AUDI'S QUATTRO FULL-TIME ALL-WHEEL-DRIVE SYSTEM DISDAINED THE HEAVY TRANSFER CASE USED BENEATH FOUR-WHEEL-DRIVE TRUCKS. BY SPLITTING POWER BETWEEN THE FRONT AND REAR AXLES, AUDI NOT ONLY IMPROVED TRACTION, BUT THE DELIVERY OF POWER TO THE ROAD SURFACE.

AUDI QUATTRO

DE LOREAN DMC12

It sounds like the story line for a Hollywood movie: Handsome, successful auto company executive quits the corporation to build his own car, the "ethical sports car," gains funding from celebrity investors, plays foreign governments off against each other in pursuit of a place to establish his factory, enlists both the world's most famous car designer and automotive engineer to craft his car and finally begins production, but his company loses money and he's indicted on charges of drug trafficking and criminal fraud, though later is cleared of any wrongdoing.

Yes, indeed it sounds like a Hollywood plot, but in the case of John Z. (for Zachary) DeLorean and his gull-winged, stainless steel-bodied DMC12 sports car, it's not movie make-believe. It really happened.

DeLorean was an automotive whiz kid and one of Detroit's leading men, an autoworker's son who studied engineering, headed research and development at Packard, then moved to General Motors and helped to create the muscle car phenomenon. He was general manager first of Pontiac, then of Chevrolet, and then quit. With help from the British government, he set up shop in Northern Ireland to build his own car, a car designed by Giorgetto Giugiaro and engineered – though technically it was actually re-engineered as best as possible – by Colin Chapman and Lotus.

Prototypes were powered by 4-cylinder Citroën engines, but even the production engine – the 2.8-liter joint-venture V6 shared by Peugeot, Renault and Volvo – proved to be barely adequate for the DMC-12 to be considered a serious sports car.

The engine provided only 145 hp and 166 pound-feet of torque. Many testers said the factory's claims of 0-60 mph (96 km/h) in 8.5 seconds and a top speed of 130 mph (210 km/h) were as optimistic as DeLorean's contention that "the long-awaited transportation revolution" had begun with the DMC-12's launch.

There were, however, revolutionary things about the car's design, such as the tiny portion of the side windows that powered down and DeLorean's insistence that the car's fiberglass body shell be covered with a veneer of stain-less steel, which proved difficult to keep clean and to repair when scratched or dented. DeLorean pitched the car as ideal "for the bachelor who's made it," and noted that there was room for a full set of golf clubs to be carried behind the side-by-side seats of the wedge-shaped, rear-engine coupe.

The car was among the first with a so-called all-electronic interior, but too often that simply meant an electrical glitch that prevented the gull wing doors from opening, leaving driver and passenger stuck inside.

Water leaking around the doors was just one of several other build-quality issues. Yet the cars certainly gained a lot of attention for their sleek shape and shinny, spacecraft shell. Some 8,500 DeLoreans were built over the course of three years and became something of a cult object among collectors.

And while DeLorean's life story had yet to be portrayed on the big screen, his car certainly was a star, in 1985 carrying Michel J. Fox and Christopher Lloyd "Back to the Future."

228 TOP HOLLYWOOD MADE AN ICON OUT OF JOHN DE LOREAN'S STAINLESS STEEL-BODIED CAR BY GIVING IT A STARRING ROLE IN THE *BACK TO THE FUTURE* MOVIES.

228-229 JOHN Z. DE LOREAN HELPED CREATE THE GTO AT PONTIAC BUT DREAMED OF BUILDING WHAT HE CALLED THE "ETHICAL SPORTS CAR."

FERRARI TESTAROSSA

This car was automotive extremism. A car with no middle ground. A car you loved or hated, and for the same reasons, for its excesses.

Just look at it. So wide, with the width of its wedge underlined, over and over again by those huge long side vents in a rear fender that begins just behind the front wheels and then climbs and widens as it works its way back through the doors, over those 10-inch wide rear wheels and all the way back to the top frame of the taillights.

Some referred to the vents as cheesegraters. Some called them egg-slicers. But they drew not only attention but also air to cool the 5.0-liter, horizontally opposed "boxer" engine that pumped out 390 horsepower, propelling this wide wedge of a car to speeds of more than 180 miles per hour (291 km/h).

To drive this car, this Testarossa, was to know how it felt to be an Olympic class sprinter, one who was especially good at the 200 meters which demanded not only speed but the ability to hold a line through the long curve, or maybe a professional American football star as he powered his way past those who would stop his progress short of the goal line. The Testarossa was named – Testa Rossa is Italian for red head, and in the color of the

cylinder head covers – for one of the most famous of all Ferrari's, the famed 250 Testa Rossa the competition spyders that won three World Sportscar Championships in four years between 1958 and 1962.

The new Testarossa had power seats and standard air conditioning. It also had hand-sewed leather through its interior and carpeting. The new Testarossa was the successor to Ferrari's 512BB (Berlinetta Boxer), and thus its designers and engineers tackled the BB's problems of a hot interior and a lack of luggage space.

To cool the big engine without overheating the car's passenger compartment, two large radiators were placed at the rear instead of a single radiator up front. This left room for some storage under the hood and lengthening

the wheelbase also left some room for a bag behind the front seats.

The engine got new four-valve heads, colored red, of course. A low center of gravity, wide track and huge rear tires gave the car a lot of grip, although the car's overall width, nearly 78 inches (nearly 1980 mm) and eight-inch front tires could make parking a challenge. But not too big a challenge, however, because fancy restaurants with valet parking were happy to have such an attention-getting, Pininfarina-design car parked right up front. "If there was ever a car that epitomized the greed-is-good excesses of the Eighties, it was the Ferrari Testarossa," writes American automotive journalist Jack Nerad. "To purists, even the name represents a sell-out. The original 250 Testa Rossa road racer was not only

shockingly beautiful, it performed beautifully on the racetrack as well… The Testarossa of the Eighties, in contrast, had no racing pedigree whatsoever. It was, impure and not-so-simple, a car designed and built to cash in on an image. And since cashing in was what the Eighties were all about, it was the perfect vehicle for its time.

"The saving grace," even such a critic has to admit, "was, it was also a damn good automobile."

230-231 MANY SPORTS CARS HAVE BEEN LONG AND LOW AND WIDE AND HAD 12-CYLINDER ENGINES MOUNTED BEHIND THE PASSENGER COMPARTMENT, BUT NONE OF THEM HAVE BEEN ABLE TO BE QUITE A TASTEFULLY OUTLANDISH AS THE TESTAROSSA.

The Making of the
Modern Car: And the
modern car company

1985/1994

Consolidation and proliferation may seem to be conflicting phenomenon. But as the auto industry approached the end of the 20th century, it found itself in a corporate culture of consolidation at the same time that it was creating new categories of vehicles, and resurrecting at least one that had succumbed years before.

Once upon a time, there were more than one hundred automobile companies, and that was just in the city of Detroit, Michigan. Some were simply too weak or too under funded or invested in the wrong technology or built too inferior a product or simply were too poorly managed to survive. Some merged. Larger companies bought up smaller ones.

And it wasn't just in Motown where this happened. It happened in Britain and Germany and France and Italy and everywhere cars were being built. Companies would come and companies would go. But never quite on the scale of the consolidation that took place near the end of the 20th century.

Manufacturers' dreams of a "world car" – a new Model T or a new Volkswagen Beetle – seemed a pipe dream, but the world car company certainly was emerging.

Germany's Daimler-Benz acquired America's Chrysler (and along with it Dodge and Jeep) and took a significant stake in Japan's Mitsubishi. BMW bought Britain's Rover and Rolls-Royce. Not to be outdone, Volkswagen added Lamborghini, Bentley and Bugatti to a portfolio that already included Audi, Seat of Spain and Skoda of Czechoslovakia.

Renault, of France, where Peugeot and Citroen had partnered, gained control of Nissan, Japan's second-largest auto producer.

Ford acquired British brands Land Rover, Jaguar and Aston Martin, and a major stake in Mazda of Japan. It also bought Volvo. Sweden's other native automaker, Saab, was enfolded under the General Motors umbrella that sheltered many American brands and parts of Suzuki and Subaru of Japan, Daewoo of South Korea and Fiat of Italy. South Korea emerged as a major auto manufacturer with Hyundai and Kia in partnership.

Somehow Toyota, Honda and Porsche remained independent, but to do so Porsche had to add a sport utility vehicle to its lineup of sports cars. The sport utility vehicle and the minivan were the part of the proliferation of vehicles offered by this consolidating auto industry. The SUV traced its lineage to vehicles created for military use in deserts, jungles or snow-covered mountain trails. But civilians – at first in the United States and Australia but soon in Europe, Japan and elsewhere – found that rugged structure, four-wheel drive and increasingly car-like interiors provided secure transportation on pavement as well. Like the SUV, the minivan was a new vehicle category created to make it possible for seven or eight people to travel in the same vehicle.

Another phenomenon wasn't something new. It was the surprising comeback of the British roadster, except this time it came from Japan. The roadster revival began with Mazda and its version of the classic British sports car of the 1950s and '60s, except Mazda's Eunos Roadster/MX-5/Miata was built with modern mechanical equipment. No oil leaks. No electrical nightmares. But just like the original roadsters, the Mazda had its engine in front and its driving wheels in back. It was light and well balanced, fun to drive and affordable. Suddenly, Mercedes-Benz, BMW, Porsche, Audi, Honda, Toyota, Nissan, Daihatsu, Fiat, Alfa Romeo, Opel, Renault, Peugeot, Chrysler, Pontiac and even British automakers MG and Lotus were building open two-seaters.

Japan also produced the other unexpected phenomenon of the late 20th century, when "Japanese luxury car" no longer was considered an oxymoron. For decades, Japanese cars had been "econoboxes," small vehicles. But with Acura, Lexus and Infiniti, the Japanese were showing that their industry had matured into a full-range producer of cars.

Mercedes-Benz, Jaguar, Cadillac and other luxury carmakers had to get in gear to keep up with companies that weren't even in their rear view mirrors just a few years earlier. And before any car company could think about engaging cruise control, China was in the passing lane and emerging as the giant of the 21st century automotive marketplace.

The Making of the Modern Car: And the modern car company

233 THE DODGE VIPER CONCEPT CAR HAD AN ALMOST CARTOON CHARACTER, BUT THERE WAS NOTHING FUNNY ABOUT THE PRODUCTION VERSION OF THE CAR, WHICH WAS POWERED BY A V10 ENGINE

235 ENZO FERRARI CELEBRATED HIS COMPANY'S 40TH ANNIVERSARY WITH A VERY SPECIAL PRESENT, THE WEDGE-SHAPED, HIGH-WINGED, 200-MILES-PER-HOUR SUPERCAR CALLED THE FERRARI F40.

1985/1994

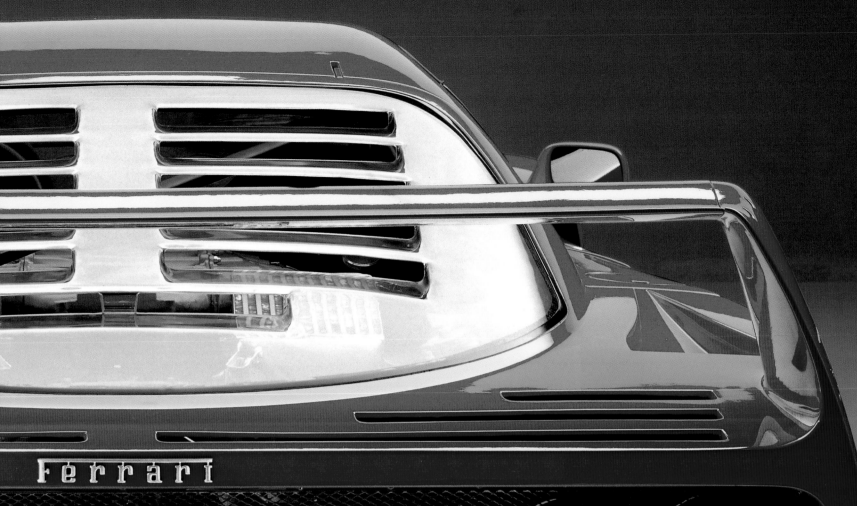

FERRARI F40

236-237 AND 237 TOP THE F40 CLAIMED THE HERITAGE OF THE FERRARI 250 GTO OF A MUCH EARLIER ERA. THE FOUR SLOTS IN THE REAR BODYWORK WERE DESIGNED TO RECALL THE SIMILAR VENTS JUST BEHIND THE FRONT WHEELS OF THE HISTORIC FERRARI.

Enzo Ferrari unveiled his last car on July 21, 1987. That car was the Ferrari F40, so named because it was designed – by Pininfarina, of course – to celebrate the 40th anniversary of il Commendatore's car company, a car company that had become the most famous in the world, and a car company whose founder would die in the summer of 1988 at the age of 90.

Where other Ferraris had been merely bold and exotic, the F40 was downright audacious and an absolutely mesmerizing siren.

Not only was it the fastest Ferrari production car ever, it was the fastest street-legal car on the planet period. And with its base price of $399,150 (by the time of its certification for sale in the United States in 1991), also seemingly the most expensive.

The F40 was the spiritual successor to Ferrari's 288 GTO, which itself was launched in 1984 as a potential entry in Group B motorsports competition and as a homage to the spirit of the original GTO, the Ferrari 250 GTO, the famed Gran Turismo Omologato of the 1960s.

Like the 288 GTO, the F40 was built as much for the racetrack as the public road. Again like the 288 GTO, the F40 was on a structure based on that of the 308 GTO road car, and beneath all those extreme body extensions you could recognize vestiges of the heritage even though the wheelbase of the tubular frame had been stretched four and a

half inches (more than 11 mm) to accommodate the F40's mechanical design and components. Because of the car's dual road/track nature, that design had the engine mounted latitudinally behind the seats with the five-speed manual transmission at the rear.

This architecture also provided room for a pair of turbochargers that empowered the 3.0-liter V8 to pump out nearly 480 horsepower. For those who might not consider that sufficient power, the factory offered a

pair of optional turbos and equipped the engine with a different set of camshafts that extracted an additional 200 horsepower.

Such power was sufficient to overcome a sedan-like 0.34 coefficient of drag and propel the lightweight sports car from a standing start to 60 miles per hour (96 km/h) in 3.9 seconds, to 124 mph (200 km/h) in a mere 12 seconds flat and all the way up to a top speed of 201 miles per hour (323 km/h).

Although longer and nearly three inches (more than 71 mm) wider than the GTO, the F40 was more than 100 pounds (nearly 59 kg) lighter thanks to its carbon and Kevlar composite body, clear plastic engine cover (with open louvers for enhance cooling) and the absence of such nonessentials as carpeting, a radio and power windows (although you could get air conditioning).

While the body weighed much less, there was much more of it with a long, aerodynamic nose, large fender extenders and that tall,

full-width rear wing that was integrated into rear quarter panels that featured four vents behind the rear wheels just like those the original GTO had just behind its front wheels.

An adjustable ride height system automatically lowered the car at speed, and high-speed stability was further aided by that big rear airfoil and the other body extensions things that

helped to keep the Pirelli P Zero tires (17s inches front and 18s in the rear, and all mounted on light, three-piece Speedline wheels) firmly planted.

The F40 also featured racecar-caliber brakes and fuel cell, and seats were custom fit to the owner It seems that Enzo saved his best – or at least his most outrageous – for last.

BUGATTI EB110

E ttore Bugatti's father, Carlo, was a famous furniture designer who moved his family from Milan to Paris late in the 19th Century. Ettore's brother, Rembrandt, was an acclaimed sculpture, especially of animal figures. Ettore also was an artist, an automotive artist. He built his first car when he was still a teenager, then worked for various German coachbuilders

before settling in Alsace, where he opened his own car-building facility at Molsheim in 1909.

Bugatti built fast racing cars and elegant road cars. His racing cars won more than two thousand events in the early years of the 20th Century and his road cars continue to command astronomical prices when they come available at collector car auctions.

In her book on the first century of automotive design, professor Penny Sparke says

Bugattis displayed "an enhanced alignment of function and beauty... Visually the cars reflected their performance capacity."

Bugatti's son, Jean, followed in his father's footsteps until his death while testing a car in 1939. Another son, Roland, tried to keep the company going after Ettore's death in 1947, but the marque disappeared until the late 1980s, when Italian auto distributor Romano Artioli, working with yet another of Bugatti's

238-239 ETTORE AND JEAN BUGATTI MIGHT HAVE RECOGNIZED THE SMALL HORSESHOE SHAPE AT THE CENTER OF THE FRONT AIR INLET AND WOULD CERTAINLY HAVE APPRECIATED ITS ARTISTIC DETAILS AND ADVANCED AUTOMOTIVE ARCHITECTURE.

turbochargers and 550 horsepower, could propel the four-wheel-drive sports car from a standing start to 60 miles per hour (96 km/h) in just 3.7 seconds and that the top speed would reach 212 miles per hour (341 km/h).

If that wasn't sufficient, a lighter Super Sport version also would be available with 611 horsepower and a 221-mph (356 km/h) top speed. Four years later, near the end of the car's production, Bugatti had a trio of EB110s on its stand at the Geneva show, and claimed speed records for each of them: one for achieving 218 mph at Nardo, another for hitting 214.2 while burning methane, a so-called alternative fuel to gasoline, and the third achieving 184.1 mph on ice.

When unveiled, the car had a carbon fiber chassis (built by French aerospace contractor Aerospatiale) with a steel roof and aluminum body panels. It featured scissors-hinged doors, wheels designed to look like those on early Bugattis and Bugatti's signature horseshoe-shaped air inlet in the center of its grille.

It also carried a price tag of $486,000 (U.S.) or for another $93,000 you could opt for the SS version. Nearly 100 EB110s and more than two dozen SS models were built, but the company didn't survive them. Artioli spent money to acquire technical excellence in the form of Lotus Engineering in 1993 and that same year commissioned Italdesign to create a four-door EB112. A concept was shown, but Giugiaro's firm withdrew from the program after not being paid, and the car didn't go into production. In fact, Bugatti withdrew from production and in 1995, it succumbed again. Three years later, however, it was reborn once more, this time with Volkswagen acquiring rights to the historic marque.

sons, Michel, resurrected it.

Artioli hired architect Giampaolo Benedini to design a spectacular new factory, which was built in Campogalliano, near Modena, Italy. Artioli hired former Lamborghini engineer Paolo Stanzani as technical director and the equally legendary Marcello Gandini as designer. Neither, however, was still around when the new Bugatti, the EB110, was unveiled. Nicola Materazzi, who had led development of

Ferrari's 288 GTO and F40, finished the work Stanzani had begun while Benedini completed the car's exotic body design.

The car took its name from Ettore Bugatti's initials and its number because it was unveiled in Paris on what would have been his 110th birthday. The new company claimed the Bugatti EB110 was the fastest road car ever built, that it's newly designed and manufactured 3.5-liter V12 engine, with 60 valves, four

In was early in 1988 that Carroll Shelby paid a visit to Chrysler's new president, Bob Lutz. Shelby, of course, was the former Le Mans race winner and creator of the Ford-powered Shelby Cobra, but after a falling out with Ford his shop had been doing work on Chrysler products. Lutz was the consummate car-guy auto executive, a former U.S. Marine Corps fighter pilot with a personal collection of exotic cars, including a Cobra replica. Their conversation included mention that someone should build a modern Cobra, a car that would disdain computerized wizardry for old-fashioned, wind in your hair, attitude in your face American sports car fun and fury.

Lutz called in Francois Castaing, Chrysler's chief engineer and a Frenchman who had spent much of his career developing cars for Grand Prix and Le Mans racing. Work already had begun on a new V10 engine with enough torque to power Dodge's big work trucks. Lutz wondered if it might be made suitable for a sports car by being cast from aluminum rather than iron and tuned, say, to around 400 horsepower.

Meanwhile, design director Tom Gale was working on a new face for Dodge vehicles... and by the 1998 Detroit auto show that face was unveiled on the Dodge Viper concept car, an outrageous, almost cartoon-like vehicle with bright red paint, a wide and bulbous

DODGE VIPER RT/10

240-241 THE DODGE VIPER RT/10 WAS A REAL THROWBACK TO AN EARLIER AUTOMOTIVE ERA. THE CAR HAD NO SIDE WINDOWS OR EXTERIOR DOOR HANDLES AND ONLY A RATHER FLIMSY.

241 TOP THE VIPER DISDAINED WINGS AND HIDDEN HEADLAMPS AND SUCH THINGS. THE POINT OF THIS PROJECT WAS TO BUILD A MODERN HOT-ROD SPORTS CAR.

nose, an integrated roll bar/wing just behind its two seats, big fat tires and prominent side exhaust pipes – and a name that unashamedly paid homage to Shelby's original Cobra.

At the time, seemingly nobody expected Chrysler to ever put such a car into production, but a Viper prototype served as the pace car for the 1991 Indianapolis 500-mile race – with 68-year-old Shelby, just months after undergoing a heart transplant – as the driver. Series production began later that year with the official unveiling at the 1992 Detroit Auto Show. The Viper RT/10 was a roadster (a coupe version was added for the 1996 model year) powered by an 8.0-liter, alloy V10 that sent its considerable power – 400 horsepower and 450 pound-feet of

torque, thanks in part to tuning help from Lamborghini, then part of the Chrysler group – through a six-speed Borg-Warner manual transmission to rear wheels that were 13 inches (33 centimeters) wide and 17 inches in diameter.

The car had a steel backbone frame and a fiber-reinforced composite body with no exterior door handles; you simply reached into the car and opened the doors from the inside. The Viper didn't have side windows, although there were side curtains that could be put into place and a folding cloth top could be stretched over the passenger compartment in the event of inclement weather.

Top speed was just 165 miles per hour (265 km/h), but this car was about acceleration, not

top end. The Viper sprinted from a standing start to 60 miles per hour (96 km/h) in just 4.5 seconds and could complete the drag racing quarter-mile in 13.5 seconds. It also could go from standing start to 100 miles per hour (160 km/h) and back to a standstill in just 14.5 seconds, thanks to all that power and to 14-inch vented disc brakes. Despite such power, the Viper could average a remarkable 17.5 miles per gallon when simply cruising down the road.

And despite its exotic performance potential, the car was priced at $50,000 (U.S. dollars), some $15,000 less that the Acura NSX or the highest performance version of the Chevrolet Corvette and more than $70,000 less than the least expensive Ferrari.

242-243 THE REAR VIEW OF THE VIPER OFFERS NO HINT OF TAIL PIPES. LIKE A TRUE OLD-FASHIONED HOT ROD, THE VIPER HAD SIDE-MOUNTED EXHAUST.

243 TOP DODGE WAS DEVELOPING ITS V10 TO PROVIDE POWER FOR LARGE,

HEAVY-DUTY WORK TRUCKS. BUT BY CASTING THE ENGINE FROM LIGHTERWEIGHT ALLOYS, AND WITH LAMBORGHINI HELPING MAKE SOME MODIFICATIONS, THE 8.0-LITER PROVIDED AMPLE HORSEPOWER AND AWESOME TORQUE FOR THE VIPER SPORTS CAR.

Though production of Jaguar's supercar didn't begin until 1992, the company's chief engineer Jim Randle starting contemplating such a vehicle several years earlier, on his Christmas holiday, when he pondered what it might take to construct a vehicle to outperform the Porsche 959.

The 959 was a technological marvel: A high-winged, wide-silled 911-based Porsche with 450 twin-turbocharged horsepower, a six-speed transmission and permanent four-wheel drive with tire-pressure monitors and a computer-controlled suspension with separate traction maps for heavy snow or mud, or ice, for wet pavement or for dry conditions. Though it looked (and was) an exotic sports car capable to speeds approaching 200 miles per hour, it also won the grueling Paris-Dakar desert endurance marathon in 1986.

Randle shared his ideas with other Jaguar engineers and designers and soon a "Saturday club" was working on the car on their own time and without any sort of official knowledge, let alone approval.

Finally, they let the company know what they were up to. Keith Helfet from the Jaguar styling studio was assigned to design an aluminum body, Tom Walkinshaw Racing, already racing at Le Mans with Jaguar power, was recruited to provide the engine and several local specialists, such as FF Developments, contributed their expertise. The XJ220 made its debut at the 1988 Birmingham motor show. Jaguar said the car was named after its anticipated top speed of 220 miles per hour (352 km/h), which would make it the fastest street-legal production car in the world. Given sufficient interest from potential customers,

JAGUAR XJ 220

244-245 FOR NEARLY SEVEN YEARS, JAGUAR'S XJ 220 WAS THE FASTEST CAR ON THE ROAD, ITS RECORD OF MORE THAN 212 MILES PER HOUR FINALLY SURPASSED IN 1998 BY THE MCLAREN F1.

Jaguar might build 220 of the XJ220s.

The original XJ220 carried a 500-horsepower, twin-turbocharged V12 and it was one very large cat. In fact, it was too big. Changes were made. By the time production began in 1992, the car was some 10 inches (25.4 cm) shorter, though still at more than seven feet (2220 mm) from wing mirror to wing mirror, it was the widest thing on British roads save, perhaps, for huge lorries and double-decker buses.

Switching from 12 to six cylinders helped shorten the car, and did so without diminishing performance, in part because the car also shed 600 pounds (272 kg). The twin-turbo V6, with four-valve heads and dry sump lubrication, pumped out more than 540 horsepower.

From standing start to 60 miles per hour (96 km/h) consumed a mere 3.5 seconds and 0-100 (160 km/h) came in just eight seconds.

In May 1991, prototypes not only turned the fastest laps ever around the long, winding and historic Nürburgring racing circuit in Germany, but hit 212.3 miles per hour (341.7 km/h) on an oval track at Ft. Stockton, Texas to claim a production car speed record (that would stand until being exceeded by the McLaren F1).

Jaguar and Walkinshaw formed a joint venture, JaguarSport, to construct the cars, with deliveries beginning in the summer of 1992. By now, the plan was to build 350 cars, and unlike some other ultra-expensive, ultra-fast vehicles that were basically racecars con-

verted for road use, the XJ220 had a full, leather-lined interior with air conditioning and other luxury appointments.

But production was tardy and prices were growing (to around $750,000 U.S., nearly double the original estimate), and many who ordered cars demanded their deposits back.

By the summer of 1993, several dozen of the cars no longer destined for paying customers were used as the basis for a made-for-television racing series that put aged racecar drivers into the brand new Jaguars. The series was called Fast Masters, but with some races on short American ovals turned into "road courses" by the presence of a coned-off chicane or two, the events too frequently resembled a very expensive demolition derby.

MCLAREN F1

246 TOP TWO DOORS, THREE PEOPLE. THE MCLAREN F1'S DOORS SCISSORED OPEN TO REVEAL THREE SEATS, WITH THE DRIVER IN THE CENTER AND SLIGHTLY TOWARD THE FRONT OF PASSENGERS ON EITHER SIDE.

246-247 EVEN THOUGH THE MCLAREN F1 COULD TRAVEL AT SPEEDS IN EXCESS OF 240 MILES PER HOUR, IT WAS EQUIPPED WITH SUCH NICETIES AS AIR CONDITIONING, CONNOLLY LEATHER SEATS, A HIGH-END AUDIO AND EVEN CUSTOM-DESIGNED LUGGAGE.

248-249 THE MCLAREN F1 GTR WAS A SPECIAL RACING VERSION OF THE CAR. A PRIVATELY ENTERED GTR WON THE 24 HOURS OF LE MANS RACE OVERALL IN 1995, WITH OTHER GTRS FINISHED THIRD, FOURTH AND FIFTH.

Like so many young men before and since, Gordon Murray's dream was to someday build the ultimate, money's-no-object car. Unlike the rest, Murray got the go-ahead.

Murray studied mechanical engineering in his native South Africa, built his own racecars (because he couldn't afford to buy those others built) and realized that his skill was in design not driving. He headed to England expecting to work for Lotus, but instead designed guided missiles until he finally went to work for the Brabham Grand Prix team, where in 1978 he created the "fan car," a car that used a large rear-mounted fan to literally draw itself to the pavement (until it was banned by a rules change). Nelson Piquet was world driving champions in Murray's Brabham BT49 in 1981 and BT52 two years later.

Murray moved to the McLaren team after the 1986 season. McLaren was at the top of its game, its drivers winning the world championship seven times in the eight seasons between 1984 and 1991 and team principal Ron Dennis was ready to develop not only the ultimate racing car but also the ultimate road car and he offered Murray the assignment.

Like a Formula One racecar, the McLaren F1 road car would be constructed of carbon fiber with a monocoque architecture (although with an overhead spine) and with its engine mounted behind the passenger compartment, which Murray designed to hold not just one or even two people but three. As in a racecar, the driver sat in the middle, and forward, but in the McLaren F1 there was a pas-

senger's seat on either side, slightly behind and out of the driver's peripheral vision.

Empowering the car was a new and specially created 6.1-liter BMW V12 engine that generated 627 horsepower and 479 pound-feet (649 Nm) of torque. That power was transmitted to 17-inch rear wheels through a custom-built six-speed transmission that, like every aspect of the car, was designed for both high speed and light weight. Still, the car came with air conditioning, power windows, a Kenwood audio system, Connolly leather-covered seats and custom luggage designed to fit into storage panels in the bodywork ahead of the rear wheels.

Murray used a pair of small fans under the car to help stick it to the road and, to supplement huge disc brakes (13.1 inches in diameter on the front wheels), an airfoil brake that rose at the rear of the car to help slow it from top speed. To create a body suitable for Murray's car, McLaren hired Peter Stevens, who had worked at Lotus after graduating from England's Royal College of Art and then

became a freelancer after Colin Chapman's death and consulted with many of the world's automakers. At 168.8 inches (4.2 meters) the McLaren F1 was about the same length as a Porsche 911, though at 71.6 inches (181.9 cm) the McLaren slightly wider, both for high-speed road holding and to accommodate the three-across seating. Access to the passenger compartment was through doors with scissors-style hinges. The McLaren F1, unveiled at the 1992 Monaco Grand Prix, was as dynamic as it was dramatic. While testing a prototype in the summer heat at Nardo, Italy in 1993, racer Jonathan Palmer achieved a top speed of 231 miles per hour (372 km/h).

Then, in March 1998, racer Andy Wallace achieved a two-way average of 240.14 mph (386.7 km/h) on the huge Volkswagen proving grounds oval in Germany for an official, all-time passenger car speed record.

Over the course of four years, McLaren Cars Limited of Woking, England, hand-built some 100 F1 cars, each priced at more than $800,000 (U.S. dollars).

Full Speed Ahead:
These are the
good old days

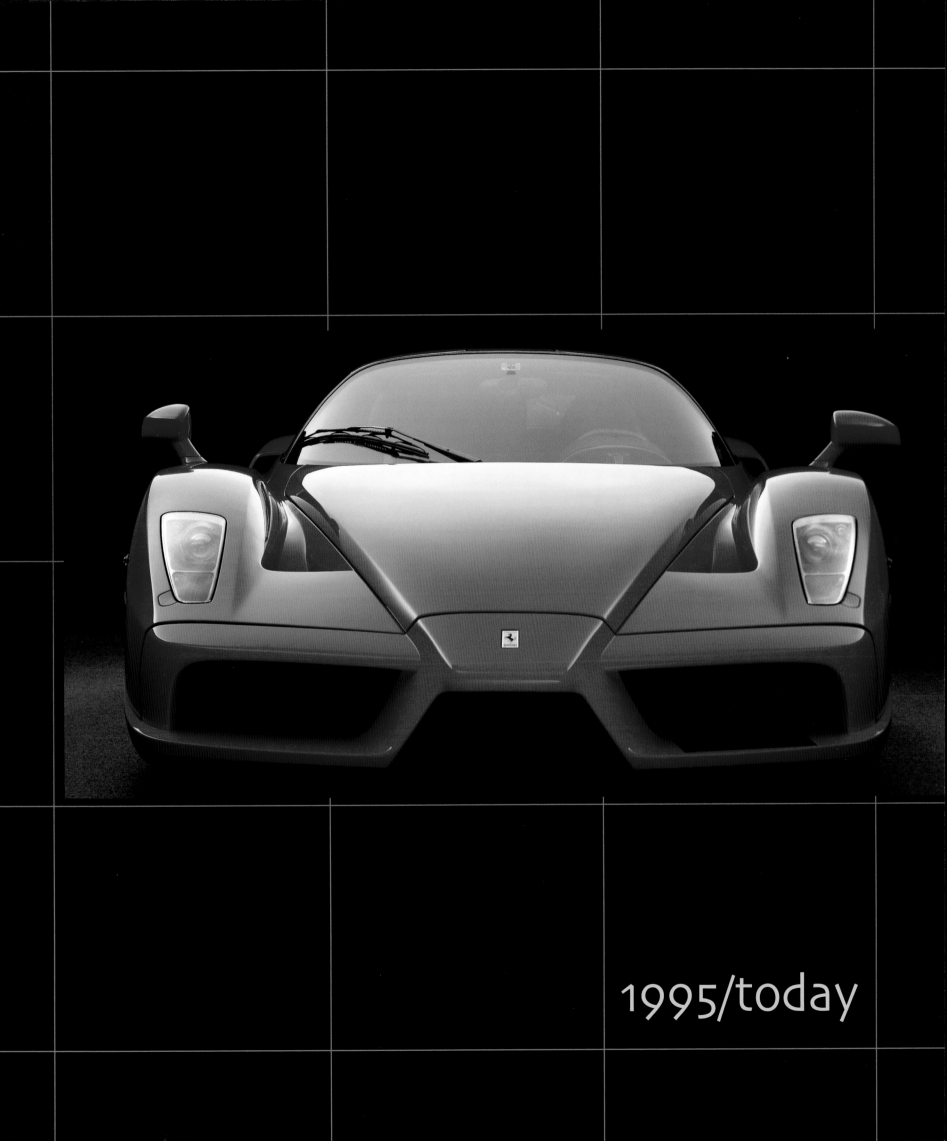

1995/today

A re we there yet? That's a question millions of parents have heard, and in many different languages, from their impatient children riding in the back seat of the family car.

But for the automakers and their executives and engineers and designers, and for their suppliers, and for government officials and environmental and safety activists, for scholars and, yes, even for everyday motorists, the

Today's cars are electronic wonder machines. While their engines still pump out power generated by burning liquid fuels, in many ways today's cars are powered by electricity. Seemingly every car that rolls out of every assembly plant around the world carries much more on-board computing power than the rocket and landing capsule that carried man of the moon. They have computers and software that control advanced technologies that help our cars run cleanly — and at speeds that used

tion were wonderful to drive? Today's economy sedans and hatchbacks are faster, and cleaner and greener, with more precise steering, superior suspension systems and much better brakes.

It wasn't long ago that 300 kilometers per hour (186.4 miles per hour) was a speed beyond most motorists' imagination. It still is, yet can buy cars from Ferrari, Lamborghini and Porsche — but also from Mercedes-Benz and Ford — that meet safety standards and emission regulations and are capable of not merely 300 km/h but of speeds in excess of 200 miles per hour (321.9 km/h), and GM and Toyota and who knows who else are giving serious study to similar cars.

Sure, such cars are expensive and come with capabilities beyond those of the typical motorist. But even the average driver can buy a technologically advanced vehicle powered by gasoline, diesel, natural gas or a hybrid powertrain that incorporates electric motors as well as an internal combustion engine. And non-polluting hydrogen fuel cells are just beyond the horizon.

Are we there yet? No, but we are getting closer.

Nikolas Otto, Karl Benz, Gottlieb Daimler, Emile Levassor and Henry Ford would be amazed to see what they set into motion... into auto motion. Leonardo da Vinci would want to know if, at last, someone would give him the keys so he could drive.

Full Speed Ahead: These are the good old days

greater question isn't: Are we there yet? It is: Where are we going? Where is this road we're following in our motor vehicles taking us as we drive deeper into the 21st century? Will there enough oil to keep our vehicles running, especially with China, India and other countries with huge populations just beginning to enter their own automotive ages?

And at what price? And at what cost to our planet, this island in space we call Earth? If the oil runs out, will we be ready with alternative fuel sources? What will it, or they, cost? What will be the new challenges that will have to be faced? Where are we going? How will we even know when we get there?

As we make the transition from the cars we drive today to those that we'll drive tomorrow, it's instructive to note where we are and how far we've already come. About the only comparison between the modern sedan and Henry Ford's Model T is that both have internal combustion engines and four wheels.

to be seen only on racing circuits.

Computerized technology uses forward-looking radar, rear-view cameras and even front-view cameras that read lane markers to help us avoid accidents. Whether the driver lets things get out of control or the weather makes driving treacherous, computerized vehicle dynamic controls can help to keep a car from spinning off the road.

Should a crash still occur, one technology inflates airbags that cushion the impact and another automatically calls for emergency medical services.

Computerized wizardry also guides, informs and entertains us as we cruise on down the road or hunt for an address in a maze of city streets. Computers make our vehicles better even before we take delivery. Computer-aided design, engineering and manufacturing have produced cars that are better built, safer and even more fun to drive.

Think the sports cars of an earlier genera-

251 WHAT IF? THAT WAS A QUESTION THE AUTO INDUSTRY FINALLY WAS IN A POSITION TO ASK. WHAT IF YOU COULD BUILD A STREET-LEGAL FORMULA ONE CAR? YOU'D HAVE THE ENZO FERRARI.

253 WHAT IF YOU COULD CAPTURE THE ESSENCE OF A CAR THAT MEANT SO MUCH TO AS MANY PEOPLE AS THE ORIGINAL VOLKSWAGEN, EXCEPT PRESENT IT IN A THOROUGHLY MODERN PACKAGE? WELL, YOU'D HAVE THE NEW BEETLE.

1995/today

Mazda may have begun the roadster revival in 1990 with its Miata MX-5 Eunos, but it was the German luxury and performance brands, which took the program to a higher level.

BMW was first, launching the Z3 as a 1996 model. Mercedes-Benz followed with its SLK, complete with a folding hard top, and Porsche with a Boxster that drew forward styling cues from the famed 550 Spyder and RS60 race-cars. BMW's roadster history traces to 1935 and the 315/1 and 319/1 models. In 1936, BMW

254 TOP DESMOND LLEWELYN, WHO PLAYED THE ROLE OF TECHNOLOGY WIZARD Q IN SO MANY JAMES BOND MOVIES, HELPED UNVEIL BMW Z3 IN CONJUNCTION WITH ITS DEBUT IN THE 1995 FILM *GOLDEN EYE*.

254-255 THE Z3 WAS THE PRODUCT OF A MODERN AND GLOBAL AUTO COMPANY. THOUGH DESIGNED AND ENGINEERED IN GERMANY BY BMW, THE CAR WAS BUILT IN A NEW FACTORY IN THE UNITED STATES.

had virtually created the modern roadster with its 328, which set performance standards on both the road and the racetrack.

BMW built the 507 in the late 1950s, and then in 1987 started production on a run of 8000 copies of the Z1, a car remembered for its power doors that retracted into the rocker panels. But the Z3 was something very different, a modern interpretation of the classic roadster. For the first time, this BMW roadster would be built in substantial numbers, and it would be built in a new BMW factory not in Germany or even somewhere in Europe but in the United States, and far from Detroit in Spartanburg, South Carolina.

The Z3 built with many components from BMW's 3 Series coupe, but its body was pure roadster with its traditional kidney grilles set into a snubbed nose at the front of a long and arching hood.

A series of louvered vents added character to the front quarter panels. The doors were well proportioned, not overly long, though entry and exit were easily accommodated. In classic roadster style, the ZE had a rounded but abbreviated tail treatment.

Power was supplied by BMW's 1.9-liter in-line four-cylinder engine, which provided 140 horsepower, enough to propel the 2700-pound car to 60 miles per hour (96 km/h) in around nine seconds and on to a maximum of around 120 miles per hour (some 190 km/h).

The concept for the Z3 began with sketches of a four-wheel motorcycle and the car that resulted was nicely balanced and fun to drive, especially in 1997 when a 2.8-liter inline six-cylinder engine was offered, bringing with it 190 horsepower.

If that wasn't enough, BMW also offered the M roadster from its Motorsport department. This version drew propulsion from a 240-horsepower, 3.2-liter six and could sprint to 60 mph in slightly more than six seconds.

To pay homage to its famed 507, BMW built a limited run of larger, Z8 roadsters in 2001, powered by the 394-horsepower, 5.0-liter V8 used in the M5 super sedan.

Then, in 1993, the Z3 entered its second generation – and BMW's new naming convention of using odd numbers of sedans and even numbers for coupes and convertibles, with the launch of the Z4 roadster with its angular and shark-like styling cues.

BMW Z3

VOLKSWAGEN NEW BEETLE

256 TOP VOLKSWAGEN'S NEW BEETLE NOT ONLY WAS CUTE, BUT IT WAS SAFE AS WELL, SCORING EXCEPTIONALLY HIGH MARKS IN CRASH-TESTING EVALUATIONS.

256-257 THOUGH THE DESIGN CAPTURES THE CHARACTER OF THE ORIGINAL VW BEETLE, THE NEW VERSION IS BASED ON THE GOLF PLATFORM AND HAS A LIQUID-COOLED ENGINE MOUNTED IN FRONT.

257 BOTTOM NEW BEETLES ROLL THEIR WAY THROUGH THE DRYING BOOTH AFTER BEING PAINTED.

Volkswagen wasn't interested in reviving its famed Beetle, even if the bug-shaped car had been the best-selling vehicle of all time. "Don't dig up old bones," they say in Germany, where der Kaefer, "the Beetle," as the original Type 1 was known, represented old bones, memories of the People's Car from the days of the Third Reich and the tough times that ensued from the late 1940s well into the following decade.

But in the United States, and in many other places on the planet, the Beetle had been a positive icon, the car that offered more than inexpensive yet reliable mobility, it was, well, just so darned cute, inspiring everything from Disney's "The Love Bug," Herbie, to hippies' psychedelicly painted "flower power" mobiles.

As is so often the case with car companies, desperation inspires innovation, and thus the timing was right when American designers J Mays and Freeman Thomas began work on the Concept 1 concept car that would be the star of the 1994 Detroit auto show.

Because of the popularity of the original Beetle, Volkswagen was selling more than half a million cars a year in the United States in 1970. But changing tastes, new competitors – both foreign and domestic – and safety and other regulations made the original Beetle obsolete and its replacement, the Golf, a squared off hatchback, never really caught on

with Americans. By 1993, VW sales had plummeted more than tenfold in the world's largest automotive marketplace. VW needed something to rekindle its brand, and that something was the New Beetle.

The Concept 1 show car had been built on Volkswagen's small Polo platform, which wasn't even certified for the American market, and was propelled by an electric powertrain designed with an eye on meeting California's zero-emissions regulations.

But none of that mattered to American car buyers, who saw only the Beetle-like shape and remembered happy times in their "bugs."

For production, the New Beetle would be built on the Golf platform, and thus would have its gasoline (or diesel) burning engine in front rather than in the back as on the original Beetle, and that engine would be a liquid-cooled inline four instead of an air-cooled boxer four, and this New Beetle would have front-wheel drive where the original was driven by its

rear wheels. Again, those changes didn't matter, because while the car technically was still a hatchback, it didn't look like any other hatchback on the road. It looked like a real Beetle, except this new one came with modern technology, from its spunky (especially when turbocharged to provide 150 horsepower) but clean-burning powertrains to its class-leading crash worthiness.

It also had a roomy and esthetically pleasing interior bathed in a light blue hue at night and with a standard flower vase, just like the original. It also had a modern HVAC (heat, ventilation and air conditioning) system instead of the original's rudimentary heater channels that quickly rusted through, leaving old Beetle drivers shivering as they struggled to see through a frosted windshield while driving in winter weather. Even before der neu Kaefer was ready for production, it had rekindled interest in the

Volkswagen brand. The introduction of the third-generation Golf, and especially of the Golf-based Jetta (Vento) sedan and the even larger Passat sedan boosted VW sales in the United States above the 100,000 mark by the end of the 1995 model year. That figure exceeded 200,000 for the 1998 model year and the launch of the New Beetle ignited a feeding frenzy with more than 350,000 Americans again buying Volkswagens.

258-259 THE SUCCESS OF VOLKSWAGEN'S NEW BEETLE SPURRED A RETRO REVIVAL IN AUTOMOTIVE DESIGN WITH MANY MANUFACTURERS NOW LOOKING TO THEIR PAST FOR STYLING CUES FOR FUTURE VEHICLES.

259 TOP VOLKSWAGEN EXPANDED THE NEW BEETLE LINEUP WITH A CONVERTIBLE VERSION FOR THE 2003 MODEL YEAR.

oon after coming together early in the summer of 2002, the team that would develop the Ford GT, the company's first true street-legal supercar and the spiritual successor to the famed GT40 racecar, put several of the world's best sports cars to the test. There was a Dodge Viper, a Chevrolet Corvette, an Acura NSX and a Ferrari 360 Modena.

Immediately, it was clear that the Ferrari was the best of the bunch, the benchmark against which the Ford GT – and all other turn of the 21st century supercars – would be judged.

The 360 Modena had been under such competitive pressure ever since it was introduced in 1999 at the Geneva auto show. The 360 Modena was to take the place of the F355, the best-selling Ferrari in history, and there were those among the Ferrari faithful who worried that the company's supercar for the street was being replaced by something closer to a luxury boulevard cruiser.

The 360 Modena was luxurious, at least by Ferrari and true sports car standards. It was the first Ferrari designed from the inside out, and with room for golf clubs between its luscious leather-covered bucket seats and the mid-mounted engine.

To make that interior so comfortable and accommodating, the 360 Modena rode on a wheelbase that was 5.8 inches (nearly 15 centimeters) longer than the F355's, and the new car was nine inches (nearly 23 centimeters) longer overall, also 1.6 inches (more than four centimeters) taller and nearly an inch (more than 2 centimeters) wider. But because of the extensive use of aluminum – for the chassis, hand-welded body and roof, suspension components, engine and even interior trim – the 360 Modena weighed in 133 pounds (more than 60 kilograms) lighter than the F355. The new car's chassis also was more than 40 percent more resistant to flex and bending, so its

FERRARI 360 MODENA

steering and suspension could be more responsive. The car was designed at Pininfarina, and honed with 5400 hours in Ferrari's wind tunnel. Its flat bottom and rear under-car ducting created a low-pressure zone that helped pull the 360 Modena toward the road. The car's design – what you saw and what was hidden underneath – generated four times the aerodynamic grip that the F355 provided.

While the 360 Modena might not match the F355's 199 miles per hour (320 km/h) top speed, it was two-tenths of a second faster from a standing start to 60 miles per hour (96 km/h) and could beat its predecessor around Ferrari's Fiorano test track by a full three sec-

onds. The F355 was powered by a 3.5-liter V8 that produced 375 horsepower.

For the 360 Modena, the engine was stroked to 3.6 liters, received a new intake manifold, variable valve timing on the exhaust side and an electronic throttle. The result: 400 high-winding horsepower that reached the rear wheels through either a six-speed manual or Formula One-style paddle shifter-controlled gearbox.

The new car might have been large and luxurious by Ferrari standards, but it was as fast as it was comfortable, and it was just as capable of setting new supercar standards as it was contented cruising to the golf course.

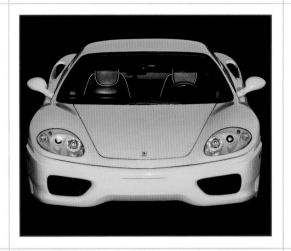

260-261 FERRARI'S 360 MODENA SET THE STANDARD FOR THE MODERN SUPER SPORTS CAR. IT NOT ONLY WAS FAST AND STYLISH, BUT IT WAS COMFORTABLE ON THE INSIDE AS WELL.

261 TOP THE 360 MODENA BROKE WITH FERRARI TRADITION BY HAVING TWO SEPARATE FRONT AIR INLETS INSTEAD OF ONE CENTRAL VENT.

262-263 THE 360 MODENA DESIGN ALLOWS A GOOD VIEW OF ITS V8 ENGINE, A 3.6-LITER POWERPLANT THAT GIVES IT EVEN FASTER ACCELERATION THAN FERRARI'S HERALDED F355.

NISSAN 350Z

264 THE INTERIOR OF THE 350Z WAS ORIENTED TOWARD THE DRIVER. TILT THE STEERING WHEEL AND THE GAUGE CLUSTER MOVED ALONG WITH IT.

In the 1970s, the world's best-selling sports car was, depending on whether you lived in Europe, Japan, the United States or Australia, the Nissan Fairlady Z or the Datsun 240Z. Regardless of its local name, the "Z" was light and nimble, sleek and sexy, quick and affordable. It was more than a car; it was a symbol of the spirit of the company that produced it.

But the Z didn't age well. Although its 1984 successor, the Nissan 300ZX, was noteworthy for being the first Japanese car powered by a V6 engine, but it, too, ultimately was just another Z wannabe that grew larger, heavier, more expensive and, while faster thanks to larger and turbocharged engines, less exciting, not nearly as much fun to drive.

Again, the car represented its maker, which had become a sluggish automotive bureaucracy that had fallen so deeply in debt that when production of the ZX ended after the 1996 model year, some at Nissan must have wondered if the company also was approaching the end of the line as well. Indeed, Nissan's survival was at stake. In 1999 the company entered a partnership with French automaker Renault, which quickly installed Carlos Ghosn as Nissan's new and non-Japanese chief executive. Ghosn was an effective and inspirational leader. His Nissan revival plan set tough, painful financial targets, but it pointed the way back to profitability.

264-265 TO HOMOLOGATE THE Z FOR RACING IN JAPAN, NISSAN PRODUCED A SPECIAL HOME-MARKET EDITION WITH A LONGER NOSE, REVISED REAR BUMPER AND SPECIAL DUCTING TO COOL REAR BRAKES.

265 TOP WORLD CLASS: A JAPANESE CAR COMPANY RUN BY A FRENCH BUSINESSMAN BORN IN BRAZIL REGAINED ITS SOUL WITH A CAR CONCEIVED IN THE UNITED STATES AND DESIGNED BY THE BRITISH-BORN SON OF PARENTS FROM INDIA.

But the company needed more than a revival plan; it needed to revive its spirit, its enthusiasm. It needed to re-identify and renew its corporate soul. "We need bread and butter cars, not toys," Jerry Hirshberg was told when he proposed that Nissan needed a new Z-car, a 240Z for the 21st century. "There was a lot of resistance."

Hirshberg was nearing his retirement as head of Nissan's North American design studio, and although he was still was still work-ing at General Motors when the 204Z was cre-ated, he recognized that the car still was the ultimate symbol of what Nissan was and could be once again. So Hirshberg and his stu-dio went to work, with Nissan's North American public relations director Jason Vines as co-conspirator and helping to provide fund-ing from his departmental budget for a clan-destine operation to develop a new Z concept car. Fortunately for their careers, Ghosn had driven a 240Z when he was a young executive at Michelin and allowed their Z Concept car to be displayed at the Detroit auto show early in 1999. The concept sparked renewed interest in Nissan and its vehicles. Within Nissan, it sparked a dialogue about just what the com-pany was all about. Now, Nissan not only had a plan, it had a purpose.

Nissan knew it needed a new Z, though not one quite as retro in design as the one on its stand at Detroit. So Nissan designers and engineers and product planners went to work, this time with full corporate support and a mandate to instill the spirit of the original 240Z into a thoroughly modern sports car.

They succeeded. Nissan showed a new Z concept at the Detroit show early in 2001, knowing that with only a few slight changes the car would be unveiled at the Tokyo show later that year as the new 2003 Nissan 350Z.

MERCEDES-BENZ SLR MCLAREN

Mercedes-Benz says its SLR McLaren is the "thrilling synthesis of tradition and innovation."

The grand turismo for the 21st century.

A car content to be used every day, but also a car capable to bringing Grand Prix technology and performance from the racetrack to the roadway, assuming, of course, that you might find a stretch of road on which to exercise this car's 207.5 miles per hour (334 kilometers/hour) top speed capability.

Should you find such a piece of pavement, Mercedes-Benz assures you that the car's carbon fiber brakes and air-brake rear spoiler combine with all sorts of computerized brake and body control technology to bring you back from the blur.

The SLR McLaren harkens to the heritage of Mercedes' famed mid-1950s 300 SL coupes with their gull-wing doors, especially the SLR versions that were so successful in interna-

tional racing competition. Thus the contemporary car includes such details as the straked checkerboard of engine air vents behind the front wheels and doors that, while not gull-winged, open upward and forward in what Mercedes terms "swing-wing" style with hinges built into the car's A pillars.

Built into the rocker panel just below those air vents on each side of the car are rectangular exhaust outlets.

This placement not only enhances the sound of the car as the drives along, but also provides for a flat under car surface that enhances high-speed aerodynamic control.

Mercedes presented its vision for its future GT at the 1999 Detroit show in the form of the Vision SLR, a concept car designed in Germany and built in Italy.

What turned vision into reality was ensuing work by McLaren, Mercedes' partner in Formula One racing and the British firm that had built its own supercar, the McLaren F1, a

266 THE REAR DECKLID OF THE MERCEDES-BENZ SLR MCLAREN INCORPORATES A SPOILER THAT NOT ONLY RISES INTO POSITION AT SPEED, BUT THAT CHANGES ITS ANGLE OF DEPLOYMENT UNDER BRAKING TO INCREASE AERODYNAMIC DRAG FOR SAFER STOPPING.

266-267 THE NOSE OF THE SLR MCLAREN CARRIES STRONG STYLING CUES FROM THE MCLAREN GRAND PRIX RACING CARS. AFTER ENLARGING ITS LARGE EQUITY STAKE IN MCLAREN, DAIMLER CHRYSLER DREW ON THE BRITISH TEAM'S EXPERTISE IN DEVELOPING THE SLR.

few years earlier. McLaren might have preferred engine placement behind the cockpit, but Mercedes wanted front-engine architecture, albeit with the engine's weight behind the front axle rather than over it.

Such front-engine design provided for more traditional GT styling, with plenty of room inside for a driver and passenger, and even 9.6 cubic feet (272 liters) of cargo space.

But McLaren got to use its expertise at car-bon fiber construction techniques, including two large carbon fiber cones designed to absorb nearly five times more energy than a steel or aluminum structure in the event of a frontal collision. While McLaren was working on the chassis and sorting out dynamics, Mercedes' wholly owned German tuning shop, AMG, was hand-building the SLR's 5.5-liter, supercharged V8 engine that provided 617 horsepower, 575 pound-feet (780 Newton meters) of torque, good enough to propel the 3900-pound (1768-kg.) car from a standing start to 62 miles per hour (100 km/h) in just 3.8 seconds, and then on to its nearly astronomic top speed. But drive the Mercedes-Benz SLR McLaren at more normal speeds and its engine provides nearly 16 miles per gallon (14.8 liters/100 km) of fuel efficiency.

Even people in position to pay $450,000 for their daily driver can appreciate that sort of performance at the pump.

268-269 THE MERCEDES-BENZ SLR MCLAREN SHOWS THE CLASSIC STANCE OF A FRONT-ENGINE GT MACHINE. WITH THE ENGINE UP FRONT BENEATH A LONG HOOD, THERE'S ROOM BEHIND FOR A COMFORTABLE PASSENGER COMPARTMENT AND EVEN A TRUNK.

270 TOP WHAT MERCEDES-BENZ CALLED "SWING-WING" DOORS MAKE THE INTERIOR OF THE SLR MCLAREN LOOK VERY INVITING AT THE 2004 TORONTO AUTO SHOW.

270-271 THE SLR MCLAREN ON DISPLAY AT THE MOTOR CITY, AND THE CAR HAD QUITE A MOTOR UNDER ITS HOOD – HAND-BUILT AND SUPERCHARGED TO PROVIDE 626 HORSEPOWER.

271 TOP THOUGH IT ONLY WENT AROUND IN CIRCLES ON ITS STAND AT THE MADRID AUTO SHOW, THE SLR MCLAREN HAS AN OFFICIAL TOP SPEED OF 207.5 MILES PER HOUR (334 KM/H).

Mercedes-Benz SLR McLaren
No sigas el ejemplo. Sigue la idea.

ENZO FERRARI

Ten years after Enzo Ferrari's death, in 1988 at age 90, Ferrari began preliminary work on a new car, a car that would go beyond the famed F40 and F50 to be an ultimate sports car, part Formula One racer, part Stealth fighter, yet a car designed for driving on public roads, albeit capable of speeds more closely associated with Grand Prix racing than even those that might be reached on open stretches of Germany's autobahn.

Work became even more focused after Ferrari ended a 16-year drought by winning the world manufacturer's championship in the 1999 Formula One season and in 2000 when Michael Schumacher became the first Ferrari driver in more than two decades to win the world driving championship.

To celebrate – and to capitalize on – such successes, Ferrari drew on both its Formula One racing team, including the organizational and technical excellence provided by Jean Todt, Ross Brawn and Rory Byrne, as well as using Schumacher as test driver, and on the racing team's key suppliers – Magneti Marelli, Bridgestone and Brembo – to help develop

272-273 WITH LINES THAT
LOOK MORE LIKE A STEALTH
FIGHTER JET THAN AN
EXOTIC SPORTS CAR, THE
ENZO FERRARI APPEARS
FEARSOME AND FAST EVEN
WHEN PARKED.

this ultimate Ferrari, a car so significant that it would carry not a number, not even the name of an important (to Ferrari and its fans) geographic location, but the name of the company's founder.

The car made its public debut in the fall of 2002 in "fly yellow" colors at the Paris auto show, where it was announced that only 399 such cars would be produced, and that they would be available only in Ferrari red, eventually specified on 80 percent of the orders, this same spectacular yellow hue or a Stealth-like black, which was selected by a mere 5 percent of the people privileged to spend $670,000 (U.S.) on such a vehicle.

For that price, you not only got the car, but the opportunity to visit the Ferrari factory to have your driver's seat and pedals specially fitted to your physique. Styling, as usual, was done at Pininfarina, with Japanese-born Ken Okuyama as lead designer.

Okuyama previously had worked at Porsche and General Motors, and after doing the Enzo would become chairman of transportation design as his alma mater, the famed Art Center College of Design in Pasadena, California, at least until early in 2004 when he went back to Italy as Pininfarina's creative director.

Okuyama's long-nosed and low bodied road car included creative and effective air ducting as well as an active spoiler that, working in conjunction with racing style tunnels beneath the car helped to generate twice the downforce of the high-winged F50. Such aerodynamic control was necessary on a car capable of speeds up to 217 miles per hour (350 km/h).

The car drew its power from a mid-mounted, 6.0-liter V12 engine that provided 660 horsepower and 485 pound-feet of torque, enough to propel the Enzo from a standing start to 60 miles per hour (96 km/h) in 3.5 seconds and to 124 mph (200 km/h) in just 9.5 seconds.

In the hands of a driver such as Schumacher, the car was a full five seconds a lap faster around the Ferrari test track at Fiorano than the heralded F50, though the Ferrari F1 car could outrun the Enzo by half a minute around the same circuit, though the ultra-light F1 racer wasn't burdened by such things as a second seat, a finished interior with air conditioning, or safety equipment such as airbags that contributed to the Enzo's 3009-pound (1365-kg.) curb weight.

"It's the fastest Ferrari road car ever," praised the editors of Britain's CAR magazine, which rated the Enzo the second coolest car of all time (behind only the legendary and gull winged Mercedes-Benz 300SL). "That edges-and-angles bodywork is bang up to date, and functional, too," they continued. "The Enzo is as cool a Ferrari as they get."

274-275 THE FERRARI F40 AND F50 HAD TALL REAR WINGS. THE ENZO'S WING STAYS OUT OF THE WAY UNTIL IT'S NEEDED, THEN IT RISES INTO PLACE TO GENERATE INCREDIBLE DOWNFORCE TO KEEP THE CAR FROM PLANTED ONTO THE ROADWAY.

275 TOP EMPOWERING THE CAR THAT CARRIES ENZO FERRARI'S NAME IS A 12-CYLINDER, 6.0-LITER ENGINE THAT PROVIDES 660 HORSEPOWER, WHICH COMES ON SO QUICKLY THAT THERE ARE LIGHTS ON THE STEERING WHEEL TO REMIND THE DRIVER IT'S TIME TO SHIFT TO THE NEXT GEAR.

276-277 AND AWESOME SIGHT: THE ENZO FERRARI WITH ITS DOORS OPEN, READY FOR YOU TO CLIMB AND LAUNCH IT DOWN THE HIGHWAY.

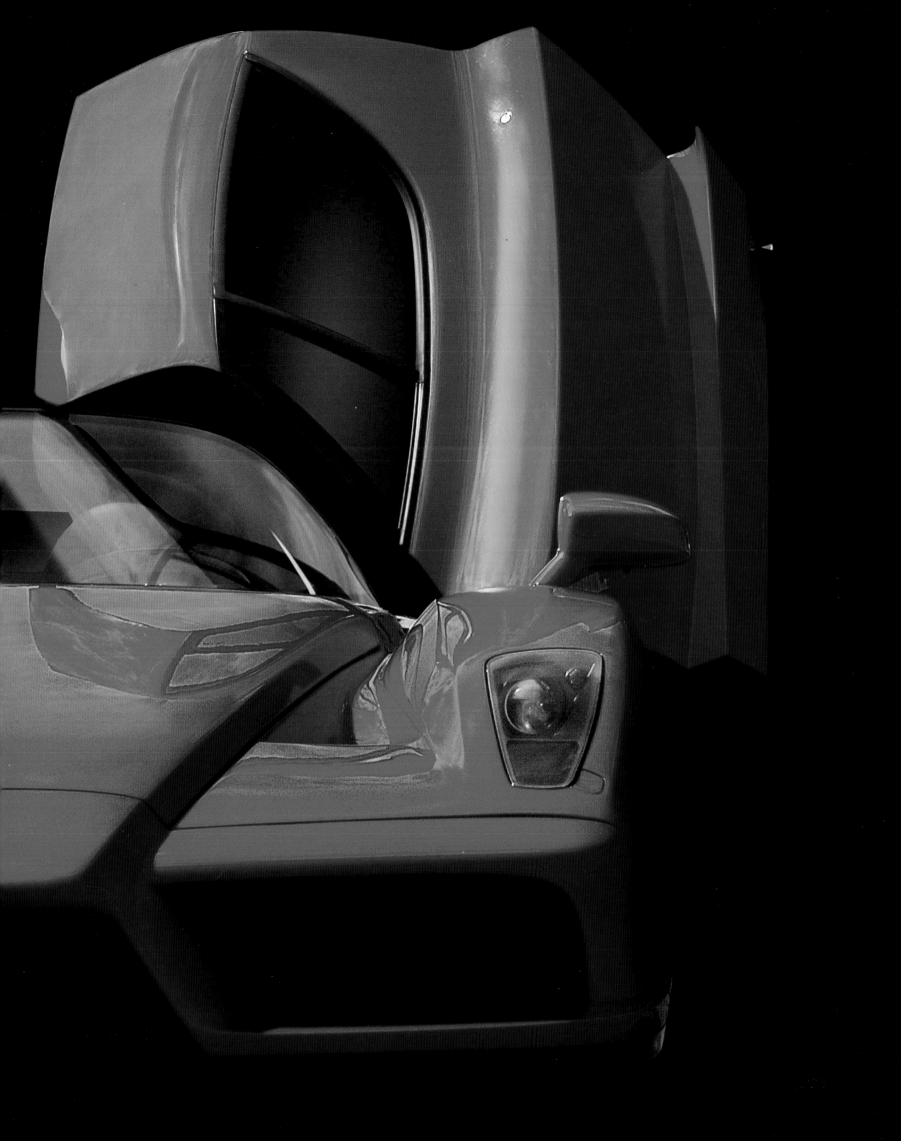

America's sports car, the Chevrolet Corvette, underwent only the fifth major revision in its long production history for the 1997 model year. This so-called C5 was hailed as the best yet, especially four years later when Chevrolet revived the Z06 version of the car.

Z06 had been a special factory-prepared racing option package designed by Zora Arkus-Duntov and made available only on the 1963 Corvette model, the famed "split-window" Sting Ray.

This special package of upgraded suspension and brakes with a 36.5-gallon (138-liter) fuel tank for endurance racing was designed to make the 'Vette competitive with Carroll Shelby's new Ford-powered Cobras.

Chevy not only created an updated Z06 package for the C5 Corvette, but instead of the usual LS1 "small-block" V8 (as if 350 horsepower might be called "usual"), this special Corvette drew its power from an LS6 "big-block" motor, a 385-horsepower, 7.4-liter engine named after the original LS6 that had been offered only in 1971.

Needless to say, Chevrolet was putting everything it had in to this new Z06, going so far as to lighten the body by some 38 pounds (more than 17 kilograms) by installing a titanium exhaust system and even lighter tires.

With its big, pushrod engine pumping out lots of torque, the new Z06 Corvette could sprint from a standing start to 60 miles per hour (96 km/h) in just four seconds and reach a top speed of 171 mph (275.2 km/h), yet such supercar figures were produced by a surprisingly affordable (around $50,000) sports car that was eager and comfortable for hours of highway cruising, thanks in part to the wheelbase being stretched more than eight inches (21.5 centimeters) compared to the earlier C4 Corvette. And the Corvette engineering team was just warming up. For 2002 it came back with an even more powerful version of the LS6 engine, now with 405 horsepower and 400 pound-feet (542 Newton meters) of torque, and a stronger clutch to deal with this newfound power.

At last the Corvette not only ran like a real sports car, it looked like one too. This newest design wasn't about body-builder bulges or add-on wings but a clean wedge-shaped profile that swelled into a tall and wide tail, with visually appealing scoops sculptured into the bodywork just behind the front wheel wells.

But as good as the Corvette had become, it looked like it might be the last of its breed, the end of the line for the American sports car. Even General Motors was having trouble justifying its development costs, at least until Cadillac underwent its stunning renaissance and engineers found a way to use the underpinnings of the Corvette sports car to produce a luxury roadster as well.

Thus for 2005 there was yet another new Corvette, the C6, and soon the Z06 offered 500 horsepower and a top speed in excess of 190 mph (305 km/h). Once again, we had the best Corvette yet.

CHEVROLET CORVETTE

278-279 HIDDEN HEADLIGHTS HAD BEEN A CORVETTE TRADEMARK EVER SINCE THE FAMED 1963 STING RAY, BUT THE FIFTH-GENERATION CORVETTE WOULD MARK THE END OF AN ERA. THE 2004 CORVETTE HAD EXPOSED HEADLAMPS.

279 TOP CUTAWAY DRAWING SHOWS THE INNER WORKINGS OF THE FIFTH GENERATION OF THE CHEVROLET CORVETTE.

P orsche's racing department was working on a new 5.5-liter, 10-cylinder racing engine for the 24 Hours of Le Mans when the program was put on hold. More pressing matters, largely in the form of the Cayenne sport utility vehicle, needed Porsche's research and development dollars.

But the price was worth it, the engineers were assured, because the success of the Cayenne would underwrite Porsche's desire to remain an independent automaker. And, besides, there might be a dividend down the road and around the corner.

One morning in October 2000, when the world's automotive press was sleeping off another night of Paris auto show parties, Porsche woke everyone very early and asked them to assemble at the Louvre, where the dividend was displayed in the form of the prototype for the Carrera GT.

This was not a racecar to challenge Le Mans. This was a road car to challenge the world's supercars.

By the time the Carrera GT would go into production in 2003, its engine had been enlarged to 5.7 liters and was pumping out in excess of 600 horsepower. But the car itself was even more advanced than its powerplant.

The Carrera GT was constructed from a fiber-reinforced plastic monocoque tub that was as structurally stiff and sound as any racecar, yet weighed only 220 pounds (100 kilograms). The first use in any automobile of a small and lightweight ceramic clutch allowed Porsche to mount the engine behind the passenger compartment and very low in the chassis. The entire design theme of the car was long and low and light, with stretched but taut lines, with aircraft-style vents providing both form and function in aesthetics and aerodynamics.

A pair of low, cross-drilled stainless steel power domes reaches back beneath safety bars just behind and above the car's seats. Again, it was form and function: the bars secured the removable roof that covers the cockpit in inclement weather. The Carrera GT's low center of gravity, combined with racing-style pushrod suspension and extensive wind tunnel aerodynamic development, provided the Carrera GT with both nimble handling and remarkable high-speed stability. The car rode on wheels that were 19 inches in diameter in front and 20 inches at the rear.

The Carrera GT certainly was capable of

280 TOP THE PORSCHE CARRERA GT CARRIES DESIGN CUES FROM THE 911 SPORTS CAR, BUT INCORPORATES A 10-CYLINDER ENGINE BEHIND THE PASSENGER COMPARTMENT.

280-281 THE CAR'S ENGINE HAD BEEN DESIGNED BY THE COMPANY'S MOTORSPORTS ENGINEERS TO POWER A RETURN TO RACING AT LE MANS.

282-283 A REMOVABLE HARDTOP ENHANCES THE CARRERA GT'S SLEEK DESIGN AND AERODYNAMICS. THE CAR IS CAPABLE OF ACHIEVING SPEEDS IN EXCESS OF 200 MILES PER HOUR.

high speeds. From a standing start it could exceed 60 miles per hour (96 km/h) within four seconds and had hit 100 mph (160 km/h) within seven seconds. In one test, the Carrera GT went from zero to 100 and back to zero in 882 feet, less than the distance of an aircraft carrier's landing deck. While the powertrain and aerodynamics were responsible for the speed, braking was accomplished by huge, nearly 15-inch (380 mm) racing-bred carbon composite brakes, a system Porsche had pioneered on its high-performance road cars.

By the way, top speed was 205 mph (330 km/h). The price: $440,000.

Even the Carrera GT's seats were made from carbon fiber, but even in this futuristic supercar, homage was paid to Porsche's racing history: The shift lever for the six-speed transmission featured a ball-shaped knob made from birch and ash wood and designed to look like the balsa-wood shifter on the famed Porsche 917 Le Mans racer.

PORSCHE CARRERA GT

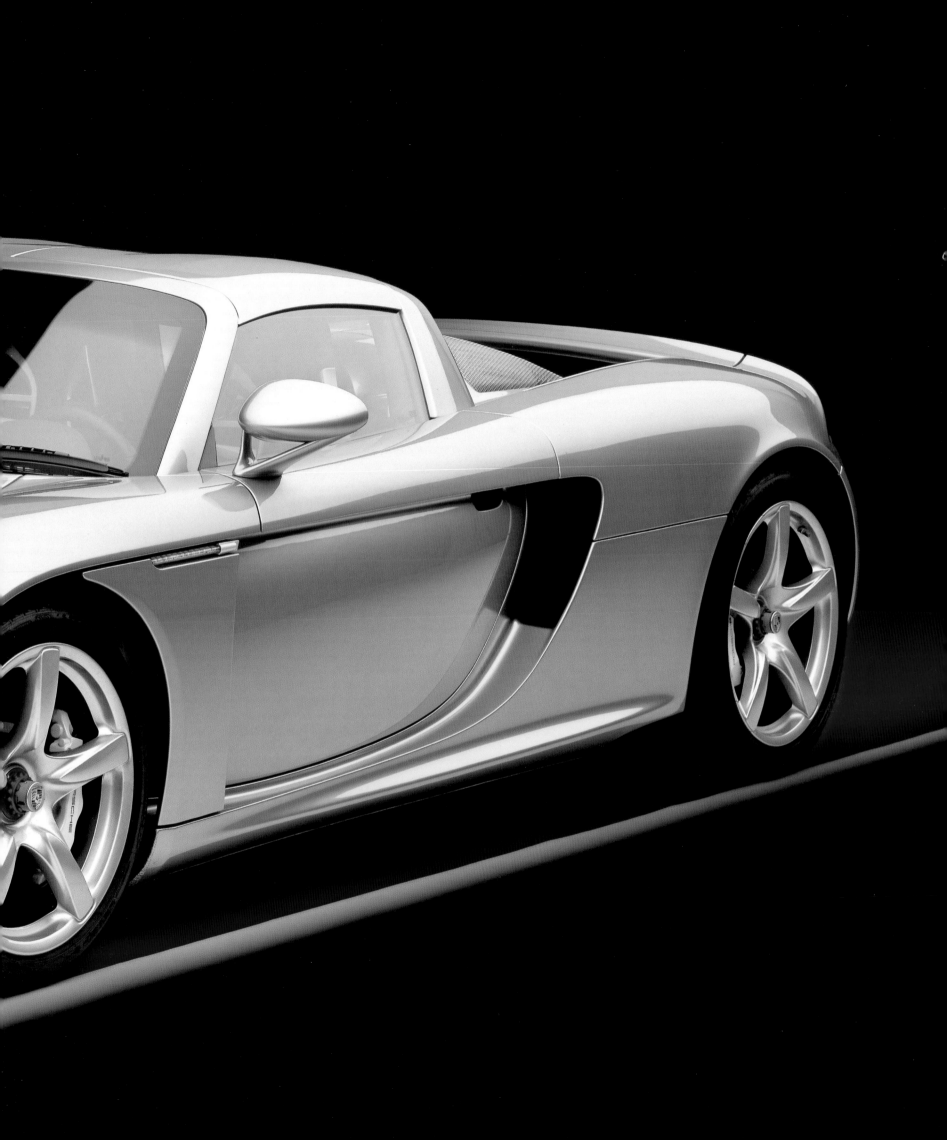

BIBLIOGRAPHY

Books

24 Heures du Mans, 1923-1992; Christian Mointy, Jean-Marc Teissedre and Alain Bienvenu. Le Mans, France. 1993.

A Century of Car Design; Penny Sparke, London, 2002

Automobile and Culture, Gerald Silk, Angelo Tito Anselmi, Henry Flood Robert Jr., Strother MacMinn, New York, 1984

AZ of Sports Cars Since 1945; Mike Lawrence, Devon, England, 1991

Bug: The Strange Mutation s of the World's Most Famous Automobile; Phil Patton, New York, 2002

Cars 1930-2000: The birth of the Modern Car; Nick Georgano, Michael Sedgwick and Bengt Ason Holm, Gothenburg, Sweden, 2001

Cars: An encyclopedia of the world's most fabulous automobiles; Martin Buckley and Chris Rees, London, 2002

Classic Cars: From 1945 to The Present; Michael Bowler, Vercelli, Italy, 2001

Classic Cars: The World's Greatest Marques; Richard Gunn, London, 2003

Concept Cars: From the 1930s to the Present; Larry Edsall, Vercelli, Italy, 2003

Ferrari: Design of a legend; Gianni Rogliatti, Segrio Pininfarina and Valerio Moretti, Milan, Italy, 1990

Ford GT: The Legend Comes to Life; Larry Edsall, St. Paul, Minn., 2004

Ford Racing Century; Larry Edsall and Mike Teske, St. Paul, Minn., 2003

Jeep Owner's Bible; Moses Ludel, Cambridge Massachusetts, 1992

Standard Catalog of American Cars 1946-1975, 1976-1999; Ron Kowalke and James M. Flammang, Iola, Wisconsin, 1999

Standard Catalog of Imported Cars 1946-2002; Mike Covello. Iola, Wisconsin, 2002

The Automobile Age; James J. Flink, Cambridge, Massachussets, 1993

The Checkered Flag: 100 Years of Motor Racing; Ivan Rendall, Secausus NJ, 1993

The Complete Book of Collectible Cars; Richard M Langworth and the auto editors of Consumer Guide, Lincolnwood, Illinois, 2001

The Complete Encyclopedia of Antique Cars: Sports & Passenger Cars 1886-1940; Rob De La Rive Box, The Netherlands, 1998

The Story of Jeep; Patrick R. Foster, Iola, Wisconsin, 1998

The Ultimate Classic Car Book; Quentin Wilson with David Selby, New York, 1995

Ultimate Sports Car; Quentin Wilson, New York, 2002

Other sources

Alfa Romeo SZ – RZ Registry

100 Events That Made the Industry, special issue, *Automotive News,* June 26, 1996

Catalog of Il Museo Dell'Automobile Carlo Biscaretti di Ruffia di Torino

Ford 100, special anniversary iisue, *Automotive News,* June 16, 2003

MX-5 Miata Anniversary Album by Barbara Houndt Beach, 1994

Museum of Modern Art (New York) catalogs for auto design exhibits in 1951 and 1953

Through Darkest America with Truck and Tank, a chapter in *At East: Stories I tell to friends,* Dwight D. Eisenhower, Doubleday & Company Inc., Garden City, N.Y., 1967

Magazine articles

100 Coolest Cars; *CAR,* May 2004

A Car, A Watch? Swatchmobile! Thomas A. Sancton and Margaret Studer, *Time,* March 28, 1994

Escape Roads, *AutoWeek,* various issues and articles written by Randy Barnett, Robert Barlow, Rick Carey, Dan Carney, Mike Covello, Larry Edsall, Patrick Foster, John F. Katz, Nick Kurczewski, J. William Lamm, Michael Lamm, John Matras, Bill McGuire, Nina Padgett, Jonathan Stein, Matt Stone, Jan Tegler, Howard Walker and Michael Worthington-Williams

Various articles from *AutoWeek* by Luca Ciferri, John P. Cortez, Matt DeLorenzo, Larry Edsall, Gavin Green, John F. Katz, Dutch Mandel, Denise McCluggage, Wes Raynal, Steve Thompson, Mark Vaughn, J.P. Vettraino and Kevin A. Wilson

Piero Dusio & the Cisitalia; Genevieve Obert, *European Car* online features

Newspaper articles

Museum Shows Army Jeep as "Work of Art," *Elyria (Ohio) Chronicle-Telegram,* August 30, 1951

INDEX

PHOTOGRAPHIC CREDITS

6613/Gamma /Contrasto: page 93
A213/Gamma/Contrasto: pages 181, 182
Alamy Images: pages 44-45, 46 , 47, 157, 190-191
AP Photo: pages 96, 270
Archivio Massimo Massarenti: pages 72 top left and right, 72 center, 72 bottom left and right
Archivio Nissan: pages 264, 264-265, 265
Archivio Porsche: pages 83, 108, 108-109, 109
Archivio Scala: pages 44, 60 top
Archivio Storico Alfa Romeo: page 131
Archivio Storico Bertone: pages 216, 217
Archivio Storico FIAT: pages 36 right, 37, 73
Artemis Images: page 222
Bernard Cahier: pages 180-181
Bettmann/Corbis/Contrasto: pages 16, 18-19, 98 top, 100
BMIHT Archive Heritage Motor Centre: pages 145, 160 top
BMW AG Historiches Archiv: pages 60 bottom, 62-63, 223, 224-225, 225
Bradley Smith/Corbis/Contrasto: page 168
Cindy Lewis Photography: page 190
Daimler Chrysler: pages 50-51
David Reed/Corbis/Contrasto: page 119
Everett Collection/Contrasto: page 228
FIAT Auto Press: page 130 top
Fotostudio Zumbrunn: pages 2-3, 20-21, 2?   5, 40, 41, 42, 43, 52-53, 64   65   68-69, 74, 74-75, 76, 76-7   9, 90, 92-93, 103 bot⁺ 117, 117, 11⁹ 139 bot⁺ 155, 1⁵

left and right, 172-173, 185, 187, 194-195, 195, 204-205, 206, 207, 208-209, 230, 235, 237, 240-241, 241, 242-243, 243, 251, 272-273, 274-275, 275
General Motors Media Archive: pages 20, 21, 35, 166 bottom, 167, 169, 183, 279
Georgeon Rossi/Gamma/Contrasto: page 106
Giles Chapman Library: page 193
Gjon Mili/Time Life Pictures/Getty Images/Laura Ronchi: page 99 top
Hulton Archive/Laura Ronchi: pages 102, 139 top
Hulton-Deutsch Collection/Corbis/Contrasto: page 158
IIHS/AP Photo: page 256
illustrazione di Sergio Zaniboni, Diabolik©Astorina: page 173
Jaguar Archives: page   op left and right, 95 center left and right
James Mann: pages 200-201, 201, 226-227, 248-249
Lat Photographic: pages 42-43, 56, 57, 62
Ludvingsen Library: page 227
Maggi and Maggi: pages 36 left, 38, 38-39
Mario Fourmy/Rea/Contrasto: page 271
Media.Ford.com: page 99 bottom
Michael Furman Photography: pages 12-13, 33, 56-57, 106-107, 110-111, 123, 146-147, 156-157, 174-175, 192-193
Museo Dell'automobile di Torino: page 23
Neill Bruce: pages 19 top, 52, 188-189
Paul Almasy/Corbis/Contrasto: page 221
Peter Harholdt/Corbis/Contrasto: pages 216-217
Peter Vann/Automedia: pages 58-59
Photos12: pages 19 bottom, 92, 143, 259
Photoservice Electa/AKG: pages 103 top, 111, 153, 177

R.A./Gamma/Contrasto: page 174
Raphael Demaret/Photonews/Gamma/Contrasto: pages 270-271
Rene' Staud Studios: pages 10-11, 125, 128-129, 130 bottom, 148, 152, 152-153, 162, 163, 202-203, 203, 210-211, 211, 212-213, 219, 246, 253, 266, 266-267, 268-269
Richard Cummins/Corbis/Contrasto: page 1
Roger Viollet/Archivio Alinari: pages 115, 124, 136
Ron Kimball: pages 4-5, 6-7, 15, 24-25, 26-27, 28-29, 30-31, 48, 48-49, 54-55, 55, 78-79, 96-97, 97, 126, 126-127, 144, 144-145, 196, 196-197, 198-199, 214-215, 228-229, 230-231, 233, 236-237, 238-239, 254-255, 258-259, 260-261, 261, 262-263, 278-279, 280, 280-281, 282-283
Schlegelmilch Photography: pages 246-247
Schwartzwald Lawrence/Corbis Sygma/Contrasto: page 254
The Advertising Archive Ltd.: pages 91, 101, 159, 166 top
The Culture Archive: pages 39, 50, 51, 98 bottom
Todd Corzett: page 61
Topfoto/ICP: pages 17, 244-245
Underwood & Underwood /Corbis/Contrasto: pages 45, 80-81
Volkswagen Media: pages 104, 107, 256-257, 257, 288
www.carphoto.co.uk: pages 22, 70, 70-71, 71, 94-95, 141, 168-169, 276-277
Zoomstock: pages 8-9, 81, 114, 114-115, 176-177, 178-179, 182-183

AKNOWLEDGEMENTS

The author is grateful to the following for their contributions to the research for this book: Leslie Armbruster of the Ford Motor Co. archives, Dave Buchko and Rob Mitchell of BMW North America, Sam Butto of Toyota Motor Sales USA, Bob Carlson of Porsche Cars North America, Dean Case of Nissan North America, Jennifer Cortez of Audi of America, Donald Davidson of the Indianapolis Motor Speedway, Jackie Jouret of Bimmer magazine, Tim McGrane of Barrett-Jackson Auctions and CurtCo Publishing, "Landspeed' Louise Ann Noeth, Peter Reed of the Museum of Modern Art, Will Rodgers of SHR Perceptual Management, Wes Sherwood of Ford Motor Company, Eduard van de Beek of the International SZ and RZ Registry, Patricia Lee Younge of the University of Houston, Corrine Young of the Automotive News Information Center, to the Phoenix Public Library and especially to former co-workers at AutoWeek magazine, including Cynthia Claes, Joe Kovach and Kevin A. Wilson for their help.

Finally, the author dedicates this work to his grandmother, Ethel Acord, who loved to drive but was an eager passenger when her grandson was old enough to take the wheel, and to his own grandson, Nicholas Russell Chester, may cars still be cool when you're old enough to drive.

The Publisher would like to thank:

Archivio Storico Fiat, Turin, Italy
Astorina Publisher for the image on page 173, Milan, Italy
Fiat Auto Press, Turin, Italy
BMW Historical Archive, Munich, Germany
Nissan Italia Press Office, Rome, Italy
Bertone Engineering Press Office, Grugliasco (TO), Italy
Porsche Historical Archive, Stuttgart, Germany
British Motor Industry Heritage Trust, Gaydon, Great Britain
Alfa Romeo Historical Archive, Turin, Italy
Volkswagen Press Office, Wolfsburg, Germany
Autogerma, Verona, Italy
General Motors Archives, Detroit, USA

288 THE LINES OF THE
NEW BEETLE LEND
THEMSELVES TO
CUSTOMIZATION OF
ALL KINDS.

© 2005 White Star S.p.A. - Via Candido Sassone, 22/24
13100 Vercelli, Italy - www.whitestar.it

ISBN 88-544-0081-5

REPRINTS:
123456 09 08 07 06 05

Printed in Singapore
Color Separation Chiaroscuro, Turin